Explorer's Notes

THE BIBLE

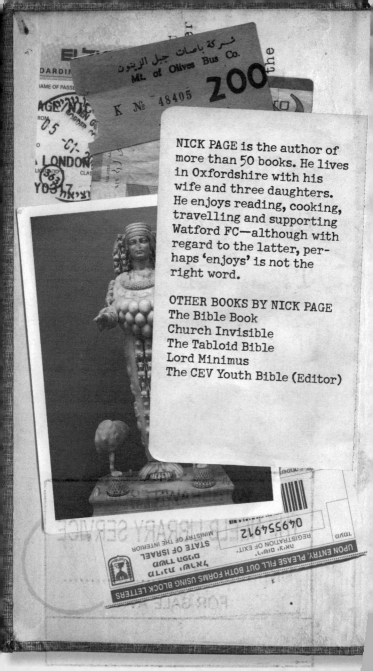

NICK PAGE is the author of
more than 50 books. He lives
in Oxfordshire with his
wife and three daughters.
He enjoys reading, cooking,
travelling and supporting
Watford FC—although with
regard to the latter, perhaps 'enjoys' is not the
right word.

OTHER BOOKS BY NICK PAGE
The Bible Book
Church Invisible
The Tabloid Bible
Lord Minimus
The CEV Youth Bible (Editor)

Explorer's Notes
THE BIBLE

Nick Page

Collins

First published in 2006 by Collins
an imprint of HarperCollins*Publishers*
77–85 Fulham Palace Road
London W6 8JB

www.collins.co.uk

Copyright © 2006 Nick Page
www.nickpage.co.uk

Nick Page asserts the moral right to be identified as the author, photographer and designer of this work.

A catalogue record for this book is available from the British Library.

1

ISBN-10: 0-00-721704-8
ISBN-13: 978-0-00-721704-5

Printed and bound in Great Britain by Clays Ltd, St Ives plc

CONTENTS

This book is dedicated to my boots,
which have taken me on thousands
of miles of pain-free exploration.
Thanks guys.

Explorer's Notes—Part 1
Introducing the Bible

The boots in front of a VIP seat in a Roman theatre

Why explore the Bible?

The Bible is the most important book ever written.

No book has exerted more influence on the world—certainly the western world. Art, literature, politics, architecture, history, law—they've all been influenced by the Bible.

More importantly, as the basis of **two of the great religions of the world,** its writings are considered sacred. Christians believe that the Bible is inspired by God, which means that the people who wrote it were passing on messages from God—messages that were not only for the people of their time, but for all people, everywhere and in any time.

Having said all that, exploring the Bible can be a bit daunting for the modern reader. We're put off by its size: **66 books, 1,189 chapters,** over **750,000 words.** We're also put off by its age; we're talking about a book written by many different authors, across thousands of years, and completed around 2,000 years ago.

And maybe we're put off by the content itself. There are passages in the Bible that lift and inspire—and there are parts that disgust and shock. It can also be dull; long family trees, even longer lists of laws, all those strange names of people and countries...

But if you do venture in, if you do try to explore, then there are wonderful things to be found. You get great **poetry,** stirring **stories,** thought-provoking **wisdom,** life-changing **truths.** You get love, sex, violence, faithfulness, bravery, cowardice, triumph and disaster.

The Bible is all about the **big issues** in life. It tells us why we're here, what we're supposed to be doing on earth, where we all came from. It tells us how we should live our lives and how we should treat other people. It talks about real people with real problems—and although they lived a long time ago, they faced exactly the same kind of problems that we face today.

Most of all, Christians believe **the Bible speaks to us.** It is one of the ways that we hear from God and understand more about him.

The Bible is the most revolutionary, most exciting, most important book ever written. **What more do you need to know?**

Where did it come from?

The first Christians did not have 'the Bible' as we know it. (In fact, the final contents of our Bibles were only agreed around 400AD.) When the early Christians talked about scripture, they were talking about the Hebrew Scriptures, or what we know as the **Old Testament**. The early Church probably sang Psalms and read the prophets to see how they pointed to Jesus.

But they also told stories and shared memories of Jesus' life and teaching, passing on these memories from group to group. After a while, the church had grown and the original eyewitnesses began to die. So people began to write down their own accounts, drawing on their own observations and the memories of the people who were there. These became the **gospels**. At the same time, leaders such as Paul, Peter and John wrote **letters to churches** helping them to solve problems and offering spiritual advice. These letters were collected and copied and passed around the early Church. Eventually, the gospels and the letters were brought together to form the **New Testament**.

The way the early Church decided what should be in the Bible was to look for writings that were attributed to apostles or people **closely associated with Jesus**. Church leaders drew up their own lists of 'recommended' reading. This was particularly important because some people had started circulating fake—and often ridiculous—gospels and **acts**, full of bizarre stories and weird teaching.

Finally, in 376AD, Bishop **Athanasius** wrote to the churches in his region, listing what he considered 'Holy Scripture'. His list was eventually confirmed by two councils, one in **Rome** in 382AD and one in **Carthage** in 397AD and that is the New Testament that we have today.

How is it organised?

The Bible is split into two parts: the Old Testament and the New Testament.

The Old Testament also forms the Jewish or Hebrew scriptures. ('Testament' means 'promise'; Christians believe that the Old Testament tells the story of God's promise to the Israelites, while the New Testament of his promise to all people.)

Each Testament is split into different sections. The Old Testament contains **History**, **Prophecy**, **Wisdom** and what some people call the **'Pentateuch'** or the **'Books of the Law'**. The New Testament is divided into two main sections: the **Gospels and Acts** and the **Letters**, from people such as Paul, John and Peter.

Each section is made up of different numbers of **books of the Bible**. (For example, the Gospels and Acts section contains Matthew, Mark, Luke, John and Acts). Some books are huge, some are just one page long. They are written in different styles. The **Psalms**, for instance, are collections of poems; **Kings** is a long history.

Each book of the Bible is broken down into **chapters**. Some bits of these appear in more than one book; **Chronicles** and Kings share a lot of the same content, as do Matthew, Mark and John.

Finally the chapters are split into individual, numbered **verses**. Again, some verses are found in more than one book of the Bible.

To find our way around we use **Bible references**—a bit like an address. So, for example, the verse John 3.16 means 'the book of John, chapter 3, verse 16'. Genesis 1.1–17 means 'the book of Genesis, chapter one, verses 1 to 17'. James 4.13,15, 5.6 means 'read James chapter 4, verse 13, verse 15 and chapter 5, verse 6'.

When you see a reference, the book name is often abbreviated (e.g. 1 Corinthians 6.3 might be shortened to 1 Cor 6.3). A list of all the books and their abbreviations can be found opposite.

OLD TESTAMENT

THE LAW or PENTATEUCH — 5 books

HISTORIES — 12 books

WISDOM — 5 books

MAJOR PROPHETS — 5 books

MINOR PROPHETS — 12 books

NEW TESTAMENT

GOSPELS & ACTS — 5 books

LETTERS OF PAUL — 13 books

GENERAL LETTERS & REVELATION — 9 books

LAW or PENTATEUCH
Genesis (Gen)
Exodus (Ex)
Leviticus (Lev)
Numbers (Num)
Deuteronomy (Deut)

HISTORIES
Joshua (Josh)
Judges (Judg)
Ruth (Ruth)
1 Samuel (1Sam)
2 Samuel (2 Sam)
1 Kings (1 Kings)
2 Kings (2 Kings)
1 Chronicles (1 Chr)
2 Chronicles (2 Chr)
Ezra (Ezr)
Nehemiah (Neh)
Esther (Est)

WISDOM
Job (Job)
Psalm (Psa)
Proverbs (Prov)
Ecclesiastes (Ecc)
Song of Songs (Song)

MAJOR PROPHETS
Isaiah (Isa)
Jeremiah (Jer)
Lamentations (Lam)
Ezekiel (Ezk)
Daniel (Dan)

MINOR PROPHETS
Hosea (Hos)
Joel (Joel)
Amos (Amos)
Obadiah (Ob)
Jonah (Jon)
Micah (Mic)
Nahum (Na)
Habakkuk (Hab)
Zephaniah (Zeph)
Haggai (Hag)

GOSPELS & ACTS
Matthew (Mt)
Mark (Mk)
Luke (Lk)
John (Jn)
Acts (Acts)

LETTERS OF PAUL
Romans (Rom)
1 Corinthians (1 Cor)
2 Corinthians (2 Cor)
Galatians (Gal)
Ephesians (Eph)
Philippians (Phil)
Colossians (Col)
1 Thessalonians (1 Thess)
2 Thessalonians (2 Thess)
1 Timothy (1 Tim)
2 Timothy (2 Tim)
Titus (Tit)
Philemon (Philem)

GENERAL LETTERS & REVELATION
Hebrews (Heb)
James (Jas)
1 Peter (1 Pet)
2 Peter (2 Pet)
1 John (1 Jn)
2 John (2 Jn)
3 John (3 Jn)
Jude (Jude)
Revelation (Rev)

How do we explore?

Get a good, modern translation

People sometimes complain that the Bible is written in a 'weird old language'. But what they actually mean is that they've been reading an old translation (usually the Authorised Version from the 17th century). The most important aid to exploring the Bible is a good, modern translation. I'd recommend the CEV, the NIV, the Good News Bible or the ESV. The Message is also excellent.

Work to a plan

The Bible is big. It contains around 750,000 words. So we have to have a plan of action to help you explore. You can work through a particular book, or follow a particular person and study their life. Or you could study a topic such as 'prayer', or 'forgiveness' or 'justice'. This book contains over 100 mini reading plans, called 'The Sights', which suggest readings on a wide range of topics.

Give it time

Take your time. You can't see anywhere clearly if you're zooming through it at 120 miles per hour. Read carefully and you'll find loads to fascinate you. It often helps to read the passage aloud. Make time for it. You can get a good grip of what the Bible is all about by reading it for five or ten minutes a day. That's probably less than the time you spend watching adverts on TV! Try not to concentrate on just one verse, but look at the passages that surround it.

Ask questions

This is really important. A lot of people feel like they shouldn't ask questions about the Bible, as if it's 'too sacred' for that. In fact, the Bible is full of people who asked God challenging questions. If you don't ask, you won't find out.

Write notes

Keep a traveller's journal as you explore. Write down your thoughts and observations. Make maps, draw diagrams. You can keep a notebook for the purpose or you can make notes in the margins of your Bible. Underline important bits. Write down how God has spoken to you. (This book has loads of bits taken from my own notebooks and drawings.)

Use some guidebooks

When I go travelling I take some things like guidebooks, maps and phrasebooks. When you explore the Bible it's good to get some help as well. There are some parts where we need an expert to give us a bit of help. You can use Bible guides and commentaries to help you delve into a lot more detail.

Learn about the history

If there is one thing that really helps people understand the Bible, it's a broad understanding of Bible history. Each book of the Bible was written at a different point in time; understanding this can help our understanding of the entire book.

Understand the culture

They did things differently in Bible times. They had different attitudes to war, women, families, relationships and other such things. If you spend a little time trying to grasp the culture it will help you understand the passage a lot better.

Don't expect to understand everything

There are bits in the Bible that even the experts don't understand. So if you find a difficult part, work at it, ask questions and then, if it's still baffling, move on. Just because we don't understand something, doesn't mean we should stop exploring.

Use your commonsense

God has given us wisdom. Some of us could do with a little more, admittedly, but we all have it. So, when you read the Bible, try to use the wisdom God has given you. Don't fly off into fanciful theories and ideas based on one verse. Try to identify when people are speaking metaphorically or literally. Use your common sense.

Be creative

Try reading the Bible in different ways. Exploring a story? Draw a picture, write it as a play, turn it into a comic book. Act it out with a friend. You'll find a lot more in there if you look at something from a different perspective.

The Bible: an overview

The Old Testament

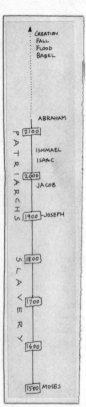

The Bible starts with **creation**. God creates the heavens and the earth. He creates a world that is good and fills it with plants and animals. He creates **Adam and Eve**—the first man and woman—and gives them a garden to inhabit. Even though they are only given one rule to obey, they choose to disobey and turn away from God. They're thrown out of the garden. **Sin** and evil have polluted God's creation.

It doesn't stop there. As humanity spreads throughout the earth, so does evil. So God decides to send a flood to wash away humanity and start again. **Noah** and his family are saved, however, and God makes a solemn promise never to destroy humanity again.

Now God takes a different approach. He decides to work through a nation and, to begin this nation, he chooses **Abraham**. God makes a **covenant** or promise with Abraham that his descendants will be a great nation and they will inhabit the land of Canaan—the **Promised Land**. He also says that all of humanity will be blessed by Abraham's descendants.

Although Abraham is in his nineties, God keeps his promises, and Abraham's wife Sarah gives birth to **Isaac**. Isaac is the father to twins, Esau and **Jacob**. After a dramatic encounter with God, Jacob changes his name to **Israel**, and it is by this name that the people will henceforth be known.

Jacob has twelve children, one of whom, Joseph, ends up in Egypt after annoying his brothers. Jacob's family flee to Egypt to escape famine where they are reunited with Joseph. The descendants of Jacob's twelve children become the **twelve tribes of Israel**.

In Egypt, the Israelites start to multiply and by the time a few hundred years have passed, the entire nation is in slavery. So God selects a leader called **Moses**, who, empowered by God, helps the Israelites escape. This escape is known as the **exodus**. They make their way back to Canaan. On the way God gives them **ten commandments** and detailed instructions on how to live and worship Him. However, when they get to the borders of

Canaan, they are too scared to cross into it. God punishes this lack of faith by exiling them for **forty years in the desert**.

Moses never makes it into Canaan. He dies on a mountain overlooking Canaan. He hands the leadership to **Joshua**, who takes the Israelites across the River Jordan and into the Promised Land. God gives his people instructions to conquer all the land, but the Israelites do not finish the task. Some of the old inhabitants—the Canaanites—remain and, with them, their own ways of worship. For the next 800 years, Israel's history is a battle between the worship of God and the worship of **false gods**.

After Joshua's death comes a troubled time of anarchy—when the country was filled with lawlessness and violence and 'each man did what he thought was right'. The **Judges**—leaders like **Deborah**, **Gideon** and **Samson**—bring only occasional light into the darkness. In the end, the Israelites ask the prophet **Samuel** to appoint a king and **Saul** becomes the first king of Israel. He is a brave, but foolish, leader and he's succeeded by **David**, Israel's greatest king. David captures **Jerusalem** and defeats the enemies of Israel while his son and successor, **Solomon**, builds a magnificent **temple**.

On Solomon's death, however, civil war breaks out, and the Promised Land splits into two countries; **Israel** in the north and **Judah** in the south. For the next 300 years, the two nations are constantly threatened by powerful enemies, while a succession of evil and foolish kings stray from worshipping God to follow false gods. God sends a series of **prophets**—like **Elijah, Elisha, Isaiah, Jeremiah and Ezekiel**—who warn the kingdoms what will happen to them if they don't change. They also talk of a **Messiah**—a 'chosen one'—a mighty leader whom God would send to save his people.

In 722BC the northern kingdom of Israel is captured and the inhabitants taken into captivity in **Assyria**. They are never heard of again. A hundred years later, the southern kingdom of Judah falls to another empire, the **Babylonians**, and all the people are exiled to **Babylon**. This period—known as **the exile**—lasts seventy years.

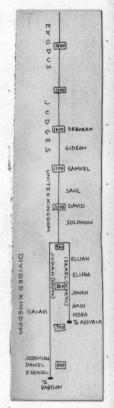

Then the Babylonian empire falls and the **exiles return** to Israel. They rebuild Jerusalem and the Temple. Israel and Judah are one country again, but the glory days have gone. God sends no more prophets and the people of Israel place their hopes in the long-awaited **Messiah**.

The New Testament

Four hundred years later, a poor teenage girl called Mary gives birth to a son, whom she calls **Jesus**. After **John the Baptist** warns people that someone special is coming, Jesus' public work begins, when he is around 30 years old. With his **disciples** he travels through **Roman Palestine**, preaching, teaching and performing miracles. He makes claims for himself that go beyond those of a teacher or even a prophet. He forgives people their sins and raises the dead; he challenges the establishment. He enters Jerusalem in triumph. Then it all seems to go wrong. Betrayed by one of his followers, Jesus is tried by the authorities, taken outside the city and **crucified**.

Three days later, his followers start to make remarkable claims. They claim that Jesus has **risen from the dead**, that he has appeared to many of his followers. More, they claim that Jesus is the Messiah, that his death has changed the world and that he has sent them a new helper, the **Holy Spirit**, to empower and inspire them.

These followers become known as **Christians**. New leaders emerge: **Peter**, the fisherman who was one of Jesus' first followers; and **Paul**, who began his career persecuting Jesus' followers and who, after a dramatic vision of Jesus, becomes one of his most outspoken followers. Gradually the stories about Jesus are written down as **gospels** and sent around the world. The followers set up local groups called **churches**. People of all nationalities start to believe in this Messiah.

Increasingly, Christians face persecution from the Jewish and Roman authorities. One such follower is John, who is sentenced to exile on a small island. While there, he has a vision of the end of time. Jesus will **return** and gain the final victory over darkness. The world will end as it began—with creation, with God creating a **new heaven and a new earth**, where all his followers will live in peace. It is an end, but also a new beginning.

Explorer's Notes—Part 2
Key Passages

The boots outside a fruit and veg shop in Bethlehem

Why is this important?

- It shows who made the world and universe
- It shows what humanity's relationship with God should be like
- It shows what humanity's relationship with the rest of creation should be

CREATION

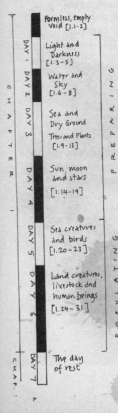

CHAPTER 1

DAY 1 — Formless, empty Void [1.1-2]

Light and Darkness [1.3-5]

DAY 2 — Water and Sky [1.6-8]

DAY 3 — Sea and Dry Ground
Trees and Plants [1.9-13]

PREPARING

DAY 4 — Sun, moon and stars [1.14-19]

DAY 5 — Sea creatures and birds [1.20-23]

DAY 6 — Land creatures, livestock and human beings [1.24-31]

POPULATING

CHAP. 2 — DAY 7 — The day of rest

Creation
(Gen 1.1–2.25)

'In the beginning God created the heavens and the earth' (Gen 1.1). Everything begins with God. This is the key message here—Genesis is talking about who put the stars in place.

There is a pattern to creation, a sense of order. The first four days prepare the place—the universe, the land, the seas, the energy source. The last two days populate the place with animals, birds, fish and, of course, humans.

There are two accounts of the creation of humans in Genesis (Gen 1.26–30; 2.7–25). Some argue for different writers, or different traditions about our origins. The first account (Gen 1.26–30) occurs within the broad sweep of creation, so the writer does not pause to describe the detail. The second account (Gen 2.7–25) is much more detailed, describing Adam's creation and his need for a partner.

God creates not a servant, but a partner. Eve is not subservient to Adam because she came second. She was meant to be a partner, and the end of the chapter indicates that this was part of the natural order: a man and a woman, joining together to become like one being.

Adam (the name derives from the ancient name for mankind) is made in the image of God—he has the same ability to moral choices. He is given control over the animals, and also responsibility for them. Adam was put into the garden to take care of it (Gen 2.15). There are rules to obey. If humanity has great power, it also bears the weight of great expectations.

Creation

The fundamental message of Genesis 1 is that this world is not
an accident. The creation of the universe was an act of will, a
deliberate action of God. Once we understand that, it follows
that we're all here because God meant us to be here. No-one
is accidental. The dark, formless void is turned into a universe
teeming with life and purpose.

There has always been a lot of argument over the account
of creation in Genesis; some argue for a **literal interpretation**, with
the seven days being actual, 24-hour days; others claim that it's
a more symbolic, metaphorical description, with 'days' merely
standing for 'periods of time'. Whatever your take on the issue,
the main message of Genesis 1 is that God did it. It all starts
with him. Whether you believe that God made the whole thing
in a week, or over many thousands of years, the key message
here is that we did not come about by accident.

Genesis is about cause rather than process. It's about **who**
made the universe, not **how** he did it. Whatever scientific process brought about man and the universe—and whatever
processes still keep the thing going—Genesis says that God's
hand was behind the whole thing.

What is also important is to understand that, within this
creation, humans occupy a unique place. God created men
and women in his own image. This phrase has been much
debated, but it seems to imply that God created beings with
whom he can communicate. These are people 'like' him, in
the sense that they can make choices. They can 'do the right
thing'.

And the right thing, in terms of creation, is to steward the
world. Genesis is quite explicit on this; we are not like the animals; we are appointed to 'rule' the earth. But just as we are
the image of God, our rule should be the image of God's rule.
That means we do what is right for the world, not what is right
for us. We are the **stewards of creation**, not the tyrants.

When God looked at creation he saw that it was very good.
And, despite what has happened since, it is still very good.
And, more than ever, it needs looking after by mankind—only
in God's way, not ours.

Why is this important?

■ It shows how evil entered the world

■ It demonstrates that all of us have a choice to follow God or not

The Fall of Man [Gen 3.1–24]

Chapter 3 of Genesis gives the Bible's answer to the question of how sin came into the world. The answer is plain: it came through the choice of humankind.

Adam and Eve are given only one rule: there is one tree, the fruit of which they must not touch—the **tree of the knowledge of good and evil**. 'Knowledge of good and evil' here does not mean knowing right from wrong. Adam did not already know right from wrong, he would not have known enough to take any notice of God's commands.

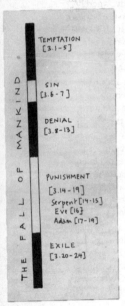

It is more a matter of who was to be in charge. The question is 'who makes the rules?' God asserts his position as the one authority—his right as creator and carer to make the rules. But he's giving Adam and Eve a choice: they can obey his rules, or choose their own path. They make their choice, eat the apple and the path leads them out of paradise and into a harsher world.

In this passage, the serpent starts by causing Eve to **doubt**, to question whether God is really telling the truth [Gen 3.1]. Doubt turns to **action** as first Eve, then Adam, eats the fruit. Although they later try to shift the blame, they are each responsible for their own sin [Gen 3.6]. The minute they eat, they experience a new feeling—**guilt**. Something has happened. Things are not the same [Gen 3.7].

This guilt leads to **separation** from God. They have chosen their own path. They cannot stay in the garden. From now on there is a separation between man and God, and between man and nature [Gen 3.8]. Yet the separation is not total. Our relationship with God is part of our very being— we are created in his image. And God still **loves**: as they leave, he gives them a gift. God does not let Adam and Eve go out of the garden without giving them warm clothes to wear [Gen 3.22].

The rest of the Bible tells of how God strove to repair the relationship and how human beings can satisfy the desire that still gnaws at every human heart: the desire to return to Eden, to live with and be loved by our true father.

Sin

Human beings are sinful creatures. **Sin** has been a part of the world, hard-wired into creation, since the fall of Adam and Eve. Before those two chose to disobey God, the world was perfect. This event is known as **the fall**, because it shows the whole of creation—not just Adam and Eve—falling from its original, untainted perfection.

The Sights: Sin
- [ ] The first sin: Gen 3.1–24
- [ ] A lamb for a sin: Lev 4.27–35
- [ ] Please wash me!: Ps 51.1–19
- [ ] A nation's sin: Isa 3.8–15
- [ ] God's warning: Psa 19.11–14
- [ ] Won't stay angry: Mic 7.18–20
- [ ] A lamb for sin: Jn 1.29–37
- [ ] Anyone seen me sin?: Jn 8.31–47
- [ ] From the inside: Mt 15.10–20
- [ ] Selfish desires: Jas 4.1–10
- [ ] He died for us: Rom 3.22–28
- [ ] God's kindness: Rom 5.1–21
- [ ] Sin's wages: Rom 6.20–23
- [ ] The right thing: 1Jn 3.4–10

They made a choice to reject God's instructions, and to do things their way. That's what sin is. It's a deliberate choice to turn away from God and do what we want.

Adam and Eve brought sin into their world and we've been copying their approach ever since. Sin came to rule the way that humans operated; to enslave humans and control them.

Through sin, death came into the world, because all who sin must die—that's the rule. Since we've all sinned, we all must die.

Except God sent Jesus to die for us. In his letter to Romans, Paul outlines the case: Adam's sin brought death to the world; Christ's death brings life. Because Adam disobeyed God we're all sinners; because Christ obeyed God we all have a shot at redemption.

Christians believe that Jesus has died for us—that he has died in our place. So, if we ask him for forgiveness, if we turn around to follow him, our sins will be wiped away and we'll be able to live with God forever. The choice of Adam and Eve can be unmade if we choose to follow Christ, and the way is clear to get back to the garden.

Noah and the ark
(Gen 6–7)

The Hebrew word used to describe Noah's boat is tebâ, which means box, or chest. ('Ark' is also old English for the same thing.) So the boat was simply an enormous, floating, waterproof crate of animals, birds and reptiles.

It had no power or steering. All it needed to do was float; God would take care of all the rest. It was made out of 'gopher' wood, which may have been cypress.

The story ends with a promise: God will never do the same thing again. The rainbow is a sign of God's love and mercy and God makes a covenant with Noah.

Noah is seen as a precursor of Christ (Lk 17.26–7) and the flood as a kind of baptism (1 Pet 3.18–22). The Old Testament also uses the word tebâ to describe the box in which Moses floated on the Nile—the only other time it is used in the Bible.

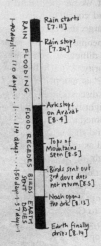

TIMING OF THE FLOOD

RAIN — 40 days
Rain starts [7.11]
Rain stops [7.24]

FLOODING — 110 days

FLOOD RECEDES — 114 days
Ark stops on Ararat [8.4]
Tops of Mountains seen [8.5]
Birds sent out 3rd dove does not return [8.5]

BIRDS SENT — 150 days
Noah opens the ark [8.13]

EARTH DRIES — 57 days
Earth finally dries [8.14]

Why is this important?

■ God is a God of judgment as well as mercy

■ It shows God's promise never to destroy the earth again

■ It introduces the '40 days' theme, which runs throughout the Bible.

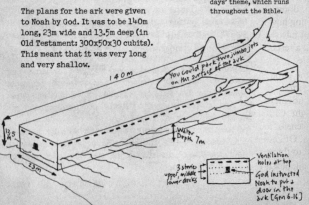

The plans for the ark were given to Noah by God. It was to be 140m long, 23m wide and 13.5m deep (in Old Testament: 300x50x30 cubits). This meant that it was very long and very shallow.

You could park two jumbo jets on the surface of the ark

140m

13.5m

23m

Water Depth 7m

3 stories upper, middle, lower decks

Ventilation holes at top

God instructed Noah to put a door in the ark [Gen 6.16]

Judgment

The Sights: Judgment
- [ ] No excuses: Psa 1.1–6
- [ ] He is coming to judge: Psa 98.1–9
- [ ] God's servant brings justice: Isa 42.1–4
- [ ] 'I don't like to punish': Joel 2.10–13
- [ ] What fruit do you bear?: Mt 7.15–23
- [ ] The son will be the judge: Jn 5.19–30
- [ ] He judges fairly: 2 Tim 4.6–8

God is a God of love. But he's also a God of **judgment**. We see this throughout the Bible, where God constantly reminds people that he's in charge; that he will judge.

Some people find the idea of a God of judgment difficult. They don't like the idea of superiority. 'What gives you the right to judge me?' is a question that is heard on every TV discussion show. To which God's answer might be 'I'm God. I made you.' The Bible is rooted in the fact that God created the heavens and the earth—He claims ownership. Jeremiah pictured God as the potter working the clay; and the craftsman has the right to do as he thinks fit with his creation [Jer 18.1–6].

But it's not just a power thing—God has the moral authority to judge. He is, after all, perfect. He is justice personified. So this is not a case of 'do as I say, not as I do'. We are all accountable to God for our actions. He put us here. He gave us tasks to do, and the resources with which to do them. He asks for our cooperation.

As human beings we have a natural hunger for justice. We hate it when things are unfair. If there is no judgment then those who commit evil deeds just get away with it. Would you really want the universe to be a place where evil is not punished, where people do not have to face up to their sins?

In the end, everyone will have to face up to the wrong things they have done. Despite the fact that he is a God of judgment, it's amazing how often in the Bible that judgment is deferred. We might have an image of a hellfire and brimstone God, but he is also a rescuer, a restorer, someone who never abandoned his people.

And the good news of the Christian gospel is that we can do that simply by saying sorry and starting again. God is a God of judgment but he's given everyone a chance to make things right. Christians believe we can come to Christ, to ask for forgiveness, to say 'sorry' and come back to a relationship with him. Of course, the repentance has to be real, but you'd be a fool to think you could fool God.

After all, he's a very good judge of people.

Why is this important?

■ It introduces the covenant—the promise between God and his people

■ It introduces us to Abraham, the great man of faith and ancestor of Israel

■ It starts the story of the nation of Israel—the people who were to descend from Abraham

God's promise [Gen 17]

This chapter is the culmination of several great promises that God makes to Abraham. It begins in chapter 12 where Abram (as he was then called) is living in Haran when God called him to go to a new land. God promises him that he will be the father of a great nation and asks him to go 'to a land I will show you'. So Abram obeys. Then in chapter 15 Abram begins to wonder what is happening with this promise. Old and childless, he wonders what is happening. In response, God shows him the stars and, in a dream, makes a covenant with him [Gen 15.12–21]. Along with the covenant ceremony, God introduces a historical perspective: he lays out the future for Abram. His people will be enslaved but will be released, and will eventually reach the Promised Land.

Now, later still, he confirms this dream with a face-to-face meeting. (Not quite face to face, because Abram falls to the floor 'face down' [Gen 17.3]).

This is a more personal agreement. There is an injunction on Abram to 'obey me and always do right' [Gen 17.1]. Abram has a responsibility as his part of the covenant. There is also the injunction to mark the covenant by circumcision, symbolising an allegiance to God. Crucially, there is also a name change, from Abram to Abraham. Part of this is to re-emphasise the promise—the longer form sounds a bit like 'father of many nations'. But part of it is to show that Abraham truly is 'under new ownership'. Kings and rulers had the right to change peoples' names—and there are plenty of instances of this in the Bible. Sarai also changes her name to Sarah—both names mean 'princess'—to signify this new start.

God outlines his plans to Abraham. Through Abraham he will establish great nations, nations that will bring a blessing to all the people of the world. In that sense, these chapters are a turning point. God has started to work through one man, and then through one people, to bring a blessing to all people.

Covenant

The solemn promise that God makes to Abraham is what was called a **covenant**.

A covenant was a legally binding agreement. In the Bible it refers to the agreement that God has made with mankind.

There are a number of covenants in the Bible. After the flood, God made an agreement with Noah never to destroy humanity in that way again [Gen 6.18]. God then promised Abraham that he would make a great nation our of Abraham's descendants. The agreement is sealed by **circumcision** [Gen 15 & 17].

> **The Sights: Covenant**
> ☐ Noah's promise: Gen. 9.7-17
> ☐ Abraham's promise: Gen. 17.1-22
> ☐ The promise to Moses: Ex 19.1-8
> ☐ It's coming: Jer 31.31-34
> ☐ It's here: Lk 22.14-20
> ☐ Celebrations: 1 Cor. 11.23-29
> ☐ Glory: 2Cor. 3.4-11

After rescuing the Israelites from Egypt, God makes a covenant with Moses. If the people obey him, they will be his people. God gives the Law, written on two large, flat stones. These stones are kept in 'the Ark of the Covenant', a special chest made out of acacia wood.

However, the Israelites never kept their side of the agreement. They worshipped false gods so God said that he would draw up a new agreement, which would not require rituals, sacrifices and circumcision, but would be written on the hearts and minds of the people [Jer 31.31–4].

This new agreement was brought into being through Jesus. He established it at the last supper [Mk 14.24] and sealed it with his death [Heb 8.8–13].

This idea is picked up in the two sections of the Bible, which use the word *Testamentum*—Latin for 'covenant'. So the two parts of the Bible are really the Old Agreement and the New Agreement.

Why is this important?

■ It introduces the Old Testament name of God—Yahweh

■ It shows God's special relationship with Moses

■ It reminds us of God's promise to rescue Israel

God meets Moses [Ex 3.1–22]

Exodus chapter 3 contains one of the most vivid and important scenes of the entire Bible. Moses is something of a lost figure. After attacking a guard who was beating a Hebrew slave, he is forced to flee to Midian, a remote region, where he is works as a sheep-farmer in the desert.

God, here described as '**the angel of the Lord**', appears to Moses in the guise of a **burning bush**. After Moses takes off his shoes—because he is on holy ground—God identifies himself and assures Moses that he has heard the cry of his people [Ex 3.7–10]. Moses is given the task of leading the Israelites out of Egypt, but the Lord will be with him. Moses asks God his name. God tells Moses that his name is '**I Am**' [Ex 3.14].

The Name of God

Yahweh is the key Old Testament name for God. It is always written in Scriptures as YHWH, and never uttered by the Jews out of reverence for God. (Some modern Jewish writers maintain this tradition and write G-d instead of God.)

Some experts believe that the name doesn't, in fact, mean anything. Others believe that it means 'he causes to be what exists' and refers to God as creator. Instead of printing Yahweh or YHWH, most modern Bibles use 'the Lord'.

The Bible uses loads of images to describe what God is like. Examples include a rock (Ex 7.1–7), a shepherd (Psa 23.1), a stronghold (Psa 18.2), a refuge (Psa 37.39) and a redeemer (Isa 41.14).

Jesus uses perhaps the most potent image, which is that of a father (Mt 6.25–27).

The name is important. God is in the present tense. He has no beginning and no end, he simply is. He is always there, dependable, reliable, faithful, present among his people. (Jesus was later to apply the phrase to himself—unmistakably identifying himself with God [Jn 8.58–59].)

The act of telling Moses his name is also important. To us, this doesn't seem such a radical action, but in Old Testament terms, names were believed to have power. To know someone's real name was to know their true nature—to *understand* them—and therefore have power over them. When God reveals his name to Moses he is entering into a deep relationship with his people. He is, to some extent, making himself vulnerable.

Moses is to return to Egypt, assemble the elders (the word used is literally 'bearded ones') and tell them that God has not forgotten them and he will take them home.

Holiness

Moses is instructed not to get too near the burning bush, and to take off his sandals, because he is standing on 'holy ground'.

It is not that the ground is special in itself. There was probably nothing special about this bush, just as, later, there was nothing inherently special about the stones used to make the Temple. What made this place special was the presence of God. Muslims still follow this practice when they enter a mosque.

'**Holy**' means 'set apart'. God is holy because he is set apart from the world and from sinful humanity. There is something different about God and that is, well, he's completely different. His holiness is seen in the fact that he is absolutely, completely perfect.

> ### The Sights: Holiness
> ☐ You will be my holy nation: Ex 19.1–8
> ☐ The holy Sabbath: Ex 31.12–17
> ☐ Be holy like I'm holy: Lev 19.1–3
> ☐ How to be holy: Psa 15.1–5
> ☐ Who compares to God?: Isa 40.25–31
> ☐ Not merely human: Hos 11.8–11
> ☐ Holy slaves: Rom 6.17–23
> ☐ Chosen for holiness: 1 Cor 1.26–31
> ☐ Made holy to do good: 2 Tim 2.20–21
> ☐ Live a holy life: 1 Pet 1.13–25

In the Old Testament, you could have **holy places** which were specially set aside for worshipping God. You could even have holy time; the **Sabbath**, for example, was a day set apart and dedicated to God. Or you could have holy people. Israel was supposed to be a **holy nation**, set apart from the rest of the people on earth and totally dedicated to God.

Pure holiness was often a frightening experience for those encountering it. Moses' first thought is to hide his face. There were times when the Ark of the Covenant—a holy object—had a dangerous, frightening power. It was raw holiness at work [1 Sam 6.19; 2 Sam 6.6–10].

Christians are called to be holy. We too have been set aside for God, to be used by Him. Our values and our behaviour must be radically different to the world around us. We have been chosen by God to be different, to follow a different set of values, to obey God's rules, to put our faith in him. We are called to pursue purity.

We are called, in fact, to be holy.

Why is this
important?

■ It shows how God
rescued Israel
from Egypt

■ It introduces
the idea of the
Passover—a
Jewish festival
still celebrated
today

The Passover [Ex 11.1–13.16]

The Israelites were enslaved in Egypt. God had sent **nine plagues** to persuade Pharaoh to let the people go. Now comes the final, most terrible punishment. God tells Moses that he will pass through the country, and the first-born sons of the Egyptians will die. God will be accompanied by another being, called simply 'the destroyer' [Ex 12.23 NIV]. The death of the first-born seems an extreme, even brutal act, but we should remember that the Pharaoh had done exactly the same thing to the sons of the Israelites [Ex 1.22].

To protect themselves, every Israelite household is to take a lamb, slaughter it, paint their doorposts with blood and then eat the meat together. Houses marked in this way will be '**passed over**' by the devastation. The Israelites obey the instructions and that night the first-born sons of the Egyptians die. Pharaoh tells Moses and his people to get out quick.

Chapter 12 includes instructions on how they are to celebrate this event in the future—possibly inserted here by a later editor. Indeed, the **Passover** became a defining ritual for the Jews. Passover (or 'Pesach' as it is called in Hebrew) is still celebrated today by Jewish families. It is followed by the week-long **Feast of Thin Bread**, commemorating the speed with which the Israelites had to leave Egypt.

Although there were long periods when the Israelites did not celebrate Passover, by the time of Jesus it had become a significant ritual. At first, the Passover was held in peoples' homes, but in New Testament times people went to Jerusalem to celebrate it at the Temple.

Passover Timetable

Passover took place in the month of Nisan (March/April)

10th NISAN

Select your animal and set aside for safekeeping. Must be an unblemished one-year old goat or lamb (Ex 12.5) or could be a calf (Deut 16.7).

14th NISAN

1. Late in the afternoon, slaughter the animal.

2. Spread blood of the animal on the doorposts and lintels of the houses.

3. Roast the animal, whole.

4. With your family or household, eat the meat, along with some bitter herbs and unleavened bread.

15th NISAN

Early in the morning, burn any uneaten meat.

Initially all this could be done at home. By the time of Jesus, it became the custom to take the animals to the Temple for slaughtering by the priests. The animal was then taken home and roasted and the meal happened as follows:

1. Eat the meat along with some herbs, a dip made of pounded nuts and fruits mixed with vinegar and four cups of wine.

2. After the second cup of wine, a son would ask the father 'why is this night different from all other nights?' and the father would tell the story of Deut 26.5–11.

3. Psalm 113 (or 113–114) would be sung.

4. After the fourth cup Psalms 115–118 would be sung.

Sacrifice

Just as God had taken away the Egyptian first-born, God instructed the Israelites to give him their first-born sheep, goats, etc. in sacrifice.

Sacrifice was a common feature of ancient religions. The idea of giving an offering to your god was widespread. The earliest sacrifices in the Bible are the gift-offerings of Cain and Abel, and the burnt-offering of Noah.

Sacrifices were generally placed on an **altar**. They were offered as thanksgiving to God, or to honour him or to make restitution for sins. After the exodus, the sacrifices were organised into a complex system with different sacrifices done at different times, for different purposes.

Although the sacrificial system continued into the time of Jesus, Christians came to believe that his advent made sacrifices unnecessary. He *was* the sacrifice for all of us. Even before then, a number of Old Testament prophets had begun to challenge the system, pointing out that what God really wanted was not the old ritual, but meaningful sacrifice. Amos pointed out that the sacrifice that God really wanted was a contrite heart.

In the end the sacrifice system ended with the destruction of the Temple in 70AD. Without a temple, there was no place to sacrifice.

18-20 in
46-51 cm

Note the 'horns'. Joab clung to the horns of the altar when seeking sanctuary (1 Kings 2.28)

STONE ALTAR
This is a sketch of a typical stone altar from Old Testament times. Made of hewn limestone, altars of this type have been found at many Old Testament sites such as Beersheba and Megiddo.

The Ten Commandments [Deut 5.1–32]

The **Ten Commandments** form the basis for most of the legal sys-
tems of our world. Not bad for something written on the top
of a mountain 3,500 years ago!

In Deuteronomy, Moses is giving a kind of farewell speech
to the Israelites, and here he reminds them of these crucial
commandments. He calls them a covenant between God and
Israel [Deut 5.2–3], a covenant like the one with Abraham, but
made with all the people, instead of just one man.

They begin with a bit of history: 'I am the Lord your God,
the one who brought you out of Egypt where you were slaves'
[Deut 5.6]. This is crucial. God is not promising to rescue the
Israelites if they are good boys and girls; he has *already* rescued
them. Obedience to God is a response to the concern and love
he has already shown.

The root of all theses commandments is the first one: '**Do not
worship any god except me**' [Deut 5.7]. No god, real or imagined, is to
take the place of the one true God.

Most of these commands are pretty straightforward, but
some need a little more interpretation. 'Respecting' your father and mother [Deut 5.16], means 'honouring', 'prizing highly',
or 'caring about' your parents. It doesn't mean they're always
right, it means that we have obligations towards them. And
'misusing the Lord's name' [Deut 5.11] means more than not using 'God' or 'Jesus' as any kind of exclamation or swear word.
It means not swearing falsely on God's name in court; nor
using it as some kind of cheap magic formula. God demands
to be taken seriously. And that means not using his name in
wrong ways.

The Ten Commandments are at the heart of Israel's relationship with God, summing up in broad strokes what God
expects of his people. In keeping with the customs of the area,
the agreement was inscribed on **two stone tablets**. These were
duplicates, the idea being that each party kept one tablet, like
copies of a contract. In Israel's case, both tablets were kept in
the **Ark of the Covenant** and carried around with them.

The Law

The ten commandments are the root of 'the law'—the rules which God gave to the Israelites to tell them how to run their lives. But why were all these rules and regulations necessary?

First, the law was about **justice**, about fair treatment for all, regardless of wealth or status, from caring for refugees [Ex 22.21] to leaving food for the poor [Lev 19.9–10] and caring for widows and orphans [Ex 22.22–4].

The laws also dealt with **health issues** such as skin diseases, avoiding eating foods such as pork and seafood and what to do with infectious people [Lev 13].

Much of the law defined **social and family behaviour**—covering such things as crime and punishment, sexual relationships, how you treat your slaves, even what to do if you borrow a donkey and it gets stolen [Ex 22.10].

There were many laws governing **worship**. Israel was not supposed to act in the same way as the nations around it; the laws about the priestly functions were to keep Israel focused on God.

A lot of the law is about offering **sacrifice** to say 'sorry' for different types of sins. There is also a great day of forgiveness, a time when the whole nation would ask forgiveness for their sins [Lev 16.1–34].

The law defined Israel. It was what made her different from all the nations around. Too often in her history, of course, she abandoned it—thus becoming just like everyone else.

The Sights: Sacrifice

- ☐ The first sacrifice: Gen 4.1–16
- ☐ The Israelites bring sacrifices: Num 7.1–89
- ☐ The sacrifices that God really wants: Ps 50.1–23
- ☐ Meaningless sacrifice: Hos 8.11–14
- ☐ The widow's offering: Mk 12.41–44
- ☐ Once and for all: Heb 7.26–28
- ☐ Our sacrifice today: Heb 13.15–16

Clean and Unclean

The law placed a great emphasis on the idea of clean and unclean. Various things made a person clean or unclean.

Contact with a dead person (Num 19.11–22) made you unclean, because the dead body represented the ultimate consequence of sin. Any **disease which affected the skin**—even their house or clothing—rendered them unclean (Lev 13–14). Certain natural bodily functions or discharges made someone unclean.

Certain **foods** like shellfish or pork—foods which even today have to be cooked carefully to avoid food poisoning—were declared unclean. For a nomadic people it was very important to keep healthy.

Generally, the **cure for uncleanness** was bathing of the body and washing the clothes, or by undergoing certain ritual healing, involving sacrifice and prayer.

Why is this importantͦ

- It is one of the most remarkable pieces of social law in history
- It introduces the idea of the jubilee—the year of the Lord's favour, picked up by Jesus
- It shapes social justice activities today—particularly in debt relief

The Jubilee [Lev 25]

Leviticus contains one of the most amazing pieces of social law in history: the **Jubilee**. Every seven years the land was allowed a year off. And every fiftieth year—that is, the year after seven lots of seven years—the entire social structure of Israel was to be reset.

The **seventh year** was a chance for the land to recover. Every gardener or farmer knows you have to allow the soil to replenish itself, and by giving the land its own Sabbath, the soil would be renewed and reinvigorated. So it's an intensely practical rule.

But this goes way beyond some kind of ancient crop-rotation. The seven-year rule was also applied to other things. Hebrew slaves were only to be kept for six years; in the seventh year they were to be freed [Ex 21.2]. Debts were also to be cancelled in the Sabbath year [Deut 15.1–11].

And then after fifty years, (i.e. seven lots of seven) came the jubilee—the year of celebration. This was a kind of 'Sabbath of Sabbaths', in which most of the property (although not houses inside walled cities) was to revert to its original owners [Lev 25.18–34]. Slaves would be released and could return to their homes. Everyone, no matter what their status, would have the chance to start again. It's like pressing the reset button on your computer. It sets everything back to how it was when you first unpacked the thing.

The aim of the jubilee was simply to eradicate poverty among the people of God [Deut 15.4]. God wants his people and their land to be radically different from those around them. Not surprisingly, this rule was hardly ever obeyed. The only time in the Bible that it is reported as occurring, the slaves were freed—and then immediately taken back into slavery [Jer 34.8–22].

Justice

The Bible is packed with verses telling us of God's concern for the poor, the refugee, the outcast, the prisoner, the despised, the hungry. It is concerned about **justice**. This is not just about looking after the poor and needy [Deut 24.19–22; 14.28–29]. It also covers things like not stealing land by moving boundary stones [Deut 19.14], or tampering with the scales so as to make more money [Lev 19.35].

The people of Israel were not very good at obeying these instructions, leading to intense criticism from prophets such as Amos and Isaiah, who condemned them for crushing the poor, while living in luxury.

Jesus echoed this by reaching out to those who were at the bottom of the pile. When he preached to the people of his home town, he chose a passage on social justice from **Isaiah** to explain why he had come [Lk 4.18–19] and he referred to the jubilee.

SABBATH

The jubilee legislation is rooted in the idea of **Sabbath**. 'Sabbath' means 'to stop work' and that's the basic point. The Sabbath day is a time to rest.

The Sabbath is also about reflection. It gives people space to think about God, to look at their lives. It reflects our priorities. The prophets were strong on their insistence on observing the Sabbath, because it was a sign of what was important.

Over time, the laws about what Jews could or couldn't do on the Sabbath became so complex that the focus of the day switched away from God and onto the rules themselves. It was this attitude that was challenged by Jesus (Mk 2.28).

The Jews were instructed to observe the Sabbath on the seventh day of the week. From very early on Christians chose to move their Sabbath to the first day of the week, in honour of Jesus rising again on a Sunday (1 Cor 16.2).

**Why is this
important?**

■ It's one of the
most beautiful
poems ever
written

■ It sums up the
caring, personal
aspect of God

■ It shows us the
idea of God as
a shepherd—an
image which was
to be used by
Jesus

The Lord is My Shepherd [Psa 23]

Psalm 23 is one of the best-loved and most famous passages in the Bible. Partly this is due to the sheer beauty of its language and imagery; like so many of the Psalms, it's a great poem which, in just a few verses, conjures up rich images of care and protection of still pools and quiet pastures, of an oasis of calm, care and trust.

But it also shows that the Psalms are more than merley poems. Israel tended to forget that the God of their people was also the God of individuals. This Psalm reminds us that the relationship was personal.

It shows this through the use of the 'shepherd' metaphor for God [Psa 23.2–4]. The shepherd was personally involved with the care of his sheep. He would lead them to good, rich pasture and provide them with still wells and pools where they could safely drink [Psa 23.2]. He would lead them along safe paths through dangerous, dark ravines [Psa 23.3–4]. He would carry a rod with which to beat off wild animals, and a staff—a shepherd's crook—to control the flock. This strong image of care and guidance was an image that was used by prophets such as Isaiah and Jeremiah and that Jesus was to apply to himself [Jn 10.11].

Then the image changes and the Lord becomes a host at a banquet [Psa 23.5–6]. Before they entered a feast, the host would anoinit the most honoured guests with perfumed oil—usually perfumes added to the finest olive oil. We are honoured guests at a banquet, where the wine overflows the cups, where those who have been attacked are vindicated [Psa 23.5] and where we live in peace and comfort forever. This heavenly image is picked up in Revelation, where the shepherd guides his sheep to springs of living water and wipes away their tears [Rev 7.17].

That's why this Psalm is so popular—it gives us a glimpse of what it means to be loved and cared for by God, and what it means to live with Him forever.

SYRIAN SHEPHERD
CARRYING A LAMB ON HIS SHOULDERS

Prayer

The Bible is full of people at **prayer**. They pray as individuals, as small groups and as nations. They pray in times of panic and distress, in times of goodness and thankfulness. Sometimes they cry aloud at God, sometimes they sit and listen.

In the Bible, prayer is more than just asking; it's also worshipping God, confessing to God, thanking God... it's really being in a relationship with God.

Prayer is relating to the father, and, as any good father will tell you, sometimes your children will ask you for things, sometimes they'll tell you things, sometimes they'll just sit on your knee.

So prayer is about more than asking. It's about spending time in God's presence. You might have things you want to talk about with God, you might have requests you want to make for other people. (If you want to see prayer in all its variety, dip into Psalms. Psalms is 'prayer unlimited'.)

The Sights: Prayer

☐ A cry for help: Psa 5.1–12
☐ Worshipping God: Psa 8.1–9
☐ Solomon prays: 1 Kings 8.22–61
☐ Prayer for success: 2 Chr 20.1–30
☐ A nation confesses: Ezr 9.5–15
☐ Job begs God: Job 7.7–21
☐ The majesty of God: Psa 104
☐ A prayer of trust: Psa 11.1–7
☐ The awesome God: Hab 3.1–19
☐ Prayer of faith: Mt 21.18–22
☐ Jesus' prayer: Jn 17.1–26
☐ How to pray: Mt 6.5–18
☐ Paul gives thanks: Col 1.9–23
☐ Good times or bad: Jas 5.13–18

Hebrew Poetry

Hebrew poetry rhymes not words but ideas.

In <u>parallelism</u>, an idea is stated and then 'rhymed' with a parallel statement balancing the first.

The Lord is a shelter for the oppressed,
 A refuge in times of trouble. (Psa 9.9)

In <u>completion</u>, the second half of the 'rhyme' completes the first part.

The Lord is my light and my salvation
 —So why should I be afraid? (Psa 27.1)

In <u>contrast</u>, the second half of the 'rhyme' contrasts with and strengthens the first half.

The LORD protects everyone who follows him,
 but the wicked follow a road that leads to ruin. (Psa 1.6)

There are other kinds of 'rhyme' within the Psalms and other poetry, but those three are the main types.

Why is this
important?

■ It shows who
made the world
and universe

■ It shows what
humanity's
relationship
with God should
be like

■ It shows what
humanity's
relationship
with the rest
of creation
should be

The Suffering Servant [Isa 53]

Isaiah is a book that is shot through with the promise of the **Messiah**—the great, anointed one who will rescue Israel.

However, the picture of the Messiah in Isaiah is not necessarily that of a **warrior-prince**, which is how most people of the time imagined him. There is a different note.

In chapter 49, Isaiah likens the nation of Israel to a bad servant [Isa 49.1–6]. He contrasts that with another servant, a strange figure, one who has come to teach, yet who is beaten and tortured, one whom Isaiah describes in a series of 'servant songs' [Isa 50.4–11]. This is a **suffering, ill-treated servant**, beaten until he looks scarcely human [Isa 52.13–53.12]. People look on him and 'think about things they have never seen or thought about before' [Isa 52.15].

This picture culminates in Isaiah 53, where this person is described in more detail. He is a figure of hatred and rejection, there is nothing about him that is attractive according to the world's values. He comes from humble beginnings [Isa 53.1–3]. And it is for *us* that he is suffering, for God's people. For **our sins** he has been wounded and crushed; to bring us back to God he took our punishment.

He is likened to a sacrificial lamb, a guilt offering [Isa 53.10; Lev 5.16]. He makes no complaint, and, although innocent, takes his place among the guilty for our sake [Isa 53.9, 12].

Isaiah 53 is the high point of messianic prediction. It throws out the old images of a mighty warrior who would drive the enemies out by force; this is a figure working at a far deeper, more mysterious level, and fighting a far more deadly enemy.

The final verse of chapter 53 contains a powerful, stunning promise: 'The LORD will reward him with honour and power for sacrificing his life. Others thought he was a sinner, but he suffered for our sins and asked God to forgive us.' This historical figure would undergo the punishment on behalf of everyone.

And his name was Jesus.

Messiah

Messiah is a Hebrew word which means 'anointed'. The Greek word for 'anointed' is christos, from which we get Christ.

For centuries, Israel had been looking for someone to rescue them from their enemies. Prophets in the Old Testament began to predict a Messiah, a special saviour sent from God to drive out the oppressors and free Israel.

They were looking for a **warrior**, a military leader, a mighty hero in the mould of **King David**, and when the Romans took over the country, their longing for a Messiah became even more acute. Before Jesus there had been others who claimed the title. All of them were failures and their revolutions were brutally suppressed.

Then came **Jesus**. His followers believed he was the Messiah, but he didn't look much like they expected. He wasn't a military leader; he wasn't leading an armed uprising. And Jesus himself tried to play down these expectations. He didn't like to be called Messiah. It wasn't because he wasn't the Messiah; it was because he wanted to distance himself from the stereotypes. He was preaching a revolutionary message and he was setting up a new kingdom, but it was not in the way that the Jews were expecting.

After his death and resurrection, the secret was out. Christians saw how the many **Old Testament prophecies** of the Messiah had been fulfilled in Jesus. Jesus really was the Christ, the anointed one, the Messiah. He rescued people from their sins. He defeated not the Romans, but death.

This door panel from the Roman church of San Sabina dates from the fifth century and is probably the earliest known depiction of the crucifixion.

**Why is this
important?**

■ It describes the
birth of Jesus

■ It shows how
Jesus came to
an ordinary
family in an
extraordinary
way

■ It's the root of
the Christian
festival of
Christmas

The birth of Jesus [Lk 1.23–2.39]

Matthew simply records that Jesus was born in **Bethlehem**.
Luke gives us the reason why he was there: his father went
to fill in the **census**. Luke assigns the census to the time when
Quirinus was governor of Syria, but this would place it in
6 or 7AD, which is probably too late. Luke could mean 'before'
Quirinus, or he could simply have got his censuses confused.
There is evidence of a similar census in Egypt some years later, and Luke is a reliable historian. The likely **date of Jesus' birth** is
around 4BC, just before the death of Herod the Great.

Luke's story emphasises the poverty of the event and those
who attended it. Luke is the most socially aware Gospel. **Mary's
song** celebrated the fact that God's grace was being showered
on someone who was poor [Lk 1.46–55]. Jesus came from poor
parents—Joseph had to offer the poor man's offering when he
visited the Temple [Lk 2.24].

Where Matthew brought us the rich, powerful **magi** [Mt 2.1–
12], Luke brings us the humble **shepherds** [Lk 2.8–17]. Just as Jesus'
birth was given to a poor family, the news is given first to some
of the poorest people in Palestine—the shepherds, sitting out
on the dark hills.

Luke's picture is of
a birth in makeshift
accommodation, of a
baby lying in the filth
of an animal's feeding
trough, of the news
being presented to the
poor and excluded. It
was good news for all
people—but especial-
ly the poor.

Incarnation

The Bible claims that God took the form of a human being; that the ruler of the universe squeezed himself into human form. What he did was called incarnation: it means simply to appear in person. God took human form and lived among humans.

Incarnation means that God **understands** what it is like to be a human, because he has been a human. Jesus was a human being like we are. He knew what it meant to be tempted, to be tired, to be lonely, to laugh, to drink, to sweat, to die.

Second, incarnation means that Jesus could **demonstrate** to us how we should live. He didn't issue a set of instructions from 'on high' he lived it out; he 'walked the talk', providing a model that we should follow.

Finally, the incarnation should **inspire** Christians to do the same. If God came and lived alongside us, we cannot stand aloof from the rest of humanity. It's the job of Christians to make God present in the world. With the help of the Holy Spirit, Christians can make God real to people through their faith and actions. God is still incarnate in the world. He walks this earth in the lives of his followers.

The Church of the Nativity at Bethlehem is one of the oldest churches in the world. It was built over the traditional site of Jesus' birth, a site which is marked by a 14-pointed 'Bethlehem' star

Why is this important?

- It shows the beginning of Jesus' ministry

- It introduces us to the work of John the Baptist

- It shows the origin of the Christian practice of baptism

- It introduces the concept of the trinity

Baptism of Jesus [Mt 3.1–17]

This is the start of Jesus' ministry. He comes to **John the Baptist**, not because he needs to repent (indeed, John feels completely unworthy to perform the baptism) but because it demonstrates to others what they ought to do and announces the arrival of the Messiah.

Baptism is a term which first appears in the New Testament. A purification ritual, it was the most prominent feature of the work of John the Baptist (hence the name). John bathed or washed people in the river Jordan; he encouraged people to make a public sign that they were asking for forgiveness and going to start again. Jesus instructed his followers to go into the world, make disciples, baptise them and teach them to follow him [Mt 28.19–20].

From the very early days of the church, baptism was seen as the entry point. If you wanted to join the early Church (from about the 2nd century onwards) you first became a *catuchemen*, which meant that you were undergoing instruction in the faith. Only after completing this were you baptised, and only then could you take part in the eucharist.

This basic pattern—of learning about Jesus, of being baptised and then joining his followers, is still followed by most Christian traditions today. Different church traditions baptise in different ways, but the act itself symbolises two main things: washing away sins and new life.

Baptism symbolises the **washing away of sin**. If you ask God for forgiveness, he will wash you clean. Baptism shows to others that you have made a conscious decision to ask for forgiveness and that God has washed away all your sins.

Baptism also symbolises **new life**. Paul said that when people were baptised, they 'died and were buried with Christ' [Rom 6.4]. In other words baptism is like washing away the old life and starting a new one. The old you has been drowned; the new you has risen from the water.

Trinity

Jesus' baptism brings together an appearance of the **Trinity**—the father speaking from heaven, the Spirit descending on the Son. By the Trinity we mean the fact that the **Father, the Son and the Holy Spirit are one**; that they are all, in fact, different aspects of God.

In fact, the Bible nowhere directly mentions the Trinity, or even use the word. But the idea is implied throughout the Bible.

Jesus claimed to be God. He forgave sins, God called him his 'son' and he used the phrase 'I Am' to describe himself. Every good Jew knew that 'I Am' was God's name, as revealed to Moses. Most of all, he defeated death and came back to life. When Thomas saw the risen Jesus, he said, 'My Lord and my God!' John's gospel makes it clear that Jesus was with God from the very start of all things.

After Jesus left earth, **the Holy Spirit came from God**. The Holy Spirit gave power, energy and guidance and Christians were told that he would be with them forever. So the early Church came to the conclusion that the Holy Spirit was an equal partner with Jesus and God the Father.

Although the Bible doesn't mention 'trinity', there are many occasions where **the three names are linked together**. At Jesus' baptism, God pronounced him his son and the Holy Spirit came to rest on him. Jesus talks about the Spirit coming from the father [Jn 15.26] and Paul also frequently links them together [e.g. 2 Cor 13.14].

The Lateran Baptistery in Rome is probably the oldest Christian building still in regular use. It was built in 440AD for baptising new believers and contains a huge octagonal marble basin which was fed by a natural spring, since the early Church believed you should be fully immersed in running water. Baptistries at this time were big, because baptisms only happened three times a year and the Bishop baptised all those in his diocese who were ready.

The Sermon on the Mount

STRUCTURE OF
THE SERMON
ON THE MOUNT

The Sermon on the Mount is not a sermon as we would understand it. Matthew describes it as 'teaching' (Mt 5.2; 7.28). It may have been delivered on one specific occasion or Matthew may have drawn together a collection of Jesus' teaching and sayings and combined them into one event.

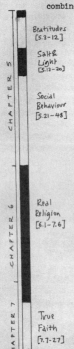

CHAPTER 5

Beatitudes
[5.3-12]

The upside-down kingdom of God, where the citizens are vulnerable, poor and humble.

**Salt &
Light**
[5.12-20]

Salt to flavour and preserve; light to scatter the darkness; the law written on our hearts.

**Social
Behaviour**
[5.21-48]

Also known as the 'antitheses', this section has statements which contrast the world's way of doing things with God's approach. 'You have heard this,' says Jesus, 'but I say this...'
Sections cover anger (5.21-6), adultery (5.29-30), divorce (5.31-2), oath-taking (5.23-7), revenge (5.38-42) and culminating in the injunction on us to love our enemies (5.43-8).

CHAPTER 6

**Real
Religion**
[6.1-7.6]

What does real religion look like? Jesus outlines what he demands of his followers, covering giving (6.1-4), prayer (6.9-13), fasting (6.16-18), wealth (6.19-24), anxiety (6.25-34) and judging others (7.1-6).

CHAPTER 7

**True
Faith**
[7.7-27]

True faith is shown in our behaviour—the 'fruit' that we produce. Not many will travel this road, or build on these foundations; but those who do will find life. Sections cover trusting God (7.7-12), choosing wisely (7.13-14), living up to the words (7.15-23) and putting Jesus' words into practice (7.24-7).

Material that is brought together by Matthew is much more widely distributed in Luke, who has a much shorter 'Sermon on the Plain'.

Matt	Luke
5.3-12	6.20-3
5.25-6	12.58-9
5.39-42	6.27-30
6.9-13	11.2-4
6.22-3	11.34-6
6.25-33	12.22-31
7.1-5	6.37-42
7.7-11	11.9-13
7.12	6.31
7.16-20	6.43-5
7.24-7	6.47-9

Why is this important?

- It's Jesus' manifesto—his programme for the kingdom of God
- It contains the beatitudes—Jesus' declaration of who really counts in the kingdom
- It contains the core ethical and moral beliefs of the Christian faith

The Kingdom of God

It was Augustine who first called it 'the Sermon on the Mount'. But it's much more like the 'Manifesto on the Mount', for it contains the rules of the Kingdom of God, the values by which the kingdom of God will overthrow the kingdom of man.

The teaching is addressed to 'the disciples', i.e. anyone who followed Jesus. Among the material included is **the Lord's Prayer** [6.9–13]——actually a misnomer, since it is the disciples' prayer—and the **'golden rule'** [7.12], where Jesus distils the entire Old Testament into eleven words!

The sermon deals with relationships—horizontal (our relationships with each other) and vertical (our relationship with God). It's a picture of God's upside-down kingdom, where the poor are blessed, the humble rewarded and the discarded and dispossessed are cherished by God.

The kingdom is a key feature in Jesus' teaching. This was a kingdom which was both present and still arriving. Sometimes He told people that they were virtually standing in the kingdom [Lk 17.20-21], other times it was clear that God's rule was still to come [Lk 11.1–4]. Significantly, Jesus likened the kingdom to **a seed growing**, or **yeast** working through dough [Mt 13.31–33]—it was small, but potent, still to reach fullness, but alive and working here and now.

And who were the citizens of this realm? They were the ordinary people, the people who lived in places like Galilee, oppressed by poverty and debt, mourning their loved ones, living with low expectations. For these, the Kingdom was not just a load of ideas; it came with **practical good news**. People were healed and freed from oppression and fed. There was equality and an inner peace born of the knowledge that it was God who really ruled the world. No wonder the authorities—the rulers of this world—were worried.

They still are. Today Christians are still God's ambassadors, representatives of His kingdom, living by a different set of rules and inviting those who feel alienated, alone and marginalised to a kingdom where they can truly be free.

Why is this
important?

■ It shows Jesus'
message of
forgiveness

■ It demonstrates
the fatherlike
qualities of God

■ It's one of the
best stories ever
told!

The Prodigal Son [Lk 15.11–31]

This is the second of the great stories that are unique to Luke
(the other one is the Good Samaritan) and one of the best
stories ever told. It continues the theme of two other parables
in this chapter—the lost sheep and lost coin—but this time it
is a person who is lost. The traditional title refers to the sons
'prodigality', an old word meaning reckless extravagance.

He gets his inheritance before his father has even died—which
is a bit unusual to say the least. And then he leaves, taking
everything, 'all he had' [Lk 15.13]. This is a final departure, he is
not coming back. Although first we find
he spends the money in 'wild living' later
on his brother is more specific [Lk 15.30].
Soon, however, the money goes, the famine bites and he is forced into working as
a pig-keeper. This, for a Jewish audience,
would have been about as low as it gets,
for pigs are unclean animals [Lev 11.7].

Then he comes to his senses. He can
return to work as a servant for his father.
Yet when he returns his father dresses
him in finery and throws a huge party to
celebrate. There are no recriminations,
just forgiveness and unwavering love and
an old man who is so happy to see his
son; the story of an old man who does
not mind looking foolish, but who rushes
towards his son and hugs and kisses him.
God does not stand on his dignity when
it comes to returning sinners.

The attitude of the elder son is the attitude of all those who want to keep the
kingdom of God for the 'right' kind of
people. It is the attitude of the Pharisees, of those who condemned Jesus for
spending time with prostitutes and tax
collectors. They said that those who ran
from God should not receive his love. Jesus shows that, if they repent, God runs
towards them.

Forgiveness and Grace

The Bible is full of people making a mess of things. It's full of the bad things in life: violence, betrayal, deceit, despair. But if there are bad things, there is also **forgiveness**. And God wants to forgive us for the bad things we do.

Repenting—saying 'sorry' to God—is the first thing you do when you become a Christian, but we need to keep on doing it. Once we turn to him, we can receive forgiveness, because God is a god of **grace**. God's grace means that we can be saved because Christ has died for us. Someone once defined Grace as 'God's Riches At Christ's Expense'. Because **Christ has died for us**, we can receive God's gift of eternal life.

> **The Sights: Forgiveness**
> ☐ God's forgiveness: Neh 9.16–31
> ☐ Confession: Psa 32.1–11
> ☐ Wash us clean: Psa 51.1–19
> ☐ How to keep friends: Prov 17.9
> ☐ Turn to the Lord: Isa 55.7–13
> ☐ Forgive and forget: Jer 31.31–37
> ☐ Love your enemies: Mt 5.38–48
> ☐ 70 x 7: Mt 18.21–35
> ☐ In your eye: Lk 6.37–42
> ☐ On the cross: Lk 23.26–43
> ☐ All the same: Acts 15.7–11
> ☐ God's gift to us: Rom 5.14–21
> ☐ Death to life: Eph 2.1–10
> ☐ For all people: Tit 2.11–14
> ☐ Forgive others: 2 Cor 2.5–11
> ☐ Living in light: 1 Jn 1.1–2.2

It's not that we've done anything to deserve this. In fact, there was nothing we could do. No, God has given us this gift because he loves us. In his letter to Ephesians, Paul writes 'You were saved by faith in God, who treats us much better than we deserve. This is **God's gift to you**, and not anything you have done on your own' [Eph 2.8].

It's God's grace that makes us right with him. God's grace is patient. He does not want to punish people, he wants to give everyone the chance to receive this gift. But people do have to choose to receive it. The result of this grace is that we will live eternally with God. No matter how much we sin, if we turn to God and say sorry, his gift will still be there.

And if we Christians have been forgiven, then we need to forgive others. Christianity means nothing if it isn't lived out in our lives and Jesus gives us several warning stories that, if God forgives us, we should forgive others [Mt 6.12,14; 18.21–35; Lk 6.37].

**Why is this
important?**

■ It shows who
made the world
and universe

■ It shows what
humanity's
relationship
with God should
be like

■ It shows what
humanity's
relationship
with the rest
of creation
should be

The Last Supper [Mt 26.17-30]

The meal that we call **the Last Supper** appears in all the Gospels, although there are some differences between the accounts. It also appears in one of Paul's letters [1Cor 11.23-26] showing that the event was well known in the early Church.

Matthew, Mark and Luke are clear that this was the **Passover meal**; John states that it was the night before. Experts are divided on the issue. Like a Passover, it was an evening meal, when the Jewish main meal was usually in the afternoon. It shares some of the same dishes, and closes with a hymn—which would have been Psalms 114 or 115–118 [Mk 14.26; Matt 26.30].

Whatever the case, it certainly has a Passover atmosphere. But it has some other key aspects. It was a meal of **acceptance**—Jesus regularly shared meals with people who were considered 'sinners'. It was a meal of **thanksgiving** (which was a part of every Jewish meal) and it was a meal to say **farewell**.

Jesus knows he is going to die. He even indicates which disciple is going to betray him—and **Judas Iscariot** slips out halfway through to organise the deed. During the supper, Jesus gives his disciples some important teaching concerning what is going to happen and how the Holy Spirit will come to help them. Before the meal, Jesus **washes the feet** of his disciples. In those days, the streets were filled with filth, there was animal dung—and worse—to be dodged, and you were only wearing sandals. So the person who had to wash the feet had one of the worst jobs. Jesus does this to indicate that his kingdom is not a place of prestige, but of service.

Jesus takes **bread** and **wine**. He says that the bread is his 'body' and the wine is his 'blood'. He asks that the disciples eat and drink these to remember him. It seems that Jesus intended his followers to copy him and that is also reflected in his choice of the elements—by choosing foodstuffs as basic as bread and wine, he made it easy for ordinary people to take part, and for ordinary people to remember that through his death, God had made a new covenant with his people [Lk 22.20].

Communion

The earliest account of the last supper actually comes from Paul's letter to the Corinthians, written around 50AD [1 Cor 10.17]. The point of the meal, according to Paul, was to bring people together in shared remembrance [1 Cor 10.17]. By then, the Church had turned this event into their most significant ritual, a celebration called **Eucharist** (from the Greek word *eucharistia*, meaning 'thanksgiving') otherwise known as the **Lord's Supper**. During the first century, it appears to have been held on Saturday evenings, moving to Sunday mornings from the second century on. Celebrants drink wine and eat bread to remember the person who had brought them all together in the first place.

In the early Church, this ritual was a part of a bigger, shared meal, which was known as the agape meal, or 'love feast'. Communal meals were a core part of the early Church [Acts 2:46; 1 Cor 11:20–32; Jude 12]. This meal was open to anyone in the community, rich or poor, high-born or low, young or old and took its lead from the many instances of Jesus sharing meals with both the socially acceptable, such as Pharisees [Lk 7:36–50] and the socially unacceptable such as Tax Collectors [Mt 9:11–12]. Meals were more than just eating—they indicated acceptance of all who shared, whatever their social background. They were all 'one body, for we all partake of one bread' [1 Cor 10:17].

Today, virtually every branch of the Christian church celebrates communion in some form or other. Like Christians in the early church, they join together in unity and equality to remember what Jesus had done for them, and to celebrate the new promise of forgiveness and salvation which God gave to them through Jesus' death.

> **The Sights: Communion**
> ☐ The place to meet: Lk 22.7–13
> ☐ Washing the feet: Jn 13.1–20
> ☐ Bread and Wine: Lk 22.14–23
> ☐ The betrayer: Jn 13.21–30
> ☐ The Holy Spirit: Jn 14.15–31
> ☐ The early church breaks bread: Acts 2.42–47
> ☐ Rules for the meal: 1 Cor 11.17–34
> ☐ Servants not Kings: Lk 22.24–30
> ☐ Testing times ahead: Lk 22.31–38

Throughout the world, in all kinds of locations, Christians drink wine and eat bread to commemorate the death and resurrection of Jesus Christ.

Why is this
important?

■ It shows
the earth-
shattering
effects of Jesus'
death

■ It introduces
the cross—one
of the key
symbols of
Christianity

■ It shows how
people of the
time reacted to
Jesus' execution

The death of Jesus [Mt 27]

The moment of Jesus' death is attended by shattering noises and startling events.

The earth shakes, like an **earthquake**. Rocks split in two [Mt 27.51]. The sky grows **unnaturally dark** [Lk 23.44]. (Interestingly, we know it wasn't an eclipse, since the moon was full the night before, and you can't have an eclipse during a full moon.) It is as if nature itself is screaming in pain. Those watching the death of Jesus know that **something unique has happened** [Mt 27.54; Mk 15.39; Luke 23.47].

There are two highly symbolic events.

First, the earth opens and **dead men walk around** [Mt 27.52–3]. Jesus' death will defeat death itself; 'God's people' have been raised to life.

Second, **the curtain in the Temple is torn in two**. This was a huge curtain guarding the most holy place—the place where only the high priest could go, where it was believed that he met with God. This curtain rips in two from the top to the bottom—not a natural occurrence, for the curtain was too high for any human to reach the top [Mt 27.51; Mk 15.38; Lk 23.45]. The symbolism is unmistakable: Jesus' death has changed things completely—now anyone can have access to God, whenever they want.

Creation screamed out against it; imprisoned spirits were released; barriers were broken. This was not an ordinary death.

Finally he is taken down from the cross and buried in a nearby tomb, borrowed from Joseph of Arimathea.

And that, so they thought, was that.

Jesus' Death

09:00
- Jesus is crucified
  (Mk 15.25)

12:00–15:00
- Darkness covers the land
  (Mt 27.45)

15:00
- Jesus cries out
  (Mt 27.46; Mk 15.34; Jn 19.30)
- He is offered a sponge filled with vinegar
  (Mt 27.48; Mk 15.36; Lk 23.36; Jn 19.29)
- He dies
  (Mt 27.51; Mk 15.37; Lk 23.46)
- His side is pierced with a spear
  (Jn 19.34)
- The curtain of the Temple is torn in two, earthquakes, tombs break open and spirits are seen
  (Mt 27.51–53)

Before sunset
- Jesus is buried in a borrowed tomb
  (Mt 27.57–61; Mk 15.42–47; Lk 24.50–54; Jn 19.38–42)

Cross

The cross is the most powerful symbol of Christianity. It reminds us of Jesus' death for us; of the way that he was willing to die the most painful death in order to bring humanity back to God. But why was it necessary for Jesus to die in this way?

Jesus' death is an **example** that we should follow. Jesus was treated unfairly and brutally, but he did not fight back and he did not complain. All Christians are called to 'take up their cross' and follow his example.

To the Romans, Jesus was a political agitator. To the Jewish authorities, he was a false messiah who was blaspheming against God and insulting their authority. The cross shows that Jesus was a **revolutionary** who stood against the oppression and injustice around him.

The New Testament says that we should be punished for our sins, but Jesus took our punishment for us. He was **sacrificed** in our place. He has served our sentence, paid our fine. We will physically die, but if we have faith in Jesus, we won't suffer punishment, because someone has already done that for us.

Finally, Jesus' death means that he **identifies** with our suffering. There is nothing we can go through that he does not understand. You cannot accuse God of not knowing about suffering; through Jesus, he lived and died and was a full part of humanity.

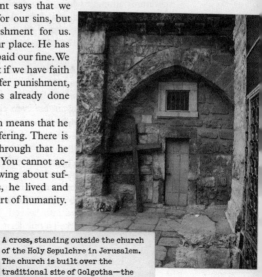

A cross, standing outside the church of the Holy Sepulchre in Jerusalem. The church is built over the traditional site of Golgotha—the place of Jesus' crucifixion.

Why is this important?

■ It tells of Jesus' rising from the dead—the key event in the Christian religion

■ For Christians, it shows that Jesus was who he said he was: the son of God

■ It depicts one of the most important days in history

The risen saviour [Lk 24]

The gospels all record the **resurrection**—the fact that Jesus rose from the dead—although they include different details. One thing they do have in common is that the event occurred on the first day of the week [Lk 24.1] which is why the early Church changed their Sabbath from Saturday to Sunday. Luke's account of the resurrection is split into three episodes.

First, **women visit the tomb** to anoint the body. They meet 'two men' who are obviously angels [Lk 24.4–5]. The angels tell them to 'remember his words'—this is one of the common themes of Luke's account; he shows people starting to remember what Jesus said and work out what has happened. The disciples, not unnaturally, struggle to take this in. They can see he's gone, but where?

The second episode switches location to outside the city [Lk 24:13–35]. Two followers of Jesus are walking to **Emmaus**. (Interestingly, Luke names one of them as Cleopas—perhaps the same Cleopas who was Jesus' uncle). They are joined by a mysterious stranger whom they don't recognise at first, but who is eventually revealed as Jesus. Again, the emphasis is on how everything was predicted in the scriptures [Lk 24.25–27]. They rush back to tell the others, only to find he's already appeared to Simon Peter [Lk 24.34].

The Sights: Resurrection

☐ His death: Mk 10.32–34
☐ Angel and stone: Mt 27.66–28.10
☐ Bribed guards: Mt 28.11–15
☐ Tell them all: Lk 24.36–49
☐ Walking: Lk 24.13–35
☐ Definitely death: Jn 19.25–37
☐ Put in the tomb: Jn 19.38–42
☐ The 'gardener': Jn 20.11–18
☐ Thomas believes: Jn 20.19–29
☐ Barbecue: Jn 21.1–14
☐ Back to heaven: Acts 1.1–11
☐ Believe in him!: Acts 2.22–41
☐ We're all raised to life: Rom 6.5–11
☐ Christ's resurrection is proof: 1 Cor 15.3–24

In the third episode, Jesus appears to the disciples [Lk 24.44–49] in the **upper room**. He proves to them that he's not a ghost, he's flesh and blood again. He even eats some fish to prove it. Again, he takes them through the scriptures. 'This is all part of God's plan,' he's saying. 'Look how it all fits together.'

Luke places the **ascension** of Jesus—when he finally goes up to heaven—in Bethany, probably on the Mount of Olives which was near that village [Lk 24:50–53]. As he blesses his disciples he is carried into heaven. The disciples have by now worked it out: Jesus has conquered death. He is more than a prophet, he is the son of God, so they 'worship him' [Lk24.52].

Resurrection

Christianity rests on one fact: that Jesus Christ rose from the grave.

'If Christ wasn't raised to life,' wrote Paul, 'our message is worthless, and so is your faith.' [1 Cor 15.14] So the resurrection is an absolutely crucial part of our faith.

But here's the good news: it happened. The evidence from the Bible is clear. A load of scared, panic-stricken people, who had seen their leader executed by the authorities, suddenly turn into a group of confident, alive, vibrant followers who perform miracles and tell everyone they have good news. What's changed them? What gave the early Church its power?

The answer is they'd met Jesus. They'd seen the risen Christ. He'd been in rooms with them, talked to them on roads, cooked fish for them by the seashore. Paul says he appeared to more than 500 of his followers [1 Cor 15.5–7]. They knew that he'd won. They realised that he hadn't been lying; that he was the truth. The person in whom they'd put their faith had proved to be God himself.

Jesus' resurrection proved he was the Messiah. It proved the claims that he made for himself. It proved that he had the power to defeat death—which is what he's done for all of us.

Jesus' resurrection was the most important day in history. On that day death was defeated, the sacrifice was made, and God opened the way for all people to be with him forever.

Resurrection Appearances

Early Sunday morning

- At the empty tomb (Mt 28.1-10; Mk 16.1-8 Lk 24.1-12; Jn 20.1-9)

- To Mary Magdalene at the tomb (Mk 16.9-11; Jn 20.11-18)

Sunday at midday

- On the road to Emmaus (Lk 24.13-32)

Sunday afternoon

- To Peter in Jerusalem (Lk 24.34; 1 Cor 15.5)

Sunday evening

- To ten disciples in the upper room (Mk 16.14; Lk 24.36-43; Jn 20.19-25)

One week later

- To eleven disciples in the upper room (Jn 20.26-31; 1 Cor 15.5)

Some time later at daybreak

- To seven disciples fishing in Galilee (Jn 21.1-23)

Some time later

- To eleven disciples on a mountain in Galilee (Mt 28.16-20; Mk 16.15-18)

- To more than 500 (1 Cor 15:6)

- To James, brother of Jesus (1 Cor 15.7)

Forty days after the resurrection

- At the Ascension on the Mt. of Olives (Lk 24.44-49; Acts 1.3-8)

Why is this important?

■ It talks about the return of Jesus

■ It warns us against people who claim to know the exact date and time

■ It introduces the theme of the end times

The return of Jesus [Mk 13:1-37]

The Temple was huge. To onlookers it must have seemed as though it would last forever. But Jesus tells his disciples that it would soon come crashing down. (He was right: in 70AD, the **Temple was destroyed** by the Romans, so completely that no trace of it can be found today.)

Later, sitting on the Mount of Olives overlooking the Temple, Jesus talks about the future. This passage—which is also in Matthew and Luke—is known as the **Eschatological discourse**. It's Jesus' teaching about **his second coming**—about what will happen at the end.

The disciples want to know what to look out for, but Jesus refuses to set out a timetable. Instead he tells them to '**watch out**'—a phrase that recurs throughout the passage. He warns of **times of persecution** and deception. **Fake messiahs** will arise, there will be international powers in conflict and natural disasters [Mk 13.5–8]. The gospel must be taken to all nations, leading to great persecution, but the Holy Spirit will give his followers strength [Mk 13.9–13].

Then he talks about '**the abomination of desolation**' which, despite the instruction 'let the reader understand', is very obscure. The phrase comes from Daniel [Dan 9.27; 11.31; 12.11], but no-one really knows what it means. Some experts think it refers to the destruction of the Temple, others that it refers to a being called the **Antichrist** [2 Th 2:3–10]. Whatever the case, the followers should escape and quickly. (Indeed, at the time of the Temple's destruction, that's what happened: the Christians in Jerusalem fled to a city called Pella in Perea.)

Whatever the case, the main point of the passage is that **Jesus will return**. There will be signs in the sky and the whole world will see him [Mk 13.24–27]. Jesus is using a poetic language here; what matters is that it will be a powerful, highly visible return. He will be seen for who he really is: the Lord of all creation.

End times

In his teaching, Jesus talks about the **end times**—the time when he will return and the world will end. Interpreting these passages is always very difficult and we should be wary of taking them too literally. Often the writers and speakers were using picture language, but we can unpack some of the features. These are what are called **'apocalyptic'** statements. Other apocalyptic writings in the Bible include **Daniel** and **Revelation**.

Jesus talks about the **destruction of the Temple**, a prediction of the events of 70AD. After rebelling against the Romans, the Jews were utterly defeated. The Temple was completely destroyed and the Jews were banished from Jerusalem. It was, effectively, the end of Israel, until the re-emergence of the modern state in the 1940s. Jesus warns of this event, but he gives **no other timescales**. All we know is that Christ will return and **all earth** will see his triumph.

And when will this happen? Amazingly, even **Jesus doesn't know** [Mk 13.32]. So Jesus advises his followers to keep on their guard. Over the years, libraries of books—from scholarly tomes to popular novels—have been written setting out exactly what will happen. But Jesus says we will not know the exact time or order of events. So we should beware anyone who thinks they can predict exactly when the event will occur. In the meantime, we have to wait.

The Arch of Titus in Rome contains a depiction of Vespasian's troops sacking the Temple in Jerusalem. They are shown carrying away the candlesticks and the tables from the sanctuary. The destruction of this temple—foretold by Christ—was a defining moment in Jewish history.

Why is this important?

■ It shows how the early church put Jesus' teaching to work

■ It introduces the Holy Spirit—the power behind the church

■ It's the origin of the Christian festival of Pentecost—the birthday of the church

The early church [Acts 2]

Something happened in the fifty days between Passover and **Pentecost** in 33AD. A group of people whom everyone thought defeated and deluded suddenly became a world-changing force. Something happened which propelled them out of hiding in a small room and on to the streets of Jerusalem.

Well, two 'somethings', actually. The **resurrection** of Jesus showed them that he was who he said he was: the son of God. And then someone else came along. Jesus had promised them the spirit and then it—or rather he, since the spirit is part of God—arrived [Acts 2.1–4].

It is the Spirit who sends them out to the streets, who gives them miraculous powers, and who binds them all together. For this is the beginning of the Church. The Jewish festival of Pentecost—originally a kind of harvest festival—becomes the birthday of the church for Christians.

Church, in the Bible, doesn't mean the building. It means simply any group of Christians who meet together regularly to worship God. Sometimes when the New Testament talks about 'Church' it's referring to all of Jesus' followers; other times it's talking about a specific group, meeting in a certain town or city.

This passage shows us something of what the early Church was like. They met to **learn together**, to join as a **family** in fellowship, to **care practically** for one another, to **remember Jesus** through breaking bread and to **show the Holy Spirit in action** [Acts 2.42–47]. Such things have been part of the church ever since.

The Sights: Early Church

☐ Jesus' instructions: Mt 18.14–20
☐ In Jerusalem: Acts 2.41–47
☐ The church grows: Acts 5.12–42
☐ Persecution of the church: Acts 8.1–4
☐ In Samaria: Acts 9.31–35
☐ In Antioch: Acts 11.19–30
☐ Paul's message: Acts 20.25–32
☐ In Rome: Rom 15.22–16.5
☐ Different gifts: 1 Cor 12.1–30
☐ Christ is head: Col 1.15–20
☐ Church leaders: Tit 1.5–9
☐ Communion: 1 Cor 10.15–17
☐ Letters to seven churches: Rev 2.1–3.22

Crucially, from the first they are a **missionary church**. Acts 2 records the first Christian preaching—Peter's speech to all the Jews who had come to celebrate Pentecost [Acts 2.14–41]. The church had been born and had burst into life. And in those few days after Pentecost, thouands of people believed.

The Holy Spirit

The Spirit is one aspect of God—the third person in the **trinity**. In Old Testament times he didn't live permanently on earth. He descended on Jesus at his baptism. After Jesus finished his work, he promised that the Holy Spirit would live with his followers forever [Jn 14.16]. So, at **Pentecost**, the Holy Spirit descended, turning the frightened, anxious followers of Jesus into a powerful, world-changing movement.

The Holy Spirit has several vital roles in the life of believers.

The Spirit **empowers** the church, and enables Christians to love each other, to forgive, to be joyful, to be, in fact, what we ought to be [Gal 5.22–3].

The Spirit **communicates** messages from God, directly or through visions [Re 2.7].

The Spirit **inspires** Christians to get out and get involved! The Holy Spirit sends people out and even tells them where to go [Acts 13.2].

The Spirit **brings gifts**, such as powers of healing, teaching, administration, helping others [1 Cor 12.28].

The Spirit is a **teacher**, bringing wisdom and insight, allowing us to learn more about God and each other [1Cor 2.13].

And the Holy Spirit can **protect** us from sinful thoughts. The more of the Spirit that is in us, the less likely we are to stray [Rom 8.5].

Why is this
important?
■ Paul explains
that faith in
God is what
really counts

■ This passage
shows how we
cannot be saved
in our own
power—only
through God

■ The passage was
crucial to the
development of
the Protestant
churches

■ It shows how
Paul began to
make sense of
Jesus' life,
death and
resurrection
and what it all
meant

Faith makes us right [Rom 5.1–11]

Romans is a very difficult letter at times. There are long, complicated arguments about circumcision and Old Testament history and the whole nature of the Law. It even begins with a single sentence that goes on for seven verses and contains 132 words.

But from the complex theological arguments there come a number of sudden bursts of light, times when Paul crafts words that are so brilliant they are almost blinding.

This section is one such moment. In it Paul sums up the core message of Romans, and, indeed, the core message of his teaching: we are **justified by faith**. We are made right with God through faith alone. It is through faith in Jesus that we are saved; through faith in him that we have access to God. That's why, Paul says, we can endure suffering and hardship, because we know that God loves us and that his Holy Spirit is with us [Rom 5.5].

Although we are sinners, **Christ has died in our place** [Rom 5.6–8]. God loved us even when we were his enemies, and now that we are his friends he will see us through to salvation [Rom 5.10]. We didn't do anything to gain this salvation—we couldn't do anything to gain this salvation—it is a gift from God.

Does that mean that we don't have to do anything? That, because we are made right with God through faith, then actions count for nothing? That's not what Paul is saying. Elsewhere in Romans [Rom 6.1–7.6; 12–15] and in all his letters, he is very careful to point out to Christians how they should live. Because Christ has given his life for us, we have a duty to him to live right.

Paul's idea of what it meant to be a Christian was, at its heart, very simple. Later in Romans he writes: 'So you will be saved, if you honestly say, "Jesus is Lord," and if you believe with all your heart that God raised him from death.' [Rom 10.9 CEV]. That's it: faith in Jesus. It's all you need.

Faith

In the Old Testament the word 'faith' is only used twice [Deut 22.20; Hab 2.4], but the topic is everywhere and is usually expressed where characters are said to 'trust' or 'believe' in God. The Old Testament is full of God's promises of salvation; promises that he will send the Messiah. Faith in the New Testament means believing that God did it: that the Messiah did, indeed, arrive, and that he died for us on the cross. So when we say 'I have faith in God', it means more than just a belief in his existence. It means that we believe God cares for us, that he has kept his promises and that we live to put that faith into action.

> **The Sights: Faith**
> ☐ Abraham's Faith: Gen 15.1–6
> ☐ Be patient and trust the Lord: Psa 37.1–40;
> ☐ The Lord can be Trusted: Isa 26.1–15
> ☐ Fools trust in their own strength: Jer 16.5–11
> ☐ The Lord will put everything right: Mic 7.8–20
> ☐ Faith brings healing: Mt 9.18–31
> ☐ Faith can move mountains: Mt 21.18–22
> ☐ Faith brings eternal life: Jn 3.16–18
> ☐ Saved by faith: Rom 4.13–25
> ☐ Faith and works: Jas 2.14–26

David says: 'I have trusted you without doubting' [Ps 26.1]. To have faith in God means simply to **believe** him, to trust that he will do what he says he will do. In this we are helped by the Holy Spirit who reminds us that we are God's children, and that we 'will share in the glory of Christ' [Rom 8.16–17]

True faith **endures**. It is not a temporary belief. There will be times when our faith is tested; all Bible characters experienced those tough times. But trusting God means just that: trusting him.

Faith is expressed in **action**. When God asked Abraham to move, he moved. James tells us that even demons believe there is only one God [Jas 2.19]. It is action that proves whether you really believe.

Faith is **factual**. The Israelites' faith in God was supposed to be a response to his acts in rescuing them from slavery. Similarly, the Christians' faith in Jesus is a response to his death and resurrection.

Why is this
important?

■ It shows what
really matters
in the Christian
life

■ It's one of the
greatest pieces
of writing ever!

■ It inspires us
all to act in a
truly loving
way

Paul talks about love [1 Cor 13.1–13]

There are times when you just hit your stride as a writer; when
the words and the images just flow and everything works. And
you can't put your finger on why it happens and you can't
replicate it, you can only hang on and enjoy the ride.

I think that's a bit like what's happening here with Paul. For
in the middle of a letter to the Corinthian church—a church
troubled by dissension and immorality—he suddenly comes
up with this fantastic hymn to the **power of love**.

Without love, he says, 'I am nothing'. I'm just a load of
noise [1 Cor 13.1]. Even if I have miraculous powers or enormous
intelligence, I'm nothing without love [1 Cor 13.2–3]. I might die a
martyr's death, but that doesn't prove anything. If I don't love
people, I am nothing.

And this love is not some airy-fairy, soft-focus feeling. He
goes on to show us how love works in real love. It means being
patient, humble, kind, forgiving, unselfish [1 Cor 13.4–7].

Nor is it a transitory thing. In today's world, where people
fall in and out of love with remarkable frequency, Paul points
to a different way. **Love never ends** [1 Cor 13.8]. All the other stuff
that happens in church, he says, all the stuff that the Corinthians are so proud of—their prophecies and miraculous gifts
and knowledge—all that will disappear. Only their love will
last.

And best of all, this earthly love is only **a dim reflection** of the
real thing. In ancient times, mirrors were made of polished
metal, so they gave, at best, a slightly blurry reflection. One
day, we will see the real thing face to face. That's real love.

As Christians, Paul says, we should have faith in Christ, and
hope of eternal life; but more than that, we should show true,
real, strong, lasting love. Because that's the greatest thing of
all [1 Cor 13.13].

Love

This is the most important thing to understand about God: **God is love**.

The Bible begins and ends with love. It begins with a God in love with his new creation and ends with a new creation filled with God's love.

God's love floods the pages of the Bible. Time and again he decides not to punish his people—even though they deserve it—because he loves them. In the end, he loves them so much, he sends his only son to die for them.

But 'love' in the Biblical world was very different to our world. We are not talking about the transient, romantic, slightly soppy stuff that fills our TV shows and movies. Love in the ancient world was more than just a 'feeling'. It was actively seeking out the best for someone. After all, most marriages weren't love-matches. Love had to be worked at. Love was something you did as well as something you felt.

Similarly, God's love is not a weak, passive thing. It's the love of a **perfect father**; a strong, passionate love; a love that demands something of its beloved; a love that is not blind, but that will forgive us when we ask and that wants the very best for God's children.

The images that he chooses to describe his love show this deliberate, sacrificial aspect. He loves Israel as a **husband loves his wife**—even an unfaithful wife [Hos 3.1 Isa 54.5–8]—as a father loves his son [Hos 11.1–3; Jer 31.9]. His love is shown in action, demonstrated by the way he **rescued Israel from slavery** [Ex 15.13; Psa 106.7]. This is an unyielding yet realistic love; it does not exclude the Israelites from punishment, but it always looks for ways to bring them back. These images were echoed in the pictures drawn by Jesus, especially of the father waiting for his errant son to return.

And this love became the key facet of the early Church. Even the enemies of Christianity recognised the way in which they cared for the poor. Their love was unmistakable. As Jesus told them; 'If you love one another, people will know you are my disciples' [Jn 13.35].

The Sights

- [ ] Tough love: Ex 34.5–7
- [ ] Love the Lord: Deut 6.1–18
- [ ] Love you can trust: Psa 86.1–17
- [ ] Unfailing love: Psa 136.1–26
- [ ] God's love for Israel: Hos 11.1–11
- [ ] Stories of God's love: Lk 15
- [ ] Basic rule: Mt 22.36–40
- [ ] Sacrificial love: Jn 15.9–17
- [ ] The extent of love: Jn 3.16–21
- [ ] Wonderful love: Eph 3.16–20
- [ ] Love the world or God: Jas 4.4–10
- [ ] God is love: 1 Jn 3.7–21
- [ ] Love is the greatest: 1 Cor 13.1–13
- [ ] God's city of love: Rev 21.1–4

Why is this important?

■ It shows us that God triumphs in the end

■ It brings us back to the beginning—but with a new heaven and earth

■ It shows a picture of what is going to happen in the future

Alpha and Omega [Rev 21]

God was there at the beginning and he'll be there at the end. At the end, all things will be made anew.

Revelation reveals that, in the end, death and hell will be no more. It is time to go back to the beginning; to reboot creation, to start again.

This passage brings the story of the Bible round in a kind of arc—we started with the creation of the earth and the heavens and we end with the creation of a **new heaven and a new earth**.

Writers throughout the Bible had looked to God's day of judgement, to the final things, to a time when God and his people would live together again [Isa 65.17–25]. John's description echoes the words of previous writers, prophets like Isaiah. They too had seen a glimpse of the perfect world that is to come. God says that he is the **alpha and the omega**—the first and last letters of the Greek alphabet. He is the beginning and the end.

God and his people will live together. As God says, 'I am making everything new' [Rev 21.5]. In the centre of this new earth is the new Jerusalem, the new 'holy city'. The city does not have a temple [Rev 21.22]; why would it need one? God is everywhere and living with his people. The gates will always be open, because all the enemies are defeated. There will be food for all, healing for all, peace for all.

Alpha and Omega—the first and last letters of the Greek alphabet. From an inscription in Ephesus.

Heaven (and hell)

Heaven is the 'home' of God, the place from where Jesus came, and to where he returned after his work on earth. It's a place of **security** and **peace**, where age and illness and pain will no longer have any part.

Jesus talked about preparing a place for those who trusted in him and the Bible contains great descriptions of heaven. Prophets caught glimpses and tried to describe it in words (like those in the book of Revelation) but inevitably words can only ever be a partial view.

There are different ideas about when believers go to heaven. Some argue they **go there immediately** after death; others argue that they 'sleep', and will all go there **at the end of the world**—at the very time described in Revelation.

The real feature of heaven is that it's a place where we will constantly be in the **presence of God**. No barriers between us any more; nothing but God and his people, together at last.

Like the descriptions of heaven, Biblical descriptions of **hell** are pictures, rather than literal descriptions. When Jesus talked of an 'outer darkness' with fire, weeping and lost, aimless people, he was painting a picture of a place of alienation, loneliness and despair.

There are three names for hell in the Bible. In the Old Testament it is called **Sheol**—a place where the soul goes after the death of the individual. There are several places where God promises to rescue those in Sheol and bring them into his presence [Ps 16.9–11].

In the New Testament, it is called **Hades**, the Greek term for the realm of the dead. Jesus also used the word **Gehenna** [Mt 10.28; Lk 12.5], which was a real place (*ge-hinnom*, the valley of Hinnom) a valley outside Jerusalem. In Jesus' time it was the city rubbish dump, where fires were kept burning day and night. It was in Gehenna that children were sacrificed to Molech [Jer 7.31]. Gehenna symbolises a spiritual wasteland, a rubbish dump for lost souls, a place marked by the absence of God.

The Sights: Heaven

- [ ] Preparing a place: Jn 14.1–6
- [ ] Isaiah sees heaven: Isa 65.17–25
- [ ] God's love: Psa 103.1–22
- [ ] Ezekiel sees glory: Ezk 1.1–28
- [ ] Treasures: Mt 6.16–21
- [ ] From heaven: Jn 3.22–36
- [ ] Jesus returns: Lk 24.50–53
- [ ] Stephen sees heaven: Acts 7.54–60
- [ ] Heavenly citizens: Phil 3.12–21
- [ ] Set your heart: Col 2.20–3.4
- [ ] John looks up: Rev 4.1–11
- [ ] New heaven, new earth: Rev 21.1–7

Need to find help?

The Bible is not just an ancient book of stories and theology. It's intended to give practical help as well. So here are some bits to explore at specific times of your life.

Where to find help when you are..:

■ **Afraid:** Psa 34.4-6; Isa 12.1-5; Matt 10.28-31; 1 Pet 3.13-14

■ **Angry:** Matt 5.22; Eph 4.25-27; 1Tim 2.8

■ **Ashamed:** Psa 32.1-11; Psa 51.1-19; Prov 17.9; Isa 55.7-13; Acts 13.38-39

■ **Bitter:** Prov 3.11-12; Eph 4.31-32; Jas 3.13-18

■ **Confused:** Psa 25.1-5; 32.8-9; 43.3-4; Prov 3.1-6; Isa 42.16; Gal 5.16-18; Eph 5.1-2

■ **Depressed:** Psa 34.1-22; Isa 35.1-2

■ **Discouraged:** Psa 41.5-11; 55.22; 150.6; Matt 5.11-12; 2 Cor 4.8-18; Phil 4.4-7

■ **Discriminated against:** Matt 7.1-5,12; Acts 10.34-36; Gal 3.26-29; Eph 2.11-22; Col 3.5-11; Jas 2.1-13

■ **Doubting:** Matt 8.23-27; Jn 20.24-29; Jude 1.21-22

■ **Feeling a failure:** Psa 73.25-26; 136.1-19; Jer 30.18-22; Rom 8.31-39

■ **Feeling let down by people:** Lk 17.3-4; Rom 12.14-21

■ **Feeling rejected:** Psa 86.1-17, 136.1-26; Rom 8.28,38-39

■ **Grieving:** Psa 119.49-52; Matt 5.4

■ **Hating yourself:** Psa 139; 1Cor 1.26-31; Col 3.12; Heb 13.5,6

■ **Impatient:** Prov 14.29; 19.11; 29.11; Rom 12.11-12; Gal 5.22-23; Heb 10.36

■ **In need of Protection:** Num 6.23-26; Psa 27.1-6,14; 56.8-13; 91.1-16; Nah 1.7

■ **Leading others:** 1Tim 3.1-7; 2Tim 2.14-26; Titus 1.5-9

■ **Lonely:** Psa 22, 23.1-6, 40.1-3; 68.5-6

■ **Needing Peace:** Lk 1.78-79; Jn 14.27-29; Rom 5.1-5; Phil 4.6-7

■ **Running out of time:** Prov 12.11; 28.19; Eccl 3.1-8; Lk 21.34-36; Titus 3.14

■ **Sad:** Psa 51.1-19; Isa 53.3-10; 61.1-7; Jer 31.15-17; 2 Cor 1.3-4; Rev 21.3-4

■ **Sick or in Pain:** Psa 38.0-22; Prov 18.14; Matt 14.34-36; Jas 5.14-15

■ **Skint:** Eccl 5.10-20; Matt 6.24-34; Lk 12.13-21; 1Tim 6.6-10

■ **Starting a new job:** Prov 11.3; Eccl 10.4; Rom 12.3-11; 1Th 5.12-18; 2Th 3.6-13

■ **Suffering:** Psa 102; 2 Cor 12.9-10; Col 1.24-2.5; 1 Pet 4.12-13,19

■ **Tempted:** Psa 1.1-6; 139.23-24; 1Cor 10.12-13; Heb 2.14-18; Jas 4.7; 2Pet 3.17-18

■ **Thankful:** Psa 100.1-5; 118.27-29; Phil 4.6; Col 3.16; 1Th 5.18

■ **Under pressure:** Ex 18.17-23; 1 Samuel 30:6; Job 19.1-27; Psa 43.1-4

■ **Weary:** Matt 11.28-30; 1Cor 15.58; Gal 6.9-10

■ **Worried:** Psa 46.1-11; 94.18-19; Matt 6.19-34; Jn 14.27; Phil 4.6; 1 Pet 5.6-7

Explorer's Notes—Part 3
The Bible Book by Book

The boots inside an old jar, among the remains of a Byzantine church.

The Old Testament

The Old Testament takes us from the beginning of creation to around 400BC. It tells the story of God's relationship with human beings. It tells how humans were created by God, how they rebelled against him and how he saved them. You can't understand what happened in the New Testament unless you get a grip on what happened in the Old Testament.

The Old Testament contains a huge mixture of different kinds of writing split into four main sections: the **Law** (or **Pentateuch**); **History**, **Wisdom** and **Prophecy** (split into the **Major and Minor Prophets**). There is a lot of great, inspiring, uplifting stuff. But equally there is a lot of confusing, strange and even downright horrible stuff. Here's why the Old Testament sometimes doesn't seem very 'Christian':

They weren't Christians. They lived thousands of years before Jesus arrived. They had great faith—and there is a lot that we can learn from their experiences and their lives. But they weren't Christians. They didn't have the whole picture.

The people in the Old Testament **lived a long time ago.** The Old Testament dates from 3,000 years ago and took around 1,500 years to put together. So, naturally, the cultures of those times were hugely different. That will affect the way they behave and the social 'rules' of the time. Generally speaking, the Old Testament times were tougher. In warfare, for example, there was no such thing as the United Nations or the International Courts—there were just a load of big people with swords. So if it seems at times more brutal, that's because it actually was more brutal.

The Old Testament is packed with **real people.** That's why they behave so badly. Real people sometimes do stupid, dumb, dangerous and evil things. Sometimes they just make mistakes, sometimes they do them deliberately; but this stuff happens. (And it still happens today.)

The Books of the Law

The first five book of the Bible are known as the Books of the law. Sometimes these are called 'the Pentateuch', from the Greek word *pentateuchos*, meaning 'five-volumed book'.

Genesis is the book of beginnings. It traces the origins of the people of Israel from creation through to people like Abraham, Jacob and Isaac. It also tells of God's promises—or covenants—with his people. By the end of Genesis, the people of Israel are in slavery in Egypt.

Exodus tells of the Israelites' escape from Egypt. The book ends with Moses receiving the Ten Commandments and the instructions for the building of the tabernacle.

Leviticus is mainly about the laws the Israelites were supposed to follow to show that they were true followers of God. Many people find it a difficult book, but there are gems inside, such as the amazing Jubilee legislation.

Numbers is so called because it's full of numbers. Amazing. But, along with a record of how many Israelites left Egypt, it also tells how the Israelites rebelled against God and ended up spending forty years in the wilderness.

Deuteronomy is a kind of summary of the other four books. It's Moses' farewell speech, given just before his death and before the Israelites' entry to the Promised Land.

The Sights: the Law

☐ Creation: Gen 1.1–2.4
☐ First Sin: Gen 3.1–24
☐ The Promise: Gen 15.7–21;
☐ In slavery: Ex 1.1–14
☐ The Burning Bush: Ex 3.1–21
☐ Passover and Escape: Ex 12.1–42
☐ The Ten Commandments: Ex 19.16–20.17
☐ The most important rule: Deut 6.1–25
☐ The Ark and Tabernacle: Ex 25.1–22
☐ The Jubilee: Lev 25.1–55
☐ The Twelve Spies: Num 13.1–33
☐ Israel's Journey: Num 33.1–56
☐ False gods: Deut 12.29–13.18

Genesis

Genesis is a 'why' book. It tells us where we came from and why we are here. Genesis is **one of the most important books of the Bible** because it introduces all the major themes that fill the rest of the Bible—**creation, sin and rebellion; love, grace and mercy**.

'In the beginning God created the heavens and the earth.'
Genesis 1.1

Who & When

Genesis was written over a long period of time. It was probably begun in the time of Moses, but later generations added other material and edited the book together. The book probably reached its final form around the time of Solomon (970–930BC).

The book is structured around the lives of several key figures, like **Adam**, **Noah**, **Abraham**, **Jacob** and **Joseph**. These are known as **'the patriarchs'**, which means 'the fathers'. They are not only the fathers of the Israelite nation, but also our spiritual ancestors. There are, of course, interludes which cover other topics, but these are the key characters.

Their stories remind us that the Bible is not just a book about God: it is a book about God and man. God is personal. He speaks, he thinks, he relates to humans. This is not some impersonal 'life-force', still less some distant, alien being. This is a 'someone', a being who wants to communicate with the world he has created. Indeed, the whole of the Bible is about God's attempts to make himself known to his creations, to inspire, cajole, correct and above all to love these people he made.

Most importantly, **God makes promises** to his people. He promises Noah that he will never again wipe out the human race; he promises Abraham that, even though he is old and childless, he will be the father of a mighty nation. These promises underpin God's relationship with his people throughout the rest of the Bible. God has promised to be with them—and he keeps his promises.

The Sights: Genesis
- ☐ Creation: 1.1–2.4
- ☐ Adam and Eve: 2.7–3.24
- ☐ Noah: 6.5–9.17
- ☐ Abram's calling: 12.1–7; 13.2–18
- ☐ Covenant: 15.7–21; 17.1–18.15
- ☐ Sodom and Gomorrah: 18.16–19.29
- ☐ Twins: 25.19–34; 27.1–45
- ☐ Jacob's ladder: 28.10–22
- ☐ Call Me Israel: 32.1–31
- ☐ Joseph: 37.1–36; 39.1–21
- ☐ In Egypt: 41.1–42.5
- ☐ Reunion: 45.1–13; 47.1–12; 50.22–26

Exodus

The title of the book means 'exit'; and the book deals with the **rescue of the Israelites from slavery** in Egypt. The Hebrew title of the book means 'These are the names', which is the first line of the book.

> ### Who & When
>
> The traditional view is that this book was written by Moses: Joshua mentions 'the Book of the Law of Moses' [Josh 8.31] and the NT claims that Moses was responsible for certain passages. Probably other, later, writers had a hand in shaping and editing the original materials. If we accept Moses started it off, it would mean that the book dates from the 13th century BC.

The book deals with the escape of the Israelites from slavery in Egypt. It includes lots of religious ceremony and legal issues, but more importantly, some vital insights into **the nature of God**, and **the relationship between God and his people**. At the centre of all this is **Moses**, the Israelite raised as an Egyptian, the first freedom fighter of his people.

Exodus tells the story of how a group of escaping slaves turned into the people of God. This is shaped by two events: the rescue from slavery in Egypt, and God's covenant with his people. Because God rescues them from the Egyptians he asks them to follow him and be his people. He gives them **the laws** for them to follow, including **the Ten Commandments** and many other laws for regulating their daily life and worship.

Exodus also contains some of the deepest, most mysterious passages of the Bible, giving us a unique insight into what God is like. He is not a distant, remote God, but one who cares for his people, who rescues them and who wants to show them how best to live. And he reveals to Moses his name—**Yahweh** or, 'I am'.

So maybe it is the book of names after all.

'I am the eternal God. So tell them that the Lord, whose name is **"I Am"**, has sent you. This is my name for ever and it is the name that people must use from now on.'
Exodus 3.14–15

The Sights: Exodus
- ☐ Slavery: 1.1–14
- ☐ Moses' birth: 1.15–2.10
- ☐ Murder: 2.11–25
- ☐ Burning Bush: 3.1–21
- ☐ Instructions: 4.1–17
- ☐ Moses v Pharaoh: 5.1–21
- ☐ Plagues: 7.14–8.32
- ☐ Final punishment: 11.1–10; 12.29–30
- ☐ Passover: 12.1–28
- ☐ Escape: 12.31–42
- ☐ Over the Sea: 14.1–31
- ☐ Manna: 16.1–26
- ☐ Ten Commandments: 19.16–20.17
- ☐ The Ark and the Tabernacle: 25.1–22

Leviticus

Leviticus takes its name from the tribe of the **Levites**, which supplied all the priests for Israel. This is essentially their handbook—a book full of the rules which they and the people are supposed to follow, rules covering subjects from sacrifice to skin diseases, from criminal justice to clothing manufacture, from health and safety to holiness.

'Dedicate yourselves to me and be holy because I am the Lord your God. I have chosen you as my people, and I expect you to obey my laws.'
Leviticus 20.7–8

Who & When

Modern experts tends to think that Leviticus is the work of someone writing much later in a 'priestly' tradition. The book, however, is full of explicit references to Moses being given the law. So, as with the other books of the Pentateuch, there is probably a core of ancient material. As to when, it depends on your view. If you view it as the work of a priestly editor or writer then it would be written around 600BC. If you view it as primarily Moses' work, then it dates from c.1400BC.

Leviticus is a book that aims to tells the Israelites **how to be holy** enough to approach God. In our culture we might find some of the methods of achieving this holiness strange or even unpleasant. For example, there is an emphasis on physical perfection which means that no-one with any blemish can serve at the tabernacle: sores, burns, skin diseases, even a woman's monthly period, were supposed to make a person unclean and force them to leave the camp.

Why, we might think, should God look down on women and those suffering from illnesses and disabilities? Why should he need all this rigmarole? The culture of the time, however, believed that only the perfect was good enough for God: perfect sacrifices, perfect animals, perfect priests.

The Sights

☐ The Priests are Ordained: 8.1–36
☐ The first Sacrifice: 9.1–24
☐ Clean and Unclean Animals: 11.1–47
☐ Rules About Sex: 18.1–30
☐ Good ways to behave: 19.9–37
☐ The Festivals: 23.1–44
☐ The Jubilee: 25.1–55

While our culture is different and while Jesus has meant that we don't have to follow all this ritual anymore, there is a lot in Leviticus which should affect our behaviour. There is stuff about behaving honestly, not making fun of blind or deaf people and respecting the elderly [Lev 19.13–17, 23]. Most of all, Leviticus includes **radical social laws** to help the poor and the needy—especially the **jubilee**, a revolutionary economic and political concept which was so far ahead of its time that even now it is used to challenge nations in the way that they treat each other.

Numbers

Numbers is largely just that: a book of statistics and accounts, a **list of the tribes of Israel** and the number of people in each tribe. The Hebrew title is *bemidbar*—meaning 'In the wilderness'—which sounds a lot more exciting.

Who & When

Traditional authorship is ascribed to Moses, but there are also passages that indicate a later writer was involved. If Moses was responsible it was only because he ordered the information to be gathered together, which would mean it dates back to c.1400BC.

Numbers tells of Israel's journey to the edge of—and failure to enter—the Promised Land. It's the story of God's faithfulness to a bickering, grumbling, disobedient group of people. God enabled them to escape from Egypt; their own sin meant that they were never to escape the desert.

But along the way there are some exciting bits. If Leviticus tells how Israel became a worshipping people, Numbers tells **how they became an army.** After the giving of the law and the creation of the **tabernacle** at Sinai, the Israelites march out to conquer the lands about them. Leviticus only covers a timescale of about a month. **Numbers covers 40 years.** Leviticus takes place in one location. Numbers zooms around the desert like a camel on steroids.

We see the jealousy of **Moses**' family and encounter the strange tale of **Balaam** and the talking donkey. We even see Moses' disobedience, and God's decision that he, too, will not enter the **Promised Land**.

So there is a lot more in Numbers than just, well, a load of numbers.

'These people have seen my power in Egypt and in the desert, but they will never see Canaan. They have disobeyed and tested me too many times.'
Numbers 14.22–3

The Sights

- ☐ The Nazirites: 6.1–21
- ☐ The Israelites begin their journey: 10.11–35
- ☐ Complaints: 11.1–35
- ☐ Jealousy in Moses' family: 12.1–15
- ☐ The Twelve Spies: 13.1–33
- ☐ The Punishment of the Israelites: 14.1–45
- ☐ Korah's Rebellion: 16.1–17.13
- ☐ Moses' Disobedience: 20.1–13
- ☐ Balaam's Donkey: 22.1–23.12
- ☐ Israel's Journey to the Canaan Border: 33.1–56

Deuteronomy

Deuteronomy is **Moses' farewell speech**. It is a reminder of all that had happened to the Israelites, of how God brought them out of slavery and, despite their own lack of faith, brought them to the verge of the Promised Land. Indeed, the name Deuteronomy means 'repetition of the law'.

> 'Today I am giving you a choice. You can choose life and success or death and disaster.'
> Deuteronomy 30.15

Who & When

The traditional view is that Moses wrote it, although obviously the introduction and the account of Moses' death were by a different hand. Jesus himself talks about Moses' authorship; indeed, the New Testament regards Deuteronomy highly—there are nearly one hundred quotations from Deuteronomy in the New Testament. If Moses was involved, it dates from around c. 1400 BC.

At the time of this speech, Moses and the Israelites are in Moab, just where the **Jordan** flows into the Dead Sea. The leadership has been handed over to **Joshua**, and Moses is saying 'farewell'. He reminds the people of the things that have happened to them and the laws they are to obey. He issues promises of blessings if Israel obeys God, and dire warnings of the consequences should they disobey. These warnings look far ahead, to a time when the Israelites would be in exile and when all the dreams of a Promised Land seemed to have turned to dust. The Lord **warns of punishment,** but he also **promises that he will bring his people back** [Deut 30.1–10].

The God that comes across in Deuteronomy is more caring and personal than he often seems in the other books of the Pentateuch. He teaches his people through their trials. In all their wanderings they never go hungry, their clothes don't wear out and they don't even get swollen feet! Now this loving God has led them to **a land of plenty** [Deut 8.1–9]. Moses knows he isn't going to make it into the Promised Land. So these speeches are his farewell gifts to the people he has led all these years. He can't go with them. He can't fight their battles any more; but he can remind them of who God is and all that he has done for them.

The History Books

All the books in the Old Testament contain some history, but the twelve books in this section are specifically about the history of Israel. They take the story on from the **conquest of the Promised Land**, through **the decline of the monarchy**, into **exile** under foreign powers and finally to the **return** from exile of the Jewish nation.

Joshua was the successor to Moses. Moses never got to enter the Promised Land—it was Joshua who led the Israelites across the Jordan. This book tells of the invasion and conquest of the land, and the division of the territory between the twelve tribes of Israel.

Judges is one of the bleakest books of the Bible. It tells of the dark, anarchic era that followed the conquest, when every man acted as he thought fit, and violence and barbarism ruled. The only exceptions were the 'judges', leaders raised by God who brought occasional order to the chaos.

Ruth is a small book telling the moving story of Ruth who, despite being a 'foreigner' from Moab, shows great faithfulness and love and is rewarded.

1 & 2 Samuel tell the story of the first kings of Israel: Saul and David. The title of the books comes from Samuel, the prophet who anointed both kings.

1 & 2 Kings starts with the reign of Solomon and then goes downhill as the kingdom splits in two, with '**Israel**' in the north and '**Judah**' in the south. Kings tell of the downfall of Israel, as a succession of bad kings get their hands on the thrones. Eventually, both kingdoms are destroyed and their inhabitants taken into slavery by foreign powers.

1 & 2 Chronicles are a condensed version of the Samuel/Kings story. The books concentrate mainly on the kings of Judah and have a particular focus on the building of the Temple and the religious ceremonies.

Esther is the story of Queen Esther, a Jew who became Queen of Persia and saved her people from extermination at the hands of their enemies.

Ezra & Nehemiah are two books telling of the return of the Jews from exile in Babylon, their struggles to rebuild the shattered city of Jerusalem, the re-establishment of the Temple and the rediscovery of the books of the Law.

Joshua

The book takes its name from the leading character, **Joshua**, son of Nun, who took over the leadership of the Israelites from Moses. After their years of wandering in the desert, the Israelites finally make it across the Jordan and conquer **Canaan**, the land that God had given them.

Who & When

Although Joshua orders his men to make a survey of the land [Josh 18.8] and he draws up commands and laws [Josh 24.25], we don't know who the author was. Some experts argue that the book was written a lot later—possibly as late as 800 years after—the events it describes. But a lot of the description of the cities use antiquated names which would have been prevalent at the time, such as 'the Jebusite city' for Jerusalem [Josh 15.8]. Probably the book dates from around 900BC, but includes material that was inserted at a later date.

The book tells of the invasion of Canaan by the Israelites, conquering city-state after city-state. In this, they are helped by God—sometimes miraculously, as in the defeat of **Jericho** and the battle at Gibeon where the Amorites are hail-stoned to death [Josh 10.1–15]! Cities were either destroyed or occupied until, finally, there was peace in the land [Josh 11.23].

When the Israelites come to settle the land, **each tribe is allocated territory** in which to live, with the exception of the **Levites**, who are given towns scattered throughout the country.

However, there is more to Joshua than meets the eye. Hidden in this list of military victories, you'll find the seeds of Israel's future problems. For it's not quite the triumph it seems; the Israelites never complete the job of clearing out the previous inhabitants and removing the false gods; some of the previous inhabitants remained, and their gods would be a temptation and a downfall for Israel for many years to come.

The Sights: Joshua
☐ Instructions: 1.1–16
☐ Rahab: 2.1–24
☐ The fall of Jericho: 6.1–27
☐ Achan: 5.1–26
☐ Israel takes over the land: 10.40–43; 11.12–20
☐ The safe towns: 20.1–9
☐ Farewell: 23.1–16; 24.29–33

Judges

This book takes us from the time of **Joshua** to the establishment of the monarchy. Its title comes from the phrase 'From time to time the Lord would choose special leaders known as judges...' [Judg 2.16] These **judges** were not only leaders in battle; they decided legal cases and even performed religious rituals.

> 'This was before kings ruled Israel, so all the Israelites did whatever they thought was right.'
> Judges 17.6

Who & When

The traditional author is Samuel, but there's no evidence of this. It is possible that he assembled some of it, but Judges is more likely the work of several hands. The book probably dates from the time of the monarchy (hence the constant refrain about Israel having no king). So probably 10th century BC. The events described in Judges take place following the death of Joshua around 1390BC.

Judges starts with a captured king having his thumbs and big toes cut off [Judg 1.6–7] and goes downhill from there. This is one of the grimmest places to visit in the entire Bible, a picture of what happens to a society when it abandons God, when everyone lives by their own laws, when '...Israel wasn't ruled by a king, and everyone did what they thought was right' [Judg 21.25].

Judges is the story of a nation who managed to forget the God who had led them to safety and turned, time and time again, to other gods. It's like a dreadful video loop: the people turn away from God; God sends a foreign nation to punish them; the people cry out to God for deliverance; God sends them a 'judge' to deliver them. Then the people turn away again...

Thankfully, it's not all despair and anarchy. There are heroes like **Samson** and **Deborah**, **Ehud** the left-handed assassin and **Gideon**. Judges is not only about the faithlessness of the people, it's also about the faithfulness of God.

The Sights

☐ Israel doesn't finish the task: 1.27–35
☐ Israel is punished: 2.6–19
☐ Ehud and Eglon: 3.12–30
☐ Deborah and Barak: 4.1–24
☐ Deborah's Song: 5.1–31
☐ Gideon is chosen: 6.11–40
☐ The army is chosen: 7.1–25
☐ Samson's birth: 13.1–25
☐ Samson's strength: 15.1–20
☐ Samson and Delilah: 16.4–31

Ruth

Set in the time of the Judges, during a period of peace between Israel and Moab, Ruth is a book about family duty, affection and friendship.

> 'Please don't tell me to leave you and return home! I will go where you go, I will live where you live; your people will be my people, your God will be my God.'
> Ruth 1.16

Who & When

The author is unknown. As the book records an incident in the history of the family of David, it is likely that it was written during the time of the monarchy.

Importantly, the person who most embodies selfless love in this book is not an Israelite, but '**Ruth The Moabitess**', a woman from Moab, a despised and hated enemy of Israel. Ruth shows that participation in the kingdom of God is nothing to do with nationality, but a matter of loving God and following his commands.

In particular, Ruth is about **redemption**—the word occurs twenty-three times in the book. Redemption means paying a price to save someone from evil. This is an important theme in the Bible because it describes what God does for all humans through Jesus. Through the death of Jesus we are bought back—'redeemed'—from slavery to sin. Through the selfless love of Ruth and **Boaz**, **Naomi** is redeemed. She is given a grandson, and through that, a future. She is brought back from hunger and homelessness to security and contentment.

The other hero of this story is **Boaz**, who protects Ruth, provides for her and eventually marries her. Boaz buys back the family property. He is described by Naomi as 'one of those who is supposed to look after us' [Ruth 2.20] and the phrase literally means a kinsman-redeemer, someone who rescues his relatives.

The Sights: Ruth
☐ Naomi and Ruth go to Bethlehem: 1.1–22
☐ Ruth meets Boaz: 2.1–23
☐ Naomi's plan: 3.1–18
☐ Ruth and Boaz are married: 4.1–22

Indeed, the marriage of Ruth and Boaz leads to **King David** and then, eventually, to **Jesus**. So this story of redemption leads ultimately to the great redeemer himself. Indeed, Ruth is so honoured that this foreign woman found a mention in the family tree of Christ [Mt 1.2].

1 Samuel

1 & 2 Samuel is actually one book, which was originally divided into two parts for the simple reason that you couldn't fit the whole thing on one scroll. They are named after the prophet **Samuel** and they cover about one hundred years, from the close of the time of the Judges to the establishment of the kingdom under **David**.

> ### Who & when
>
> It is not known who the author was—it may well have been edited together from a variety of original sources. Samuel mentions one such source—The Book of Jashar [2Sa 1.18]—but there are others mentioned elsewhere, such as The Book of the Annals of King David [1 Chr 27.24], The Records of Samuel the Seer, The Records of Nathan the Prophet and The Records of Gad the Seer [1 Chr 29.29] Whoever the author was, he probably lived after the death of Solomon since he refers to the two kingdoms, which only came into existence after Solomon's death.

> 'Does the Lord really want sacrifices and offerings? No! He doesn't want your sacrifices. He wants you to obey him.'
> 1 Samuel 15.22

The first book of Samuel is a tale of three people: **Samuel**, one of the great prophets of Israel and the man given the job of appointing the kings of Israel; **Saul**, the first king of Israel, a man who should have had it all, but who constantly relied on his own judgement, rather than obeying God's commands; and **David**, the young shepherd/harpist/giant slayer who has been chosen by God to replace Saul.

The first book centres mainly on the kingship of Saul and the emergence of David. Saul starts well, but as the book continues, he becomes an increasingly unstable figure, prone to wild mood swings and ever more desperate to hold on to his kingdom. But God has already promised it to someone else and the first part ends with Saul dying in battle against the **Philistines**.

> ### The Sights: 1 Samuel
> ☐ Samuel's calling: 3.1–21
> ☐ We want a king: 8.1–22
> ☐ Saul is king: 10.1–27
> ☐ The Lord rejects Saul: 13.1–16
> ☐ David is chosen: 16.1–13
> ☐ David v. Goliath: 17.1–58
> ☐ Saul v. David: 18.6–30
> ☐ David lets Saul live: 24.1–22
> ☐ Saul talks to a ghost: 28.1–25
> ☐ Saul dies: 31.1–13

2 Samuel

'Now I promise
that you
and your
descendants
will be kings.'
2 Samuel 7.11

2 Samuel is the story of **David's triumph**—and of his downfall. It's the tale of how Israel's greatest king gained control of the kingdom, only to lose control of himself and his family. Yet it is also the story of how he was to discover new depths of God's love and forgiveness.

Who & When:

See 1 Samuel p.75

The first seven years of David's reign are spent in civil war. David battles against Saul's supporters, led by the late king's son, **Ishbosheth**. Finally, David defeats Ishbosheth, captures **Jerusalem** from the Jebusites and becomes king of the **United Kingdom of Israel**.

But he doesn't leave it there. He goes on to defeat the enemy nations around Israel and develop the nation into a kind of small empire. He transforms Jerusalem into the capital of the country, brings the **Ark of the Covenant** in place and starts to plan a magnificent **temple**.

And then it all goes wrong. David commits adultery, tries to cover it up with murder and his family is torn apart by the consequences.

Faced with his own actions, he throws himself on God's mercy. Perhaps that's the key message of 2 Samuel. Yes, it's about national success and glory, but it's also about personal failure and forgiveness. David defeated Israel's enemies, but he also discovered more about Israel's God, a God who promised that his family would reign in the land for ever more.

The Sights: 2 Samuel

☐ David becomes king and brings the
    sacred chest to Jerusalem: 5.1–12;
    6.1–23
☐ God's promise: 7.1–29
☐ David and Bathsheba: 11.1–27
☐ Nathan reveals the truth: 12.1–23
☐ Absalom rebels: 15.1–31
☐ Absalom is killed: 18.1–33
☐ David's final sin: 24.1–25

1 Kings

Like Samuel, Kings is really one book, split into two parts because, originally, you couldn't fit it all on one scroll. The first part covers the period from the accession of **Solomon** (975BC) to the split of the kingdom after his death.

> ### Who & When
>
> The author of Kings is not known, but he worked from a wide variety of sources and was familiar with Old Testament books such as Deuteronomy. Kings was probably written sometime after 561BC, when the Jews were in exile in Babylon.

1 Kings focuses mainly on Solomon, who makes Israel a powerful kingdom and builds a magnificent **temple** of God in **Jerusalem**. But his reign ends badly, with this wise king lured by his many wives into worshipping foreign gods.

After his death, the kingdom of Israel splits into two (due mainly to the way Solomon used the northern tribes as forced labour in the building of the Temple.) The **southern part** is called **Judah**, and is made up of the two tribes. The **northern part** contains the other ten tribes and retains the name **Israel**.

Kings goes on to tell the tale of the many rulers who governed these two kingdoms. In each case, the author decides whether they are a good king or a bad king, which is decided not by military success, foreign policy or expanding trade, but whether they stayed faithful to God. Every king is measured according to whether he obeyed the commands of the Lord. Mostly, the kings chose to worship foreign gods instead.

The other major characters in Kings are the **Prophets**. In particular, 1 Kings introduces **Elijah** and **Elisha**. Elijah opposes **King Ahab** and **Queen Jezebel** of Israel, the northern kingdom. At the time he seems almost a lone voice; it's Elijah v. the Rest. It shows what a difficult job it was to be a prophet. It took courage, commitment and huge faith in God to confront wickedness and speak out for God in a world that did not wish to hear what its maker had to say.

> 'Elijah stood in front of them and said, "How much longer will you try to have things both ways? If the LORD is God, worship him! But if Baal is God, worship him!" The people did not say a word.'
> 1 Kings 18.21

> ### The Sights: 1 Kings
> ☐ The death of David: 1.1–2.12
> ☐ Solomon's wisdom: 3.1–28
> ☐ The building of the Temple: 5.1–6.14
> ☐ The dedication of the Temple: 8.1–66
> ☐ Solomon's stupidity: 11.1–13; 41–43
> ☐ The split of the kingdom: 12.1–20
> ☐ Asa–a good king: 15.9–24
> ☐ Enter Elijah: 17.1–24
> ☐ Elijah v. Baal: 18.1–46
> ☐ The Lord appears to Elijah: 19.1–21

2 Kings

The second book of Kings continues the story of the long plunge to disaster. Even a prophet as great as **Elisha** can't bring the nations back to the straight and narrow, and after he departs from the scene, **Israel** and **Judah** pretty much go into free fall.

Who & When
See 1 Kings, p.77

'The people of Judah and Jerusalem had made the LORD so angry that he finally turned his back on them. That's why these horrible things were happening.'
2 Kings 24.20(b)

King after king ignores God and follows **false and evil gods**. Despite the many warnings from the prophets, they refuse to change their ways. They're not all bad though. Among the thirty-six or so kings of Judah and Israel after Solomon, there are a couple of glimmers of hope in the form of **King Hezekiah** and **King Josiah**. However, they're more or less the only good ones. (And two out of thirty-six is not a good ratio.)

The first kingdom to fall is the northern kingdom of **Israel**. In 722BC the **Assyrians** invade and completely conquer the kingdom. The capital city of **Samaria** is demolished and all the people taken into captivity. They are never heard of again.

Judah, the southern kingdom, staggers on for another 150 years or so. But in 586BC another huge and powerful empire—the **Babylonian**—invades and systematically dismantles the entire country. Jerusalem is completely destroyed and the majority of the population taken away to Babylon.

The Sights: 2 Kings
☐ Elijah departs: 2.1–18
☐ Naaman: 5.1–27
☐ Elisha v. the Syrian Army: 6.8–23
☐ The tears of a prophet: 8.7–15
☐ The death of Jezebel: 9.1–37
☐ Elisha dies: 13.14–21
☐ Destruction of Israel: 17.1–23
☐ Hezekiah: 18.1–4; 19.1–37
☐ King Josiah and the Law: 22.1–20; 23.21–3
☐ The destruction of Jerusalem: 25.1–30

During this period prophets such as **Isaiah, Jeremiah, Ezekiel, Amos** and **Hosea** were at work. Although they are rarely mentioned in the text of Kings, we can supplement the tale told here by looking at the writings they left behind.

1 Chronicles

Chronicles aims to answer a simple question: 'Does God care about Israel any more?' Just as Kings was written to explain their history to the Jews in exile, Chronicles is addressed to those who have returned.

Who & When

According to tradition, Ezra is the author of Chronicles (not to mention Ezra and Nehemiah). It seems likely that the author was a priest, since the theme of the priesthood and temple runs through these books. Many experts assign the writing of these books to the same hand, who they call 't he Chronicler'. It was probably written around 400BC after the Jews have returned to Jerusalem.

Chronicles' aim is to express the **continuity** of God's relationship with his people, from the time of **David** through the divided kingdoms and on into the post-exile state. That is why it begins with so many genealogies. Because only by going right back to the beginning can Israel look to the future.

The book argues that the Israel which was re-established after the exile was the same nation it had been before. It followed the same practices, worshipped the same God and was led by the same royal line. Thus, the book places a great emphasis on **the importance of the Temple** and the **priesthood**. These, too, were part of the continuity. The modern kings were the successors of David. The rebuilt temple was the successor of **Solomon's temple**, and **Moses' tabernacle**. The priesthood were the successors of **Aaron**. The line was continuing.

A lot of 1 Chronicles is found in 1 Samuel. Both books tell the story of King David, although from a slightly different perspective. In 1 Chronicles, David is given the hero's treatment. He's the person who made **Jerusalem** great, who planned the Temple and who brought the **Ark of the Covenant** into the city. He's powerful because he trusted in the Lord.

'I will make sure that your son and his descendants will rule my people and my kingdom forever.'
1 Chronicles 17.14

The Sights: 1 Chronicles
- ☐ The Death of Saul: 10.1–14
- ☐ David becomes king: 11.1–9
- ☐ The return of the Sacred Chest: 15.1–29
- ☐ David's song: 16.7–36
- ☐ 'Your descendants will be kings': 17.1–26
- ☐ The plans for the Temple: 28.1–21
- ☐ Solomon takes over: 29.21–30

2 Chronicles

2 Chronicles is mainly about the life of Solomon and the building of the Temple. It also gives us accounts of kings like those we get in 1 and 2 Samuel.

Who & When
See 1 Chronicles, p.79

Mainly, this is a book about **the Temple**. Indeed, it seems that the writer of Chronicles is almost obsessed with rites and rituals, about who did what and when. Perhaps the reason is that he was probably writing for an audience who had just returned from **Babylon** and who were, themselves, struggling to rebuild the Temple. By telling them the history of the first temple he was giving them a model, something to aim at. He saw the Temple as the symbol that God was with Israel and Israel worshipped God.

1 Chronicles built a picture of **David** as comparable with **Moses**. Similar comparisons are drawn here, with the importance of **Solomon** and the builder **Huram-Abi** likened to **Bezalel** and **Oholiab** in Exodus [Ex 35.30–36.7]. (Indeed, the only other reference to Bezalel in the Old Testament is found in Chronicles.)

The point here is to establish and reinforce the continuity of the history of Israel. Just as God gave instructions for the building of the **Tabernacle**, he has also given instructions for the building of the **Temple**. That's also why we get so many names and tribes. To the people who had returned from exile they needed to know the role that their ancestors, their tribe, had played. Thus the history was personalised for them. They were urged to continue the work that had been given to their ancestors.

'But if you or any of the people of Israel disobey my laws or start worshipping foreign gods, I will pull you out of this land I gave you.'
2 Chronicles 7.19

The Sights:
2 Chronicles
☐ Solomon's wealth: 1.1–17
☐ Building: 3.1–17
☐ Solomon dedicates the Temple: 7.1–22
☐ Queen of Sheba: 9.1–12
☐ The split: 10.1–19
☐ Uzziah: 26.1–23
☐ Hezekiah: 31.1–21
☐ Josiah and the law: 34.1–33
☐ Passover: 35.1–19
☐ An end and a beginning: 2 Chr 36.17–23

Ezra

Ezra is the account of the **return of the exiles**, showing how God's promises were fulfilled, and the land restored to his people.

Who & When

Ezra is really 3 Chronicles. The beginning of Ezra is virtually identical to the end of Chronicles; it's likely, therefore, that Ezra is a continuation by the Chronicler' taking Israel past its exile and into the return. Whether the author of all three books was Ezra, we don't know, although the use of Ezra's memoirs and the first person 'I' offers some support. Some sections of the book are lists from official sources and the usual genealogies. It would have been written around 400BC.

> 'Everyone started shouting and praising the LORD because work on the foundation of the Temple had begun.'
> Ezra 3.11

God promised through the prophets that the land would be restored to his people and Ezra tells how this was achieved, using foreign kings (**Cyrus, Darius** and **Artaxerxes**), Jewish leaders (**Joshua, Zerubbabel, Ezra** and **Nehemiah**) and prophets (**Haggai** and **Zechariah**).

The first part tells how the Jews returned to **Jerusalem** and started rebuilding. Faced with the opposition of some of the people who had settled in the area while the Jews were in captivity in **Babylon**, their initial enthusiasm wanes.

The second half of the book deals with the return of Ezra. He stops the people from inter-marrying with the tribes around them and calls them back to focus on God.

Early manuscripts put both Ezra and Nehemiah together into one book. However the beginning of Nehemiah [Neh 1.1] indicates that they are two separate documents, although both cover similar ground.

The Sights: Ezra

- ☐ Return: 1.1–11
- ☐ Rebuilding and opposition: 3.7–4.5
- ☐ Haggai gets them going again: 5.1–6.5
- ☐ The Temple and the Passover: 6.13–22
- ☐ Ezra returns: 7.1–27
- ☐ The problem: 9.1–15
- ☐ The solution: 10.1–17

If you want to read Ezra in chronological order, read it like this:

The return: Ezra 1.1–4.5

Work stops: Ezra 4.24

Work starts again: Ezra 4.24–6.22

Work stops again: Ezra 4.6–23

Ezra Returns: Ezra 7.1–10.44

Nehemiah

The rebuilding of **Jerusalem** related in the book of Ezra has ground to a halt. Nehemiah, a high-ranking Jewish official at the Persian king's palace, decides to act.

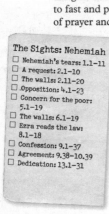

'But we kept on praying to our God, and we also stationed guards day and night.'
Nehemiah 4.9

Who & when

The author is unknown. Probably the book was begun by the same person who compiled Chronicles and Ezra, which would make the time of writing around 400BC. However, it also incorporates later material, since we know that the high priest Jaddua [Neh 12.11,22] was high priest around 330BC.

Nehemiah is the King's cup-bearer—an important and trusted position. While he is in the **Persian** city of **Susa**, he hears that Jerusalem is in danger. The city's walls are broken and the defences are useless. The city is under threat.

So Nehemiah takes steps. He approaches the king and gets permission to return. **Artaxerxes** even gives him some building supplies. Once at Jerusalem, Nehemiah has to overcome opposition from local enemies, but eventually the walls are finished and dedicated. Like **Ezra**, Nehemiah also calls the people to remain totally dedicated to God.

Nehemiah is about **prayer and action**. Nehemiah makes plans and puts those plans into action; but he also prays. The first thing he does when he hears the bad news about Jerusalem is to fast and pray. Everything that Nehemiah does is grown out of prayer and dedication to God.

The Sights: Nehemiah
- ☐ Nehemiah's tears: 1.1–11
- ☐ A request: 2.1–10
- ☐ The walls: 2.11–20
- ☐ Opposition: 4.1–23
- ☐ Concern for the poor: 5.1–19
- ☐ The walls: 6.1–19
- ☐ Ezra reads the law: 8.1–18
- ☐ Confession: 9.1–37
- ☐ Agreement: 9.38–10.39
- ☐ Dedication: 13.1–31

Esther

Esther is a book about **liberation** and **rescue**. It shows how God worked behind the scenes to rescue his people. This rescue is still celebrated today in the **festival of Purim**, which is described in the final chapter of the book.

Who & When

We don't know who wrote the book, but the evidence suggests a Jew living in a Persian city, around 460BC.

The tale of a Hebrew girl who becomes **queen of Persia** and who rescues her people, Esther has a certain fairy-tale quality about it. What is unusual about Esther is that the book doesn't once mention God (although some scholars argue that the Jewish letters for God YHWH (Yahweh) are hidden in the book in the form of an acrostic, reflecting the way that God's purposes are hidden from us, woven into the strands of history). This—and the fact that Esther marries a non-Jew—led to many rabbis having reservations about including the book in the final list of Hebrew scriptures.

However, it has become one of the most popular books among Jews, particularly because it is commemorated in the Jewish festival of **Purim**, a celebration of national deliverance. Its story of persecution and deliverance has given strength to many Jews in similar circumstances down the centuries.

> 'If you don't speak up now, we will somehow get help, but you and your family will be killed. It could be that you were made queen for a time like this!'
> Esther 4.14

The Sights: Esther

☐ Esther becomes queen: 2.1–18
☐ Mordecai saves the king: 2.19–23
☐ Haman's plot: 3.1–15
☐ This is your moment!: 4.1–17
☐ The tables are turned: 6.1–7.10
☐ The Jews defence: 8.1–17
☐ Purim: 9.20–32

The Wisdom Books

The Hebrew word for wisdom has a meaning similar to 'life skills'. So the books which make up this section of the Old Testament are not full of airy-fairy theory, but practical advice to help you live your life. They are focused on God, on his relationship with humanity and how all wisdom and knowledge is based on a proper respect for him and his works.

Collecting wisdom was very important to the people of ancient times. It was important to listen to people who were considered wise, to collect their observations and learn from their experiences.

Five books in the Bible—**Psalms**, **Job**, **Proverbs**, **Ecclesiastes** and the **Song of Songs**—are extremely varied in their subject matter. All human life is here. Pain, pleasure, love, hate, sex, anger, cynical boredom, wild jubilation—all the emotions and attitudes which fill our days can be found in these five books.

In many ways they are the most 'human' books of the Bible. They ask difficult questions and reflect bleak and often depressing moods, but just as they talk about the bad things, they also celebrate the good. There is often an almost awe-struck appreciation of the physical world and what it means to be human. **Job** is a long examination of the problem of suffering. Job is a good man, but he ends up suffering. How can that be right?

Psalms is a collection of 150 poems or songs, written by many different authors. Psalms is a kind of spiritual journal, reflecting on all the ups and downs of a believer's life.

Proverbs is a collection of wise and insightful sayings to help you live your life right.

Ecclesiastes is a dark, almost depressive meditation on the futility of life. The book recognises God's greatness, but the mood is pretty sombre and bleak.

Song of Songs is a love poem, about how good it is to fall in love. It's about men and women and the joys of a physical relationship. Not to mention gazelles.

Job

Job deals with one of the most profound of all human problems—**why do good people suffer?**

Who & When

Most likely a later author brought this story together from a variety of sources. As to when the book was written, it could have been any time from the reign of Solomon to the exile. But the hero figure dates from the time of the patriarchs, around 1500–2000BC.

Job is a genuinely good man, rich in livestock, living to a great age and blessed with a big family. Then disaster strikes. His family die, his riches are wiped out, he catches a horrible disease and he's reduced to sitting on a rubbish heap.

Job lives in '**the land of Uz**' which is 'somewhere in the East'. In other words, he's not an Israelite. The point is that all people can worship God, and all people have to face the problem of suffering.

Yet throughout it all, Job holds on to two facts: God exists and there must be some kind of explanation. Despite the 'advice' of **his friends**, who are certain that Job must have done something to deserve his suffering, Job remains resolute. He hasn't sinned, and he wants an explanation.

Job and his friends want a nice solution to why suffering occurs, but they don't get one. Instead they come face to face with God; and in the light of that they accept that some questions just have to be put aside. The book may be concerned with the problem of suffering, but in the end it doesn't actually answer the question. In the end, God sweeps in, washing away all the arguments and the shallow theories with the reality of his power and presence.

'I know that my Saviour lives, and at the end he will stand on this earth. My flesh may be destroyed, yet from this body I will see God.'
Job 19.25–26

The Sights: Job

- ☐ Job loses all: 1.1–22
- ☐ The scrapheap: 2.1–13
- ☐ I wish I'd never been born!: 3.1–26
- ☐ Why do we suffer?: 7.1–21
- ☐ Sick of life: 10.1–22
- ☐ Bildad accuses Job: 18.1–21
- ☐ I will see God: 19.1–29
- ☐ Dig for wisdom: 28.1–28
- ☐ Enter Elihu: 32.1–10; 33.1–33
- ☐ God interrupts: 38.1–41
- ☐ Out of the storm: 40.1–24
- ☐ Job's response: 42.1–17

Psalms

Psalms is **a collection of poetry**. Each 'chapter' is a separate poem, composed at a different time, for a different purpose, and often by a different person. 'Psalms' is a Greek word which comes from the psalterion, a kind of ancient stringed instrument. (Nowadays it would be like calling the book 'Guitaros'.)

'You, LORD, are the light that keeps me safe. I am not afraid of anyone. You protect me, and I have no fears.'
Psalms 27.1

Who & When

There is a lot of debate about the authorship of Psalms. Notations such as 'a Psalm of David' might mean 'written by' or they might equally mean 'concerning' or even 'for the use of'. And 'David' might even mean 'of the house of David' i.e. applied to the royal family. However, David was a lyricist and songwriter, so it is not unreasonable to assume that his works had been preserved for many years. If we take the traditional approach, authorship of the Psalms breaks down as follows: David: 73; Asaph: 12; Sons of Korah 11; Solomon 2; Moses 1; Heman 1; Ethan 1; Anonymous 49.

The collection was brought together over at least 400 years. It was probably finalised in the third century BC, where it served as a prayer book for use in the Temple and synagogues.

The Sights

- ☐ Praise the creator: Psa 8
- ☐ Close to death: Psa 13
- ☐ David's escape: Psa 18
- ☐ The glory of God: Psa 19
- ☐ So alone: Psa 22
- ☐ The Lord is my shepherd: Psa 23
- ☐ Trust in God: Psa 27
- ☐ The hunted deer: Psa 42
- ☐ God's blessing: Psa 46
- ☐ Forgiveness and mercy: Psa 51
- ☐ Saving thanks: Psa 66
- ☐ God's promise to David: Psa 89
- ☐ Joyful worship: Psa 95
- ☐ Intense suffering, intense faith: Psa 102
- ☐ The glory of creation: Psa 104
- ☐ The return of the exiles: Psa 107
- ☐ The great king: Psa 110
- ☐ The joy of the law: Psa 119
- ☐ Pilgrimage song: Psa 121
- ☐ Song of exile: Psa 137
- ☐ Praise God: Psa 150

The book of Psalms is like a diary or a **spiritual journal**, the emotional outpouring of real human beings. Although the Hebrew title is 'Praises', not all the Psalms praise God. More than perhaps any other part of the Bible, the Psalms reflect wishes, hopes, anger, desperation, joy, sadness and much, much more. The questions they ask, the honesty with which the Psalmist confronts God are universal experiences of mankind. Perhaps this is why **Jesus**, dying on the cross, screamed out a line from a psalm.

Above all, people still respond to the Psalms because they reflect a relationship with God, in all its different moods. The Psalms are incredibly honest. They Psalms reflect how life is.

Different types of Psalms

Many psalms are **cries for help**: direct, passionate, emotional prayers. Bones break, bodies crumble, waters rise over peoples' heads, savage beasts pounce. There are declarations of innocence [Psa 7, 12, 26], and even complaints to God for his apparent forgetfulness [Psa 9, 10, 22, 44]. Many, however, end with renewed faith and confidence that the prayers have been heard [Psa 6, 22, 69, 140].

Other Psalms **thank God** for answers to prayers: for a danger averted; for a successful harvest; for victory in battle; or for God's goodness to the writer.

Although most of the psalms **praise God** in some way, there are many which specifically focus on his **greatness and power**. Some celebrate God's reign over all [Psa 47, 93, 95–9], others compare God's rule with the rule of earthly kings [Psa 2, 20–21, 45, 72, 89, 101, 110, 115, 118, 144].

A few psalms are **pilgrimage songs** or 'songs of ascents'. These were sung by people climbing up the hill into **Jerusalem**. They may have been sung by pilgrims going to the city for one of the three annual festivals of **Passover**, **Purim** and **Succoth**.

Then there are **wisdom psalms**, which are closer to the style of Proverbs, and which aim to teach to the reader or listener.

Finally, there are a handful of **revenge psalms**. From a Christian point of view, these are tricky. The psalmist wants to wash his feet in his enemy's blood [Psa 58.10], or asks the Lord's blessing on anyone who smashes a Babylonian child's head against a rock [Psa 137.9]. They seem outrageously bloodthirsty, but we must remember that the writers felt passionately about the **rule of God**. They want to see God punish evil doing—now.

Proverbs

The Hebrew word for 'proverb' can also be translated 'taunt'. In some ways that sums up this book; it's full of 'provocations', nuggets of wisdom to make us think.

'Respect and obey the Lord! This is the beginning of knowledge. Only a fool rejects wisdom and good advice.'
Proverbs 1.7

Who & When

These proverb collections are attributed to a number of writers, including Solomon, Agur the son of Jakeh, King Lemuel and a being known only as 'the Oracle.' If we assume that Solomon had a hand in the book, it dates from the tenth century BC. The mention of 'Hezekiah's men' implies it was edited some time between 715 and 686BC, which would tie in with Hezekiah's interest in the writings of David and Asaph [2 Chr 29.30].

The book does not develop an argument, or narrate a story. It is, rather, a series of collections of practical advice about the way we should live. Proverbs advises us to act justly, to tell the truth, to work hard, to avoid damaging relationships. In the eyes of the writers of Proverbs, behaviour like this is what it means to 'fear the Lord'.

Proverbs urges us to **gather up and treasure wisdom**. A personal collection of wisdom is the best investment a person can make. Among the recurring themes, we are urged to **avoid bad influences** and choose true, wise friends, to **help the poor** and fight for justice. The reader is advised to **use words carefully**, not only giving up gossip, lies and foolish talk, but welcoming the right 'word of correction' from a friend. We are urged to **get out of bed** and **work hard**. And we are warned against **sleeping around**, avoiding adultery, prostitutes or even sleeping with people who don't see anything wrong with their actions [Prov 30.20].

The Sights: Proverbs
☐ Instructions: 1.1–7
☐ Friends: 1.8–33
☐ Value of wisdom: 3.13–35
☐ Lured away: 7.1–27
☐ Words of wisdom: 8.12–36
☐ The Lord sees all: 15.1–33
☐ Language: 26.17–27.7
☐ True friendship: 27.17–27
☐ The poor: 28.1–28
☐ Lemuel's mum: 31.1–31

Ecclesiastes

Ecclesiastes is one of the most surprising books of the Bible; a cynical, weary summary of the **apparent pointlessness of life**.

Who & When

The author—'Quoheleth' or 'teacher'—is identified as 'son of David, King of Jerusalem' which is usually taken to mean Solomon. However, it could mean a king from the line of Solomon, or even an ideal, archetypal king. It was probably written around 400BC, but if the author was Solomon, then it dates from c.900BC

'Nothing makes sense! Everything is nonsense. I have seen it all—nothing makes sense!'
Ecclesiastes 1.2

Despite this apparent cynicism, Ecclesiastes does have moments of humour and lightness, not to mention passages of startling and moving beauty. But still, the overriding feeling is one of weariness. This is why there have been many disputes as to what Ecclesiastes is doing in the Bible. Many Christians feel uncomfortable with its corrosive cynicism, its penetrating rejection of superficial optimism and cheerful platitudes.

Others argue that that is exaclty what gives Ecclesiastes its unique strength. It represents the thoughts of many, many people; people who are close to despair, who believe life to be without purpose—the kind of people we pass every day in our modern towns and cities.

Whether this book is the genuine record of one man's anguish, or a more artificial, measured attempt to portray a way of thinking, is difficult to judge. Either way this book calls to us to do all we can to help people who are trapped in the worldview of Ecclesiastes. Life is not meaningless; life is purposeful even if, sometimes, it really doesn't feel that way.

The Sights: Ecclesiastes

- ☐ Nothing makes sense: 1.1–18
- ☐ Wisdom helps: 2.12–26
- ☐ All in time: 3.1–8
- ☐ Worship with care: 5.1–20
- ☐ Better wise than stupid: 9.13–10.20
- ☐ Work hard: 11.1–6
- ☐ Remember while you're young: 11.7–12.14

Song of Songs

The full title of the book is 'The Song of Songs which is Solomon's' or 'The Most Beautiful of Songs'.

Who & When

Traditionally ascribed to King Solomon (although which wife he is addressing is not made clear), but that is probably a later addition. The language of the book is more typical of a later period than Solomon's, probably the third century BC.

Song of Songs is a celebration of **spontaneous and natural love**. Not surprisingly, many commentators have found this difficult to come to terms with and have sought alternative explanations. Many Jewish rabbis saw the song as an allegory of the love between **God and his people**, while Christian teachers saw it as an allegory of the love between Christ and his church, or even between **Christ and the believer's soul**. (In fact, for a thousand years this interpretation was the official line as the second council of Constantinople in 553AD condemned the literal interpretation.)

The problem with these theories is that there is no hint of them in the book itself, nor is a similar allegory or image found in the rest of the Bible.

The Bible has a lot to say about the bad side of love, about degradation, lust, perversion and even rape. Song of Songs celebrates what is good about **physical love**. In this, the most powerful voice in the poem is, perhaps, that of the woman. It is she who speaks most profoundly of love, who affirms its spontaneity, power and mystery.

Song of Songs is about love, both physical and emotional. Those who are uncomfortable with that will always be uncomfortable with this book.

The Sights: Song of Songs

☐ Love is better than wine: 1.1–2.7
☐ The wedding: 3.6–5.1
☐ Dream lover: 5.2–16
☐ Wedding Dance: 7.1–13
☐ If only...: 8.1–14

The Books of the Prophets

The section of the Bible called 'The Prophets' contains seventeen books. The first five are known as the **major prophets**; the remaining twelve are called the **minor prophets**. (The distinction refers not to their importance, but to their length. Some of the minor prophets are only one chapter long, whereas the longest of the major prophets—Isaiah—contains sixty-six chapters.)

Prophets played a significant part in the life of Israel. Although many were abused and ignored, they were accorded respect and allowed to exercise their gifts, even if that made for uncomfortable listening. It was also a risky business. If a prophet's words were not proved to be true, they could be taken and stoned.

Prophecy is often confused with **prediction**, with the ability to see the future. Prophets certainly did predict the future—a major theme of the prophets is the impending destruction of Israel and Judah and the salvation that was to come though the Messiah—but if they looked to the future, they also **challenged the present**. They challenged injustice and oppression and idolatry in the here and now. They argued with kings, berated the people and tried to pass on what they knew to be true.

Biblical prophecy is fundamentally about **passing on a message from God**. Descriptions of the prophetic experience in the Bible are often physical. Prophets shake, their message burns inside them, they cannot help but speak. Their message bursts out in **outrageous language and actions**, shocking people into listening, and reflecting a passionate God who will do anything to make his people turn around.

Isaiah is a long book warning of the judgment of God, but also looking to the **Messiah** and the world that is to come.

Jeremiah prophesied during the final days of the doomed country of Judah.

Lamentations is a short, sad poem about the **fall of Jerusalem**.

Ezekiel contains a series of powerful (and even bizarre) visions warning the people in Jerusalem to change their ways and urging them to stay faithful in exile.

Daniel is part prophecy, part the story of a **Babylonian exile** who refused to compromise his faith.

Isaiah

'I am creating new heavens and a new earth; everything of the past will be forgotten... I will celebrate with Jerusalem and all its people; there will be no more crying or sorrow in that city.'
Isaiah 65.17-19

Isaiah's core themes are judgment and redemption. God would judge his people for their sins, but he would also rescue them from captivity.

Who & When

Isaiah's name means 'the Lord saves'. We know that he was married with two sons, Shear-Jashub [Isa 7.3] and Maher-Shalal-Hash-Baz [Isa 8.3]. He lived mainly in Jerusalem, reportedly wrote a biography of King Uzziah [2 Chr 26.22] and, according to Jewish tradition, died a particularly gruesome death during the reign of King Mannasseh: he was sawn in half. (Heb 11.37 makes reference to this). He began his ministry in, 'the year that King Uzziah died' i.e. 740BC [Isa 6.1] and lived at least until 681BC, when the Assyrians were defeated. Many experts believe the book is the work of three different 'Isaiahs' rather than just one, basing their claims on stylistic differences between different sections. However, it must also be argued that there are similarities between different sections as well, and phrases that crop up throughout the book, which are not found elsewhere in scripture.

The book of Isaiah is not chronologically arranged. We are constantly thrown forward and backward in time. Political observations and historical accounts jostle with visions of the far-future and calls to repentance. Signs of the near-future mingle with announcements of the **Messiah**. The Messiah— the anointed one who would rescue Israel and usher in a new age of peace and wholeness—is a major feature of Isaiah's visions. Isaiah constantly emphasises **God's power and might**—he is a 'fire' that will scorch the earth. But if he is a fire in judgment, he is also a stream in the desert, and a road back from exile.

Isaiah contains some of the most inspiring, moving and powerful pictures of God's reign in all its glory, when the exiles are brought back home, when the Lord will create a new world, free of suffering, sadness and pain.

The Sights

☐ Justice, not religion: 1.1-20
☐ The vineyard: 5.1-30
☐ Isaiah's vision: 6.1-13
☐ The Messiah: 8.16-9.7
☐ Homecoming: 11.1-12.6
☐ Victory: 26.1-27.1
☐ Punishment: 28.1-29
☐ The Assyrians: 36.1-22
☐ Message to Hezekiah: 37.21-38
☐ Hope: 40.1-31
☐ Lord's Servant: 42.1-9
☐ Suffering servant: 53.1-12
☐ True Religion: 58.1-14
☐ The new world: 65.17-25

Jeremiah

God is going to punish the people of Judah for their evil. And Jeremiah has the job of telling them about it.

Who & What

Jeremiah, son of Hilkiah the Priest lived in Anathoth, about three miles north of Jerusalem. He began his career in the reign of Josiah and his work breaks into three broad periods:

- 627–605BC Prophecies while Judah was threatened by Assyria and Egypt.
- 605–586BC Proclaims God's judgment against Babylon.
- 586–580BC Prophesied in Jerusalem while the city was captured.

'Here is the new agreement that I, the Lord, will make with the people of Israel: I will write my laws on their hearts and minds. I will be their God, and they will be my people.'
Jeremiah 31.33

Jeremiah lived through a succession of increasingly ineffective and appalling monarchs. Few people in the Bible have led lives of such conflict; he was forever being thrown into jail, or tried for his life, or forced to flee. He was publicly humiliated by false prophets and even thrown into a sewer.

The reason for this harsh treatment is simple: those in power simply did not want to hear his message. Jeremiah told them that, unless they changed their ways, **the kingdom of Judah would be destroyed**.

Time and time again, Jeremiah calls the people to repent; time and time again he is ignored, reviled or abused. The reward for his prophecies is beatings, exclusion and imprisonment. And all the time the forces of destruction are gathering and waiting to pounce.

Jeremiah is a very honest book. The prophet was originally a timid figure and, despite promises that he would receive strength from God, he often struggled with his calling (not surprising when you see what happened to him). He often calls for vengeance on his enemies and he often breaks down in tears. Yet he does remain strong. He keeps the memory of his first calling close to his heart and he keeps going. While all around him collapses, Jeremiah's foundations remain firm.

The Sights: Jeremiah

- ☐ God chooses Jeremiah: 1.1–19
- ☐ First message: 2.1–37
- ☐ In the Temple: 7.1–26
- ☐ Slaughter valley: 7.27–8.17
- ☐ Jeremiah complains to God: 12.1–17
- ☐ Dirty underwear: 13.1–27
- ☐ Tough message: 16.1–18
- ☐ Enemy action: 18.18–23
- ☐ Seventy years: 25.1–14
- ☐ The false prophet: 28.1–17
- ☐ The new agreement: 31.1–40
- ☐ Buying a field: 32.1–44
- ☐ Down the sewer: 38.1–28
- ☐ The end: 39.1–14

Lamentations

Jerusalem fell to the **Babylonians** in 588BC. Lamentations consists of five poems, written by **Jeremiah** as the city of **Jerusalem** was descending into chaos and defeat.

> 'The Lord's kindness never fails! If he had not been merciful, we would have been destroyed. The Lord can always be trusted to show mercy each morning.'
> Lamentations 3.22–3

Who & When

Traditionally, Jeremiah, although no authorship is mentioned in the book. It was written after the fall of Jerusalem, around 588–587BC.

While the prophet understands that Jerusalem's suffering is deserved, he questions whether they really deserved this much. There is an awful feeling that **God has deserted them**, that he is on the side of their enemies, that he and his people are no longer even on speaking terms. It is not merely that Jerusalem is crushed, not merely that their own sins have brought them to this, it is that feeling that the Lord has turned his back on them.

Yet despite this feeling, the prophet knows that this will not last. The Lord will build up his city and his people again. There is hope among the rubble.

The first four chapters of Lamentations are written as **acrostics**. In Hebrew, each verse of each chapter begins with successive letters of the Hebrew alphabet (chapter three has three verses for each letter). It's as if you wrote a poem in which the first sentence begins with 'A', the second with 'B', the third with 'C' and so on. Perhaps the prophet is indicating that the suffering of the people has gone from A–Z, across the complete range of experience.

The Sights:
Lamentations
☐ The lonely city: 1.1–22
☐ The angry God: 2.1–22
☐ Hope in the ruins: 3.1–66
☐ Jerusalem's punishment: 4.1–22
☐ Have mercy: 5.1–22

Ezekiel

Ezekiel has been deported to **Babylon**, along with many others from Jerusalem. While there he sees a series of powerful visions of what is going to happen.

Who & When

A younger contemporary of Jeremiah, Ezekiel was a priest (Ezk 1.3) and, apparently, was among the first group deported to Babylon in 597BC. A later tradition asserts that he was murdered in Babylon and was buried there. The most popular view is that the book was edited soon after the prophets death—some time around 570BC.

There's a thin line between 'prophet' and 'nutter' and, at times, it seems as though Ezekiel has crossed that line. He's one of the Old Testament's most bizarre, outrageous figures. He ate a scroll. He lay for 390 days on his left side, and then lay for only 40 days on his right side. He knocked a hole in the wall of his house and climbed through. Not what you'd call well-balanced behaviour.

But Ezekiel was **a shock-tactic prophet**, bringing people messages from God in a way which they couldn't fail to notice. Indeed, at times his message is couched in a language that is almost obscene (for example, chapter 16). Ezekiel is passionate, because **God is passionate**. He shocks people because God wants to shock people out of their apathy; to get them to open their eyes.

Ezekiel warns the people remaining in Jerusalem to change their ways; he calls on his fellow exiles to recognise the faults that led to their captivity and he urges them to keep faith with the Lord. He will bring them through this. Ezekiel didn't only see visions of doom; he also saw visions of glory. His career as a prophet began with a dazzling vision of God and in the final section of the book—after the final fall of Jerusalem—God gave Ezekiel a vision of a **future Jerusalem**, with an **ideal temple** where God will once again be worshipped in peace and security. The people would return, God will bring his people back to him.

> 'I, the Lord God, promise to open your graves and set you free. I will bring you back to Israel, and when that happens, you will realise that I am the Lord. My Spirit will give you breath, and you will live again.'
> Ezekiel 37.12-14

The Sights: Ezekiel

- ☐ Ezekiel is chosen: 1.1-2.10
- ☐ Eat the scroll: 3.1-27
- ☐ Acts of destruction: 4.1-17
- ☐ Through the walls: 12.1-16
- ☐ Jerusalem sleeps around: 16.1-43
- ☐ The rusty pot: 24.1-27
- ☐ The fall of Jerusalem: 33.21-33
- ☐ Good and bad shepherds: 34.1-31
- ☐ The valley of bones: 37.1-28
- ☐ The stream from the Temple: 47.1-12

Daniel

Daniel is an odd mix of narrative and prophecy. It tells the tale of a group of Jews in exile in Babylon, but also recounts prophecies that point to future times.

'Daniel's faith in God had kept him from being harmed.'
Daniel 6.23

Who & When

It was written by Daniel—or by someone a lot later, depending on your point of view. Few books have excited so much discussion as Daniel. Some experts argue that the book is a 'modern' invention, written around 165BC. They point to things like its language and style, and supposed innaccuracies in its historical references. Others argue for its authenticity, claiming that the book shows a detailed knowledge of Babylonian culture and arguing that some of the modern terms could well have been in use at an earlier date. Fundamentally, the argument is about the predictive powers of prophecy. If you believe that the kind of detailed prophetic statements in Daniel are impossible, then you will always have problems with the book. If, however, you believe that they are perfectly possible, then the other issues become less difficult.

The first half of the book is a narrative set in the reigns of the **Babylonian** emperors **Nebuchadnezzar** and **Belshazzar**. They feature Daniel and his friends and their struggle to keep their integrity under pressure. Daniel is **a kind of Joseph**, rising to power and influence in a foreign court through his God-given wisdom and insight and granted prophetic visions of future empires. The second part of the book details Daniel's own prophecies of the future.

One central theme of the book is the **pressure to conform**, to change our customs and practices. Babylon was a 'multi-cultural' empire that had absorbed knowledge and customs from those it had conquered. But Daniel is all about **integrity**—retaining a purity of worship in the face of enormous pressure to conform and to change. In today's multi-faith, relativistic world, Daniel has an important message about the struggle to stay faithful, and the way that God will support us in that struggle.

The Sights
☐ A vegetarian diet: 1.1–21
☐ Nebuchadnezzar's dream: 2.1–49
☐ The fiery furnace: 3.1–30
☐ The writing on the wall: 5.1–31
☐ The lion's den: 6.1–28
☐ The four beasts: 7.1–28
☐ Seventy years: 9.1–19

Minor Prophets

This section consists of twelve books. The phrase **'minor prophets'** refers not to the contents of these books, but to their length; some of these books are only one chapter long.

Most of these men prophesied during **the decline of the kingdoms of Israel and Judah**. The themes they deal with are similar to those of the major prophets—themes such as the unfaithfulness of the people, social injustice and oppression, the future redemption of God's people, and the coming of a **Messiah**, a person chosen by God who would rescue his people from their foes.

Hosea is a tale of one man's love for his unfaithful wife, a love which mirrors the merciful, forgiving love of God.

Joel is a short book that tries to explain why Judah has been laid waste by a huge plague of locusts.

Amos is a powerful book that condemns the hypocrisy, idolatry, corruption and injustice of Israel.

Obadiah is only one chapter long, and deals with the destruction of Edom.

Jonah is more a story than a book of prophecy. It deals with God's offer of forgiveness to the hated, evil Assyrians.

Micah moves between condemnation of Israel's unjust conduct and prophecies of a great, future hope.

Nahum talks about the destruction of Nineveh, the capital of the Assyrian empire.

Habakkuk is a kind of mini book of Job, and asks why God is allowing bad things to happen to his people.

Zephaniah warns that those who follow false gods will face the judgment of God.

Haggai and **Zechariah** are associated with the return to Jerusalem after the exile, and aim to encourage the people to continue working on restoring the Temple. Zechariah talks of a king who will one day return to Jerusalem.

Malachi is the last book of the Old Testament. Malachi reminds people of their obligations to God and their purpose in his plan.

Hosea

Hosea is a dramatic tale. The prophet is told to marry Gomer, a prostitute. Her unfaithfulness to him, and his love for her, is a powerful image of God's enduring love for Israel.

'I'd rather you were faithful and knew me than offered sacrifices.'
Hosea 6.6

Who & When

Hosea lived in the northern kingdom of Israel. (Indeed, Hosea is the only Old Testament book from the northern kingdom of Israel.) He prophesied around 750–715BC, in the troubled, final years of Israel, before it fell to the Assyrians. He prophesied for around forty years, but nothing is known of him outside this book.

The Sights: Hosea
☐ Hosea's family: 1.1–2.1
☐ Punishment and hope: 2.2–3.5
☐ False priests, false people: 4.1–19
☐ Pretend worship: 6.1–11
☐ My child: 11.1–11
☐ Terrible fate: 13.1–16
☐ Future forgiveness: 14.1–9

Hosea loves his **unfaithful wife**; God loves his **unfaithful people**. He doesn't want to punish them, but the way they have 'slept' with other gods gives him little choice. The people are dishonest; the priests are idol worshippers; the kings are corrupt. Hosea condemns social injustice and the false gods and fake worship that bring it forth.

Other prophets performed dramatic acts to get their message across to the people, but Hosea's *whole life* was a prophetic act: marrying an unfaithful prostitute, naming his children 'not pitied' and 'not my people', this was a man who truly lived his message.

Joel

The country of Judah has been ravaged by a plague locusts. Joel sees this as foreshadowing the day of the Lord.

'I am merciful, kind, and caring. I don't easily lose my temper, and I don't like to punish.'
Joel 2.13

Who & When

Joel, son of Pethuel. He probably lived near Jerusalem, around ninth century BC.

Locusts were a sad feature of life in the ancient Middle East. One swarm sweeps through Judah, devastating Jerusalem and

The Sights: Joel
☐ The locusts and the army: 1.1–2.11
☐ Turn around: 2.12–32
☐ Judgment Valley: 3.1–21

Joel asks 'why?' He interprets it as a warning from God, a forerunner of the day of judgment. Joel uses the locusts as a picture of a real army; an army that would be far more devastating. And the only insect repellent that will work against this army is for the people to return to their God.

Amos

Amos was a farmer from **Judah** who went north into **Israel** to condemn the behaviour of the leaders and people.

Who & When

Amos was a shepherd and fig-grower from Tekoa. His name meant 'burden'. Although his home was in Judah, he went to preach in Bethel, the then capital of Israel. He preached in the reign of King Uzzia, sometime around 760–750BC.

Amos starts by attacking other nations but then narrows the focus of his attack to deliver a stinging attack on Israel and their **skin-deep religion**. They pretended to be holy, but their society was crawling with idolatry, corruption and injustice.

Amos has a true prophet's passionate commitment to the truth, a deep respect for God and an understanding of the significance of all that God has done for his people. He has seen God at work and heard him speak. Now he must pass that message on, an ordinary person who has been suddenly promoted to the prophet's ranks. As he says, 'Everyone is terrified when a lion roars, and ordinary people become prophets when the Lord God speaks' [Amos 3.8].

> 'No more of your noisy songs! I won't listen when you play your harps. But let justice and fairness flow like a river that never runs dry.'
> Amos 5.23–4

The Sights: Amos
- ☐ Judgment on nations: 1.1–2.5
- ☐ Judgment on Israel: 2.6–16
- ☐ You fat cows! 4.1–13
- ☐ Start doing right: 5.1–15
- ☐ I hate your religion: 5.21–27
- ☐ The crumbling house: 9.1–10
- ☐ New roots: 9.12–15

Obadiah

Only one chapter long, this book deals with the **destruction of Edom**, a nation south of the Dead Sea.

Who & When

Obadiah. His name means 'worshipper of the Lord'. If verses 11–14 refer to a Philistine invasion, that means Obadiah was writing in the ninth century BC; if it refers to the Babylonian invasion, he lived two hundred years later.

Obadiah pronounces judgment on a nation who had stood by while Judah suffered. The book is also about all those who stand passively by while evil is committed, all those who are rejected by God for their sin and their callous disinterest.

> 'The day is coming when I, the Lord, will judge the nations. And, Edom, you will pay in full for what you have done.'
> Obadiah 15

The Sights: Obadiah
- ☐ Edom's pride: 1.1–14
- ☐ Israel's victory: 1.15–21

Jonah

This little book contains one of the most famous stories of the Bible. And its four chapters have given rise to almost as much debate as the first four chapters of Genesis.

' You are a kind and merciful God, and you are very patient. You always show love, and you don't like to punish anyone, not even foreigners.'
Jonah 4.2

Who & When

Traditionally the book is believed to have been written by Jonah himself, but it may come from the same source as the tales of Elisha and Elijah. The action takes place around 800–750BC. Some date the book later, after the exile, or at least after the fall of Nineveh in 612BC. However, it would certainly make more sense to have the prophet go to an active superpower, rather than one that had just collapsed.

Jonah features elsewhere in the Bible, [2 Kings 14.25] where he predicts success to Jeroboam II, and the the restoration of the land of Israel to its ancient boundaries. These prophecies must have made Jonah very popular in Israel. However, one of the key factors in Israel's military success was the fact that Damascus—the country with which Israel had been at war—was only quietened because it had been attacked by the Assyrians.

And it is to the Assyrians that Jonah is sent. The startling fact about Jonah is not that he ran away; it's that God wanted to forgive the Assyrians. They were the Nazis of their day, a frightening, brutal people who destroyed countries and deported people. No one in their right mind would go to Nineveh, their capital, and then tell them to repent. Israel believed that the truth was theirs alone and they wrapped it in ritual and rite and sanctimonious piety. But God says that the hated, feared Assyrians were his children as well. And when they repented and listened to his message, he forgave them.

In one sense it is wrongly placed, for unlike the rest of the Prophets, it is a narrative about a prophet, rather than the contents of his message. Indeed, we only have one line of prophecy from Jonah in the whole book and that consists of one simple message: 'Forty days from now, Nineveh will be destroyed!'

The Sights: Jonah
☐ Jonah prophesies for Jeroboam: 2Kings 14.25
☐ Jonah runs away: 1.1-17
☐ In the belly of the fish: 2.1-10
☐ The Assyrians repent: 3.1-10
☐ All people matter: 4.1-11

Micah

Crying out against injustice and trying to get the people to change their ways, the seven chapters of Micah move between condemnation of Israel's conduct and great prophecies of a future hope.

Who & When

Micah was a resident of Moresheth, a small town in southern Judah. He prophesied between 750 and 768BC, during the reigns of three kings: Jotham, Ahaz and Hezekiah. He was a contemporary of Isaiah and Amos.

Micah uses strong, vivid language: people shave their heads 'as bald as vultures' [Mic 1.16]; mountains melt like wax. There are images of people sitting at peace under their own vine, and majestic images of **a future King** who will shepherd his people into a time of great peace.

'The Lord God has told us what is right and what he demands: See that justice is done, let mercy be your first concern, and humbly obey your God.'
Micah 6.8

The Sights: Micah
- ☐ Judgment: 1.1–16
- ☐ Evil rulers: 3.1–12
- ☐ Out of Bethlehem: 5.1–5
- ☐ Empty inside: 7.1–7
- ☐ Come and lead us!: 7.14–20

Nahum

The theme of the book is the destruction of **Nineveh**—and by Nineveh, Nahum means the entire **Assyrian empire**. This cruel, oppressive empire was to be destroyed and, indeed, the book ends with the destruction of Nineveh.

Who & When

Nahum was a resident of Elkosh. His name means 'comforter'. He worked around 620BC, making him a contemporary of Zephaniah and a young Jeremiah.

God is depicted in Nahum as slow but sure. He is 'slow to anger' but he will not leave the guilty unpunished. Evil will not triumph.

'The Lord is powerful, yet patient; he makes sure that the guilty are always punished. He can be seen in storms and in whirlwinds; clouds are the dust from his feet.'
Nahum 1.3

The Sights
- ☐ When God gets angry: 1.1–6
- ☐ The messenger is coming: 1.7–15
- ☐ Doom to the crime capital!: 3.1–19

Habakkuk

Habakkuk lived in troubled times. **Judah** was in turmoil and everything was falling apart. So Habakkuk's question to God is simple: why are you allowing this to happen?

'The Lord gives me strength. He makes my feet as sure as those of a deer, and he helps me stand on the mountains.'
Habakkuk 3.19

Who & When

Habakkuk prophesied around 605BC—the same time as Jeremiah. He predicts the Babylonian invasion of Judah and the attack on Jerusalem in 597BC.

Habakkuk raises the same questions as **Job**, but from a slightly different perspective. Whereas Job asks, 'How could you let this happen to me?', Habakkuk asks, 'How could you let this happen to us?' The book is set out as **a dialogue** between man and God. Habakkuk tries to understand God's actions, which seem to him meaningless and mysterious. God replies to Habakkuk and the prophet responds with a moving and passionate declaration of faith.

The Sights: Habakkuk
☐ The first conversation: 1.1–11
☐ The second conversation: 1.12–2.20
☐ Praise the Lord: 3.1–19

Zephaniah

Judah was to be **judged**. Those who were following false gods would face the judgment of the one, true God.

Who & When

Zephaniah was a distant member of the royal family; his great-great-grandfather was King Hezekiah. He prophesied during the reign of King Josiah (640–609BC), probably in the early part of his reign.

'If you humbly obey the Lord, then come and worship him. If you do right and are humble, perhaps you will be safe on that day when the Lord turns loose his anger.'
Zephaniah 2:3

Zephaniah talks about '**the day of the Lord**'. The people of Judah believed that this would be their moment, the day when the Lord would wipe out all their enemies. But Zephaniah tells them that Judah too would get what it deserved.

The Sights: Zephaniah
☐ Judgment on Judah: 1.1–2.3
☐ Judgment on other nations: 2.4–15
☐ Turn to the Lord: 3.1–20

Zephaniah prophesied during the reign of **King Josiah**, who was a good king and a reformer [2 Kings 22.1–23.30; 2 Chr 34–5]. This raises the possibility that Zephaniah himself might have been that even rarer thing: a prophet who was listened to.

Haggai

It's 520BC. The Jews who had been in **exile in Babylon** have been allowed to return home to **Jerusalem**. But life is hard, and the Temple is still in ruins.

Who & When

Haggai was an exile in Babylon and returned to Jerusalem in the second wave of returnees. We can date his prophecies precisely, though, to 520BC: 21 September, 17 October and 18 December to be precise!

When Babylon was captured by **Cyrus the Great**, the excited exiles were allowed to return to Jerusalem and re-inhabit the land. Then reality set in. Weariness and hardship, combined with local opposition, had led to the abandonment of the **Temple rebuilding project**. Haggai calls Israel to reconsider its priorities. The Temple is more than a building project; it is a sign that the land will be dedicated to God.

Zechariah

Demoralised people in a damaged city, Zechariah inspires the people to see the Temple to completion.

Who & When

Zechariah was the grandson of Iddo (possibly the Iddo who returned from exile in 536BC [Neh 12.4; Ezr 2.2]). Probably a priest, he was a contemporary of Haggai, and his first vision occurred about mid-October, 520BC. His work continued for at least two years until 518BC [Zec 7.1].

Few books of the Bible are as **difficult to interpret** as Zechariah—it's right up there with **Revelation**. However, no prophet has more to say about the **Messiah**, or points more clearly to **Jesus**. Zechariah saw a wounded King, a shepherd for whom all creation was waiting. He saw what was coming and his excitement and awe is found on virtually every line.

The first part contains eight strange visions. The second section consists of a series of **messages to Israel and its leaders** as well as a final, awe-inspiring vision of the far-future. Much of the imagery in Zechariah reappears in Revelation.

'But cheer up! Because I, the LORD All-powerful, will be here to help you with the work, just as I promised your ancestors when I brought them out of Egypt.'
Haggai 2:4–5

The Sights: Haggai
☐ Rebuild the Temple: 1.1–15
☐ I'll be here: 2.1–23

'So once again, I, the Lord All-Powerful, tell you; See that justice is done and be kind and merciful to one another!'
Zechariah 7.8–9

The Sights: Zechariah
☐ Back to God: 1.1–17
☐ Plumb line: 2.1–13
☐ Ruling branch: 6.9–15
☐ Did you do it for me?: 7.1–14
☐ Enemies punished: 8.1–23
☐ Wounded shepherd: 13.7–9
☐ Streams of life: 14.1–21

Malachi

The Temple is rebuilt, sacrifices are being offered again, but times are difficult. The old sins of Israel are creeping back.

'But for you who honour my name, victory will shine like the sun with healing in its rays, and you will jump around like calves at play.'
Malachi 4.2

Who & When

His name literally means 'messenger'. Malachi could be a name, but equally could be simply a title. He was probably the last prophet of Old Testament times. This prophecy probably comes from Jerusalem, after the exiles have returned, in 433BC. He was a contemporary of Ezra and Nehemiah.

The Sights: Malachi
- ☐ God loves Israel: 1.1–5
- ☐ The false priests: 1.6–2.9
- ☐ The Lord will come: 3.1–4
- ☐ Don't cheat God: 3.5–18

God's laws were being disobeyed, his instructions ignored, the people were once again on the receiving end of injustice and greed. The glory prophesied by **Zechariah** and **Haggai** had not come about. The Temple, far from being a spiritual powerhouse, was a place where they simply went through the ritual.

Malachi was an intense, sometimes severe patriot. Faced with a disheartened and disobedient people, he reminded them that religious ritual is no good on its own. It only has value if it is a **true expression** of sincere belief. The law is important. The priests should guard it carefully. But more than that, they should obey it.

God has a purpose for these people—a particular role for them to play. By weakening their culture they were hindering that purpose.

Between the Testaments

By the final pages of the Old Testament the Israelites have **re-established the kingdom of Israel** after exile in Babylon. But between the last book of the Old Testament and the first book of the New, there is a gap of **about four hundred years**.

So what happened in between?

Although people like **Nehemiah** and **Ezra** rebuilt Israel it was always a weak country, and for the next few centuries the country was owned by a number of different empires. First there were the **Greeks** under their leader **Alexander the Great**, one of the greatest leaders in history. Alexander invented a policy known as **Hellenisation**, which meant he tried to impose the Greek culture on all the lands he conquered. He established many Greek-style cities throughout the Middle East.

When he died, his massive empire was split between his generals. Two of them—**Ptolomy** and **Seleucis**—founded families which each had turns in ruling Israel. The Ptolomies went to Egypt and ruled Israel for about one hundred years. Then the Seleucids had their turn … and here's where Hellenisation really starts to kick in. A Seleucid ruler called **Antiochus IV** tried to wipe out the Jewish faith. He tried to destroy every copy of the **Hebrew Scriptures** and he forced people to make offerings to **Zeus**. He even marched into the Temple, set up a statue of Zeus and sacrificed a pig—an unclean animal.

The Israelites revolted. An uprising led by a soldier called **Judas Maccabeus** drove out the Seleucids and led to **one hundred years of Jewish independence**.

And then the **Romans** came along. In 63BC a Roman general called **Pompey** took Jerusalem after besieging Temple Mount for three months. He massacred priests and even marched into the **holy of holies** in the **Temple** (which he was baffled to find completely empty).

And that's the situation at the beginning of the New Testament. Israel is under foreign occupation, controlled by the Romans.

The Apocrypha

The **Apocrypha** is the name given to Old Testament books found in some Bibles but not in others. **Catholic and Orthodox** Bibles include these texts, but most **Protestant** Bibles do not.

For these reasons, we have to go back to 382AD, when **Jerome** was commissioned by the Pope to make a Latin translation of the scriptures. He went and worked in Palestine—in Bethlehem, in fact—to look at copies in the original languages. He discovered that some versions of the Hebrew Scriptures had fourteen extra books. He called these books the 'Apocrypha' which means **'hidden things'**, because he believed they had been hidden away, or that they had hidden meanings.

From the start there were arguments over whether or not these books really were scripture. Some early Church writers quote from them, indicating that the first Christians read them, but they gradually came to be accorded a sort of second division status. And that is largely how they are viewed today. They can be interesting, instructive and moving, but they are not on a par with the rest of the Bible.

Anyway, if you have a Bible with the Apocrypha, this is what you get:

1 and 2 Maccabees tell the story of the **Maccabean** wars, where the Jews revolted against their Greek rulers. It talks about the desecration of the Temple, the successful wars and the period up to 61BC, when Pompey and the Romans invaded. It also tells the story of the Jewish festival of **Hanukah**. Although they are linked together, the books are quite different. 1 Maccabees is a complete book, while 2 Macabees summarises another, much longer work.

1 and 2 Esdras are what is known as 'apocalyptic' books as they talk about the end times. But they also seek to explain certain aspects of Jewish history.

Ecclesiasticus (also known as **The Wisdom of Jesus ben Sirach**) is a wisdom book a bit like Proverbs. It does include a famous passage which begins, 'Let us now praise famous men' [Si 44.1–50.31] in which the author includes himself!

The Book of Wisdom (or the **Wisdom of Solomon**) is another wisdom book, which seems to be a kind of positive reply to **Ecclesiastes**. (Given that Solomon is the traditional author of Ecclesiastes, he appears to be talking to himself.) It talks a lot about the uses of wisdom, particularly in preparing a soul for life after death.

Tobit is a book that tells the story of a Jew living in **Nineveh**. This man—the Tobit of the title—is a devout, faithful man who is now blind. In response to his faithfulness, God sends an angel to cure his blindness and reward his family.

Judith is a bit like Esther. It tells of a Jewish woman living in Jerusalem when the city is under attack by the **Assyrians**. She sneaks into the enemy camp, seduces the Assyrian general and cuts off his head, leading to an amazing victory. It is set in the time of 'Nebuchadnezzar who ruled over the Assyrians in the great city of Nineveh' [Jdt 1.1]. Since Nebuchadnezzar was Babylonian and not Assyrian, you could say that its grasp of history is a bit shaky.

As well as entire books, the Apocrypha also includes additions to existing books of the Old Testament.

There are four extra parts of the Book of Daniel. **The Prayer of Azariah** and **The Song of the Three Children** are inserted into Daniel, chapter three, where the young men are thrown into the fiery furnace. **The History of Susanna** is perhaps the earliest detective story in the world and tells of a woman unjustly accused of adultery, whose innocence is revealed by Daniel. It usually becomes Daniel chapter thirteen. **Bel and the Dragon** (which becomes Daniel chapter fourteen) tells how Daniel escapes from a plot to put him to death.

There are **additions to the Book of Esther,** which include Mordecai's dream, letters from the emperor and various prayers.

The **Book of Baruch** (who was Jeremiah's secretary) is an add-on to Jeremiah and contains a letter to the Jews in exile, as well as some prayers, poems and passages of wisdom literature.

The **Prayer of Manasseh** apparently relates the prayer of King Manasseh who, after a lifetime of wickedness, repents of his sins before he dies.

The New Testament

The New Testament is probably the most influential book in the world. For nearly 2,000 years, those inspired by its teachings have changed the lives of millions of people, through their teaching, their preaching, their care for the outcast and the poor.

It is made up of two main sections. The **Gospels and Acts** are biographies of **Jesus** and the story of what happened immediately after his death and resurrection. The four gospels were not the only accounts of Jesus. There were probably other histories and collections of sayings. Indeed, not all the sayings of Jesus made it into the gospels. Paul quotes Jesus in Acts 20.35: 'It is more blessed to give than to receive' but it doesn't appear in any gospel, so he must have got it from another collection of Jesus' sayings.

The **Letters**, which answered questions, explained Jesus' teaching and reminded the followers of Jesus what he had said. There are various collections of letters. Most influential, perhaps, are the **letters of Paul**, but there are also letters from **John**, **Peter**, **James** and others. This section also includes the book of **Revelation** which is a vision of the future seen by John while he is a prisoner on the isle of Patmos. It's not really like anything else in the New Testament. Or the rest of the Bible for that matter...

The New Testament writings all date from the second half of the first century AD. They were intended to be read aloud—this was an age before printing, before mass education.

When reading the New Testament we should bear in mind that they didn't have all that we have now. The early followers, therefore, saw Christianity as **the fulfilment of Judaism**. They didn't know they were founding a new religion; they thought they were completing the old one. That's why the New Testament is so full of references to the Old Testament: they weren't starting a new book, they were finishing the old one.

The Sights: New Testament

- ☐ Sermon on the mount: Mt 5.1–16
- ☐ The ideal prayer: Mt 6.5–15
- ☐ Good news for the poor: Lk 4.16–30
- ☐ Born again: Jn 3.1–18
- ☐ Loving your enemies: Lk 6.27–36
- ☐ The servant king: Jn 13.1–20
- ☐ The risen saviour: Mt 28.1–20
- ☐ The Holy Spirit: Acts 2.1–47
- ☐ Conversion of Saul: Acts 9.1–31
- ☐ Faith makes us right: Rom 5.1–11
- ☐ The Lord's Supper: 1 Cor 11.23–34
- ☐ Many people, one body: Rom 12.1–8
- ☐ Love: 1 Cor 13.1–13
- ☐ Christ sets us free: Gal 5.1–26

The Gospels

At first there were only the stories.

After Jesus died, stories of his life and works were remembered and recounted. Jesus himself left no writings, but he was such an amazing figure that his most **famous sayings** and actions were passed on from person to person.

As Christianity spread, its followers needed a more permanent record. Those who saw and knew Jesus were dying and the new recruits in the church wanted to know what had happened. So four writers—**Matthew**, **Mark**, **Luke** and **John**—wrote accounts of Jesus' life, drawing on all the evidence and the material they could find.

Most experts agree that **Mark** was the earliest of the gospels to be written. It is simple and short and ends rather abruptly. Both **Luke** and **Matthew** used Mark as one of the main sources for their own works.

Out of the four gospels, **Matthew, Mark** and **Luke** are noticeably similar, covering many of the same events and narrating the history in roughly the same order. This has led to them being dubbed the **synoptic gospels** (*syn* = 'together' and *optic* = 'seeing'). They see things, as it were, with the same eyes.

However, they also drew on **memories and recollections**. Most of the people Jesus met did not read or write, but they were used to memorising facts, stories, important sayings. Then there woud have been **fragments of writing** and **early 'gospels'**. Although Mark is the first we have, there may well have been earlier accounts. There was probably **a collection of Jesus' sayings** in circulation. Matthew and Luke certainly drew on this. Experts call this document '**Q**' (from the German 'Quelle' = 'Source').

Finally there would have been **divine inspiration**. The gospel of **John**, for instance, includes reflections and comments from the writer himself; it delves a lot deeper into the mind and thoughts of Jesus. John had obviously spent many years thinking about and praying over what he had heard and seen. His gospel, therefore, includes ideas that came to him direct from God, rather than from other sources.

Matthew

'Go to the people of all nations and make them my disciples. Baptise them in the name of the Father, the Son, and the Holy Spirit, and teach them to do everything I have told you. I will be with you always, even until the end of the world.'
Matthew 28.19–20

Matthew is writing mainly for the **Jewish followers**, explaining that Jesus was the Messiah they had been looking for.

Who & When

The traditional view is that this was written by Matthew the disciple. Whatever the case, the author was Jewish, probably living in Palestine and addressing a Jewish audience. Some say the gospel was written as early as the late 50s AD, others argue for the 70s or even later.

Because Matthew's gospel is aimed mainly at a Jewish readership, it emphasises the way that **Old Testament prophecy** leads to Jesus and uses a lot of **Jewish terminology** (e.g. calling Jesus the 'Son of David'). Matthew quotes from the Old Testament more than any other gospel writer. He aims to prove that **Jesus is the Messiah**, the promised one, and to do that he includes a family tree to show Jesus' descent from **King David**.

Because Christ is a king, Matthew talks about his kingdom, or as he calls it '**the kingdom of heaven**'. This is a kingdom that is carried everywhere in the hearts of believers. Wherever two or three people gather for prayer, Christ is with them; and the kingdom bursts into life.

If you've got a kingdom and you've got a king, you've got to have rules. So Matthew also talks a lot about what the people must do to be a part of the kingdom. There is the famous **sermon on the mount** and the golden rule—'Treat others as you want them to treat you' [Mt 7.12].

Although it is aimed at Jewish readers, Matthew's gospel is not a narrow gospel. The kingdom is open to all, from whatever nation. He tells a series of parables, which show that the Jews have not recognised the **Messiah** and that now the Gentiles will have the opportunity. At the end of Matthew's Gospel there is what is known as **the great commission,** where the disciples are told to go and spread the good news throughout the world [Mt 28.18–20].

Mark

People are asking questions. They want to know who this Jesus was. Mark, who knows both Peter and Paul, decides to give them a simple, action-packed account.

> 'Don't be alarmed! You are looking for Jesus from Nazareth, who was nailed to a cross. God has raised him to life, and he isn't here.'
> Mark 16.6

Who & When

The gospel is traditionally attributed to John Mark, the friend of Paul and Peter, who lived in Jerusalem with his mother Mary during the early church times [Acts 12.12]. Papias of Hierapolis, writing in 130AD, records that an old man told him that Mark wrote down Peter's recollections in Rome while Mark was working alongside Peter [1 Pet 5.13]. This is backed up not only by references from the early church historians, but also by the amount of Latin terms that creep into the gospel. The date is usually given as some time between 58–65AD.

Mark's is the most **action-packed Gospel**, mainly because it is the shortest It was also, probably, the **first gospel written**.

Mark's aim is to get over the simple facts. So, there is nothing in his gospel about Jesus' birth and upbringing, and no details about his age or the length of his ministry. The Gospel opens with a bang—with **John the Baptist** and **Jesus' baptism**. If it starts abruptly, it also ends rather quickly, with no resurrection appearance, just two women, an empty tomb and an angel with a message from God. (Although some versions of Mark include alternative, longer endings.)

The simple facts then: Jesus Christ is the **Son of God**. Mark was probably writing for a mainly Gentile, Roman audience. So he is careful to explain Jewish customs and translate Aramaic words and phrases and he includes testimonies from people such as the **Roman Centurion** who was present when Christ was on the cross. There are also many accounts of healings and miracles—sure signs, according to Mark, that Jesus' power came from God. But he also emphasises the difficulties, the way that Jesus suffered. The new life that we get through Jesus isn't easy; it's a life of service and suffering.

The Sights: Mark

- [ ] John the Baptist: 1.1–13
- [ ] The work begins: 1.14–45
- [ ] The crowds respond: 3.1–35
- [ ] Seeds of faith: 4.13–41
- [ ] Sending out the apostles: 6.1–13
- [ ] Who am I?: 8.22–38
- [ ] True glory: 9.2–29
- [ ] Who's the greatest?: 9.33–50
- [ ] Entering Jerusalem: 11.1–33
- [ ] The key commandment: 13.28–37
- [ ] The plot against Jesus: 14.1–26
- [ ] The arrest: 14.27–72
- [ ] The death: 15.6–41
- [ ] The return: 16.1–8

Luke

Luke was an educated man, a doctor and historian who writes a life of Jesus based on a careful collection of all the sources.

'So I made a careful study of everything and then I decided to write and tell you exactly what took place ... I have done this to let you know the truth about what you have heard.'
Luke 1.3–4

Who & When

The author's name—as in all of the gospels—does not appear in the book, but it is certain that the same author wrote Acts. Traditionally, this book has been ascribed to Luke, Paul's companion. It was probably written around 65–70AD, although many experts argue for a later date, around 80–85AD. If the 't heophilus' to whom to book is addressed was a high-ranking Roman official, the book was probably written in Rome.

Luke aims to write a proper history. The book is addressed to someone called **Theophilus**, who may have been a high-ranking Roman official. Luke is **making the case for Christ**. He's looked at all the accounts, examined all the evidence and this is his report. So he includes stories and songs that had been handed down among the early Church, such as the songs of Mary [Lk 1.46–55], Zechariah [Lk 1.68–79] and Simeon [Lk 2.29–32].

The result is not some dry, stuffy history, but a joyful, optimistic account. In Luke's account, the **poor and the marginalised** get the full blast of the good news. His Gospel is packed with tax collectors, prostitutes, lepers and thieves. The news of Jesus' birth comes to humble, despised shepherds. Luke's Gospel also shows **a respect for women** that is highly unusual for the time. Here, women—who were also second-class citizens in Bible times, like the shepherds—play key roles.

Luke is also **writing for a gentile audience**. He was a gentile himself living in **Philippi**. So his gospel also features gentile 'heroes' such as **Centurions** and **Samaritans**. Like Matthew, he includes a genealogy, but his goes back to Adam, the father of all.

Luke's gospel is the first part of a two-part work. He also wrote the book of Acts, which takes the story forward from the resurrection of Jesus through the spread of the early church.

John

The others had shown what Jesus did and said, John set out to explain what it all really means...

Who & When

Tradition has it that this book is the work of the Apostle John. He is not named in this gospel, but referred to as 'the disciple that Jesus loved' [Jn 13.23; 19.26; 20.2; 21.7], which would be natural if he was the author. Some argue that the book is the work of several hands, a sort of 's chool of John'. Clement of Alexandria claimed that John wrote his gospel as a supplement to the other three and tradition places this as the last of the gospels, dating from around the end of the first century AD. However, some experts believe it was written earlier—around 70AD.

> 'God loved the people of this world so much that he gave his only Son, so that everyone who has faith in him will have eternal life and never really die. God did not send his Son into the world to condemn its people. He sent him to save them!'
> John 3.16–17

John's gospel is very different to the other three. There is more **interpretation** and more **reflection** than the other Gospels. When John recounts episodes that we find in the other gospels, he doesn't use the same language. He is seeing the same event, but from **a different perspective**. Mark, Matthew and Luke might tell us of Jesus' authority to forgive sins, but John tells us where this authority came from. In the other gospel Jesus' claim to be God in human form is shown through his actions. In John it is right there on page one, line one.

John is concerned with who Jesus is. He calls Jesus **'the Word'**, the power by which God created everything there is. Jesus, from the very start of John's gospel, is much more than a human being; he is God, and he always has been.

This theme is also picked up in the gospel, where in seven key speeches Jesus begins by saying 'I am...' Indeed, in one crucial incident he just calls himself, **'I am'**, a phrase that the Jews recognised as the most sacred name of God. Jesus also performs seven miraculous signs, each of which tells us more about his nature and origins.

John is the work of one who was with Jesus and knew him intimately. It is also the work of one who, prayerfully and over many years, asked God what it all meant. And what it meant was life. Life in all its fullness, life in all its power, life everlasting.

The Sights: John

- ☐ In the beginning: 1.1–18
- ☐ The wedding: 2.1–12
- ☐ Born again: 3.1–21
- ☐ At the well: 4.1–42
- ☐ The healing of the son: 4.43–54
- ☐ Feeding 5000: 6.1–15
- ☐ Water walking: 6.16–21
- ☐ Bread of life: 6.22–59
- ☐ Light of the world and the great 'I am': 8.12–59
- ☐ Blind man sees: 9.1–41
- ☐ The gate and the good shepherd: 10.1–42
- ☐ The raising of Lazarus: 11.1–44
- ☐ Washing feet: 13.1–20
- ☐ A new rule: 14.15–31
- ☐ The way, the truth and the life: 14.1–31
- ☐ The true vine: 15.1–17
- ☐ Jesus and Pilate 18.28–19.16;
- ☐ Crucifixion: 19.17–42;
- ☐ Resurrection: 20.1–29

Acts

Jesus promised his followers that he would send them the Holy Spirit. This book tells that story and what happens next.

> 'Jesus was taken up to sit at the right side of God, and he was given the Holy Spirit, just as the Father had promised. Jesus is also the one who has given the Spirit to us, and that is what you are now seeing and hearing.'
>
> Acts 2.33

Who & When

The traditional view is that this is the second book written by Luke the doctor, who also wrote the gospel of Luke. Whoever wrote it was a companion of Paul—the historian starts to use the word 'we' from around chapter 16, indicating that he is taking part in the events. There seems no strong reason to doubt that Luke wrote this book. It was probably written about 64 or 65AD. It ends a little after Paul's imprisonment in Rome but does not give any result of his trial, which it surely would have done had the result been known.

Luke had written an account of Jesus' life; now he tells the story of the **early Church**, from the resurrection of Jesus in Jerusalem to the imprisonment of Paul in Rome.

The fact that the early Church grew so quickly brought it into conflict with the **Jewish** and **Roman** authorities, and Acts features several episodes where followers of Jesus are **martyred** for their beliefs. Christianity was a dangerous, life-changing faith, and nothing illustrates that better than the conversion of Saul, who went from being Christianity's greatest enemy to its staunchest follower.

Saul—who became **Paul**—played a crucial role in some of the key issues facing Christianity. There were many arguments within the church itself as to what the Church should be like. Was the Church a part of the **Jewish faith**, or was it something new? Should they try to recruit **Gentiles**—non-Jews—to the cause? And how should the Church organise itself?

So Acts is the history of the first decades of the church. But Acts is a kind of biography of the **Holy Spirit**, who is a constant figure in the background, inspiring, protecting, punishing, informing, pushing the first Christians to ever greater lengths as they spread the good news of Jesus Christ.

The Sights: Acts

- ☐ The Holy Spirit 2.1–47
- ☐ Stephen's death: 6.8–8.3
- ☐ The Ethiopian 8.4–40
- ☐ Saul's conversion: 9.1–31
- ☐ Clean and unclean: 10.1–48
- ☐ In Antioch: 11.19–30
- ☐ Paul's first journey: 13.1–12
- ☐ Council meeting: 15.1–35
- ☐ In Philippi: 16.11–40
- ☐ Berea and Athens: 17.10–34
- ☐ God, not goddesses: 19.21–41
- ☐ Paul's arrest: 21.17–36
- ☐ I want to go to Rome: 25.1–27
- ☐ Arrival in Rome: 28.16–30

Letters

This section contains **letters** written to churches and individuals in the very early years of Christianity. Most of these letters were written by **Paul**, the great evangelist and teacher. The rest were written by other **Apostles**, and by one, unnamed writer.

Paul's Letters

Romans, written by Paul to introduce himself to the church at Rome and to share some of his core beliefs.

1 and 2 Corinthians were written to challenge and correct the sinful behaviour of the church at Corinth.

Galatians was written to a group of churches planted by Paul on his first missionary journey.

Ephesians emphasises the need for unity and summarises Paul's ideas and beliefs.

Philippians is a thank-you letter from Paul. He encourages the church at Philippi to keep going.

Colossians was written to a church that Paul had heard about from a friend. He encourages the church to focus on Jesus.

1 and 2 Thessalonians are early letters written to encourage new converts to Christianity.

1 and 2 Timothy are letters written to Paul's helper Timothy, dealing with practical issues of running a church.

Titus was written to one of Paul's most trusted associates and deals with practical church matters, holiness and honesty.

Philemon is a short letter written on behalf of a runaway slave.

General letters

Hebrews deals with the relationship of Christianity to the Old Testament Law.

James is a practical guide on how to live as a Christian.

1 and 2 Peter challenge false teachers and encourage those facing persecution.

Jude rejects false teaching.

1, 2 and 3 John deal with false teaching and the need for Christians to live right.

Revelation is a massive, powerful, vision of the future, filled with mystical imagery and symbolic numbers.

The Sights: Letters

☐ Introduction: Rom 1.1-15
☐ Building: 1 Cor 3.10-23
☐ Pull no punches: Gal 3.1-20
☐ His own hand: Gal 6.11-18
☐ Stop arguing: Phil 4.2-9
☐ From jail: Col 4.9-18
☐ Timothy: 1 Tim 6.11-21
☐ Plea for a slave: Philem 1.1-25
☐ Be brave!: Heb 10.19-39
☐ No favourites: Jas 2.1-26
☐ Paul is difficult: 2 Pet 3.1-18
☐ The same commandment: 1 Jn 2.7-27
☐ Letters to churches: Rev 2.1-29

Romans

Paul writes to introduce himself and more imprtantly, his key
ideas, to those in Rome—probably in preparation for a visit.

> 'The good news
> tells how
> God accepts
> everyone who
> has faith, but
> only those who
> have faith. It
> is just as the
> Scriptures say,
> "The people God
> accepts because
> of their faith
> will live".'
> Romans 1.17

Who & When

Written by Paul to the church in Rome, probably around 57AD. It was probably
written in Corinth, since there are references in the letter to people living there.

Paul describes himself as an **apostle**, chosen to spread the good
news to the **gentiles**. And the message that he has been given is
that all who put their faith in Jesus are saved.

He doesn't say anything very much about the Roman
church for the simple reason that he didn't know much about
it. However, he does know a lot of people there whom he has
met elsewhere—the letter ends with a long list of 'hellos'.

The subject of the letter is **faith in Jesus Christ**. Although Paul
is writing to introduce himself, he uses the letter to set out his
core beliefs; his understanding of what the basis of Christianity is. Salvation comes to us not through what we do, but from
whom we put our faith in. It is God's forgiveness and love that
rescues us, not our own efforts. This is particularly vital in that
it reflects difficulties between **Jewish and gentile Christians** over exactly what Jewish customs Christianity should incorporate.

So the theme of justification through faith, not through
works, occurs frequently in Paul's letters. We've all fallen short
of what is required and there's nothing we can do for ourselves
to gain salvation. It is God's gift to us. That's not to say that
it does not matter what we do. As followers of Jesus we are
obliged to live lives of love, hope and sacrifice. But, Paul argues, we do this as a **response** to salva-
tion, not in order to obtain it.

1 Corinthians

Paul challenges the behaviour of the Corinthian church. He calls on them to **stop arguing** and urges them to value the only thing that really counts: **love**.

> 'For now there are faith, hope, and love. But of these three, the greatest is love.'
> 1 Corinthians 13.13

Who & When

Written by Paul, around 55AD, towards the end of Paul's time in Ephesus [Acts 20.31].

Paul's relationship with the followers in **Corinth** was not an easy one. Partly this was due to the atmosphere of the city itself. Corinth was a wealthy sea port with a reputation for sexual immorality, so much so that the Greeks used the word 'corinthianise' as a verb: if someone was doing a bit of 'corinthianing', they were sleeping around.

This atmosphere of immoral behaviour infected the church, turning it into a group of followers infected by **wealth and sex**. The Corinthian church had many of the signs of a true church, but they were behaving like spoilt brats, rather than children of God.

Although this is called '1 Corinthians' Paul is following up a previous letter, which we no longer have [1 Cor 5.9]. Perhaps Paul's meaning in the first letter had not been clear, but there were still **arguments** in the church and accusations of **sexual immorality**. So he wrote from Ephesus and dispatched Timothy to try to deal with the situation.

Paul was especially concerned with the amount of arguments and splits in the church. They treated each other differently according to wealth and position; they split into **factions**. So Paul encourages them to change their ways; to worship God as he should be worshipped.

Above all, he talks about **love**. In one of the greatest passages ever written he argues that love is the most important thing [1 Cor 13]. If they only loved one another, then the splits and the arguments would disappear.

The Sights: 1 Corinthians

- ☐ Gang warfare: 1.10–31
- ☐ Grow up!: 3.1–23
- ☐ Sexual immorality: 5.1–13
- ☐ A slave for everyone: 9.1–27
- ☐ Rules for worship: 11.1–34
- ☐ One body: 12.1–31
- ☐ Love: 13.1–13
- ☐ Help each other: 14.26–40
- ☐ We will be raised: 15.1–34
- ☐ Death is dead: 15.35–58

2 Corinthians

Paul writes to correct rumours about himself and to encourage the church to deal with troublemakers.

'We never give up. Our bodies are gradually dying, but we ourselves are being made stronger each day. These little troubles are getting us ready for an eternal glory that will make all our troubles seem like nothing at all.'
2 Corinthians 4.16

Who & When

Paul wrote this around 55–56AD, less than a year after his first letter.

This second letter was probably written from northern Macedonia. Paul had only been able to visit Corinth (maybe making a quick trip from Ephesus) for a short, difficult visit, not the 'long stay' he'd promised [1 Cor 16.6]. He'd promised to return, but decided that another painful visit would serve no purpose, so he returned to Asia. His opponents seized on this, claiming that Paul didn't keep his promises.

The result is one of Paul's **most personal letters**. He argues that he stayed away because he wanted to see if his instructions were being followed. He **defends his work** for the gospel and he promises to visit the Corinthians again. We feel the weight of his anxiety for the Corinthian church, and the depth of his concern for them. We also see a **vulnerable side** of Paul—a side that feels the need to assert his own integrity and honesty. Finally, we begin to understand the **sheer cost** that his work has meant to him, the hardship and suffering that he has had to endure.

2 Corinthians refers to a '**severe letter**' that Paul had sent to the Corinthian church. Some experts claim that chapters 10–13 are, in fact from the 'severe' letter. They point to the sudden change in tone, the fact that the flow of the letter has been completely interrupted; one moment Paul is encouraging the Corinthians to give generously, the next moment he is criticising them and threatening them with punishment. It would certainly explain some of the references within those chapters. However the earlier chapters indicate that the criticism of Paul has not entirely disappeared, so Paul may simply be reinforcing the message from the 'strong' letter.

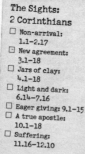

The Sights:
2 Corinthians
☐ Non-arrival: 1.1–2.17
☑ New agreement: 3.1–18
☑ Jars of clay: 4.1–18
☐ Light and dark: 6.14–7.16
☐ Eager giving: 9.1–15
☐ A true apostle: 10.1–18
☐ Suffering: 11.16–12.10

Galatians

Paul writes to combat the ideas of those who thought Christians still had to be circumcised. They need faith in Jesus, not outward shows of obedience.

Who & When

Written by Paul around 49AD, making it the earliest of the New Testament writings.

Galatia is a region. Paul here is writing to the churches in south Galatia that he had established on his first missionary journey—churches in **Derbe**, **Lystra**, and **Iconium** [Acts 13].

Something has happened to these churches. They have been infiltrated by '**Judaizers**'—people who believe that all Christians should follow Jewish religious laws and get **circumcised**. Even prominent 'pillars' of the church like Peter are giving in to their pressure. (Eventually there was to be a **major council** meeting which decided the issue in Paul's favour [Acts 15]). These people claimed that Paul was not a 'proper' apostle, and that he was toning down the requirements of the **Jewish Law** in order to make the gospel acceptable to Gentiles.

Paul's anger at what these people are saying is evident for all to see. He even argues that they shouldn't just go for circumcision, they should cut off the whole lot [Gal 5.12]! He recognises that this isn't some side-issue—it's crucial to his message of grace. So he writes in very strong, passionate terms, asserting his right to be called an **apostle** and arguing that the gospel is a gospel of **love and grace**, not of rules and regulations. In what is his most strongly worded letter, Pauls makes the case for **freedom**—not to do what we want, but to serve Christ [Gal 5.1–15].

> 'If you are a follower of Christ Jesus, it makes no difference whether you are circumcised or not. All that matters is your faith that makes you love others.'
> Galatians 5.6

The Sights: Galatians

☐ A true apostle: 1.1–24
☐ A bit of biography: 2.1–21
☐ Foolish people!: 3.1–14
☐ True freedom: 5.1–6.10

One of the few remains of Lystra is this stone, which mentions 'Lustra'— the Latinised name of the city.

Ephesians

Paul emphasises the need for **unity**. The walls of hatred between Jew and Gentile have been broken down.

'We have only one Lord, one faith, and one baptism. There is one God who is the Father of all people. Not only is God above all others, but he works by using all of us, and he lives in all of us.'
Ephesians 4.4

Who & When

Paul was probably writing from prison in Rome in the early 60s. The letter may well be a sort of circular—an inspirational newsletter sent to other churches as well as the one in Ephesus.

The letter to the churches at Ephesus brings together many of the **major themes** of Paul's teaching, as a kind of summary of his thoughts. It's a sort of general introduction to Paul's ideas; it emphasises especially the need for unity. Followers of Jesus need to recognise that we are all **joined together** and that we should all work for and support one another. Christ has brought together **Jew** and **Gentile**, we all have our role to play, and no one is more important than another.

Paul was probably in prison when he wrote this letter. He reflects on his role in the **great plan** that God has put into action, and he writes to the Ephesians to urge them to stay together.

Paul has an almost breathless tone of wonder at God's kindness, wisdom and love. The overriding theme in this letter is the way in which God has planned all this from the start. Christ has **died to give us freedom** [1.7–8], and the same Christ now sits with God and rules over all things. Christ has given us **life** and he has given us a **future** [2.4–6]. This is **God's gift** to us. There is nothing we can do to earn it.

The Sights: Ephesians
☐ God's plan: 1.1–14
☐ Unified by Christ: 2.11–22
☐ New life: 4.1–24
☐ Living for God: 5.6–20
☐ The fight: 6.10–24

Ephesus, looking down the main street towards the library and agora. The city was one of the greatest in the Roman world and Paul spent two years preaching and teaching there.

Philippians

This is a thank-you letter. Paul thanks the Philippian church for their gift and urges them to keep **running the race**.

> ### Who & When
>
> Paul was writing from imprisonment in Rome, some time around 61AD. Some have argued for an early date—and an earlier imprisonment—but it does seem to fit well with the account of Paul's imprisonment in Acts 28, when he was under house arrest in Rome.

The Philippians, hearing of Paul's imprisonment, had sent him a gift. Paul is writing to thank them, but along the way he takes the opportunity to **encourage** them and to warn them about possible pitfalls. He encourages them to keep on running, because the race is not yet won.

The Philippian church was always very special to Paul. He founded it around 50AD on his **second missionary journey** [Acts 16]. It was probably the first church founded on European soil. **Luke** stayed in **Philippi** after Paul left, which may be because it was Luke's home town.

In return, the Philippian church had always taken an active interest in Paul's work. This is reflected in their support for him while he is in prison. This, perhaps, is why his prayer for them is so **full of joy** [Phil 1.3–11]. This church doesn't need correcting or rebuking; Paul encourages them to continue in their faith, despite the persecution they face.

'I run towards the goal, so that I can win the prize of being called to heaven. This is the prize that God offers because of what Christ Jesus has done.'
Philippians 3.14

The Sights: Philippians

- ☐ Paul's prayer: 1.1–11
- ☐ Prison life: 1.12–30
- ☐ True Humility: 2.1–18
- ☐ Run the race: 3.1–21
- ☐ How to be satisfied: 4.10–23

Colossians

Paul introduces himself to the church at Colossae. He tells them to forget false ideas and practices and focus on Jesus.

> 'Each of you is now a new person. You are becoming more and more like your Creator, and you will understand him better.'
> Colossians 3.10

Who & When

Paul is probably writing from Rome where he was awaiting trial. Around 61AD.

Paul was in jail when he met **Epaphras** who told Paul about the faith of the **Colossians**. Epaphras had probably founded the church at Colossae, as well as churches in Laodicea and Hierapolis [Col 4:12–13]. Around this time Paul also met Onesimus the runaway slave, also from Colossae [Col 4:9; Philem 10].

Epaphras told Paul that his flock was confused. They seem to have been lured into some kind of **Judaism** mixed with **mystical pagan festivals**, a pick'n'mix menu of Jewish dietary laws, angel worship and new moon festivals. The Colossians had a syncretistic religion, mixing ideas from Christianity with ideas from other philosophies and religions which are viewed as equally true.

Paul writes to urge them to stick to what they know and not get lured down a load of theological blind alleys. He urges the Colossians to **root themselves in Christ**, in the fundamental truth of Jesus.

The Sights: Colossians

Colossae today. The mound on which the main buildings of the city stood (it can be seen against the mountains) has never been excavated. Colossae was famous for its purple wool, which was commonly called **colossinus**. By Paul's time the city was overshadowed by the richer **Laodicea**, just a few miles away. A severe earthquake hit this region around 60AD and it may have been the threat of earthquakes that made the people move eventually to the nearby town of Chonae (Honaz).

1 Thessalonians

Paul encourages new converts to Christianity and explain some key issues—especially those concerning the future.

Who & When

Dating around 50AD, this may have been the first letter that Paul wrote to a church (although some experts place Galatians earlier). Written only twenty years after the death and resurrection of Christ, this letter is probably earlier than the gospels.

Paul arrived in **Thessalonica** in the winter of 49AD, after a difficult experience at Philippi. He only stayed for a short while, because of the fierce opposition [Acts 17.5–10]. So, this is a letter of support, dealing with some issues that had arisen and repeating some of his teaching. Paul is writing to address two main issues: **when the Lord will return** and **what to do while waiting**. The letter is full of Paul's delight in the church. He's like a father watching his child take their first, faltering steps He's full of joy at their efforts, while still concerned that they don't fall over.

'Christ died for us, so that we could live with him, whether we are alive or dead when he comes. That's why you must encourage and help each other, just as you are already doing.'
1 Thessalonians 5.10–11

The Sights:
1 Thessalonians
☐ Their faith: 1.1–10
☐ Paul's work: 2.1–20
☐ The good life: 4.1–12
☐ The Lord's return: 4.13–5.11
☐ Final instructions: 5.12–28

2 Thessalonians

Paul encourages the Thessalonian church to keep going.

Who & When

Some experts question the authenticity of 2 Thessalonians, but the letter had a lot of support from early Christian writers. Assuming we accept Paul's authorship, the letter dates to 51 or 52AD.

Someone in Thessalonica claims to have a letter from Paul saying that the Lord has already returned. Someone is using Paul's name to back up their own ideas. So Paul writes again to the Thessalonians to go into more detail about **the second coming**. He warns them against laziness, and assures them that the **trials** they are going through are not punishments but **tests of their faith**.

'God our Father loves us. He is kind and he has given us eternal comfort and a wonderful hope. We pray that our Lord Jesus Christ and God our Father will encourage you and help you always to do and say the right thing.'
2 Thessalonians 2.16

The Sights
2 Thessalonians
☐ The Lord will bring justice: 1.1–12
☐ He hasn't returned yet: 2.1–12
☐ Be faithful and keep praying: 2.13–3.18

1 Timothy

Paul writes to instruct his 'son' on various aspects of church life and teaching.

> 'Be careful about the way you live and about what you teach. Keep on doing this, and you will save not only yourself, but the people who hear you.'
> 1 Timothy 4.16

Who & When

Paul, probably around 65–66AD. Some experts doubt the authenticity of these letters, arguing that the language is different to Paul's earlier letters and that the issues he deals with date from a later time (around the second century AD). Supporters of Paul's authorship argue that the language varies in Paul's other letters, and the issues are exactly the same facing those in places like Colossae—not to mention the early Church as described in Acts.

The Sights:
1 Timothy
☐ False and true teaching: 1 Tim 1.1–20
☐ How to pray: 1 Tim 2.1–15
☐ Church leaders: 1 Tim 3.1–13
☐ Instructions: 1 Tim 4.6–16
☐ True wealth: 1 Tim 6.3–21

Paul had known **Timothy** for years and regarded him as a kind of son. Timothy was now at **Ephesus**, helping to lead the church there. Paul writes to him giving guidelines on how to **choose church leaders** and how to **combat false teaching**.

2 Timothy

Paul asks for help and encourages Timothy to be strong.

Who & When

See above. Around 65–66AD, probably in Paul's last—and fatal—imprisonment.

> 'Everything in the Scriptures is God's Word. All of it is useful for teaching and helping people and for correcting them and showing them how to live.'
> 2 Timothy 3.16

Paul was writing from a **prison**, most likely in **Rome**. This seems to be his final imprisonment and he had no illusions about the future: he realised that his race was almost run.

This, Paul's final letter, is **intensely personal**. Paul was lonely. In jail in Rome, Paul's friends have deserted him—only **Luke** remains faithful. At this time, more perhaps than any other, Paul is missing his 'dear child'.

Paul reminds Timothy how he had been **specially commissioned** for the work he was to do and how he **prays constantly** for Timothy. He encourages Timothy to continue in his work. **Keep running**, he says, right until the point you reach the finishing line.

The Sights:
2 Timothy
☐ No shame: 2 Tim 1.1–1.18
☐ Do your duty: 2 Tim 2.1–26
☐ Keep running: 2 Tim 3.10–4.8

Titus

Paul advises Titus on leadership, holiness and honesty.

Who & When

Paul probably wrote this between 63–65AD, around the same time as 1 Timothy.

Titus worked with Paul on several of his journeys. Paul appointed Titus to oversee the work in **Crete** and he is writing to encourage him and advise him. **Church leaders** should be people of good reputation and personal behaviour. **Arguments and disputes** should be avoided. Above all, it matters how we conduct ourselves. We used to be evil and stupid and disobedient, but that behaviour should have gone now. We have been given **new life through Jesus**, and that means new ways of behaving.

> 'We are filled with hope, as we wait for the glorious return of our great God and Saviour Jesus Christ. He gave himself to rescue us from everything that is evil and to make our hearts pure. He wanted us to be his own people and to be eager to do right.'
> Titus 2.13–14

The Sights: Titus
☐ Church leaders: 1.1-16
☐ Good examples: 2.1-15
☐ Doing good: 3.1-15

Philemon

Paul is writing an appeal on behalf of a **runaway slave**.

Who & When

60–61AD. Paul was in Rome, where he was under arrest. The letter was probably written around the same time as his letter to Colossians.

Under Roman law, **Onesimus** was a dead man. A runaway slave who had stolen money, he deserves to die. But Onesimus has become a Christian, like his master **Philemon**, who probably ran a church in his home in **Colossae** [Col 4.9,17]. So Paul tries to make peace between the two.

Paul's letter is light-hearted and very personal. This is an appeal for mercy. He knows that the law says Onesimus should die, but he offers to pay the money back himself.

> 'Onesimus is much more than a slave. To me he is a dear friend, but to you he is even more, both as a person and as a follower of the Lord.'
> Philemon 16

The Sights: Philemon
☐ The same as me: 1.1-25

Hebrews

Some Jewish Christians were wavering. The Jews had history, a temple and a high priest. What did Christianity have?

> 'Faith makes us sure of what we hope for and gives us proof of what we cannot see.'
> Hebrews 11:1

Who & When

The author is not known. Some people have suggested Barnabas or even Apollos. Whatever the case, it was probably written in the late 60s AD. It was almost certainly written before the destruction of Jerusalem in 70AD. When the writer refers to the Temple, he uses the present tense.

Hebrews argues that Christianity is the fulfilment of Judaism. The old system is completed by the new. The rules and regulations have been superseded, the barriers torn down.

It's all about **faith**. Faith makes us sure of what we hope for, gives proof of things that we can't see. To prove this, the writer scrolls through centuries of Jewish history, looking at all the heroes and showing how they were characterised by faith. But even heroes like **Aaron**, **Moses**, **Abraham** and **Joshua** must bow to their superior, the one true **high priest**, **Jesus Christ**.

The Sights: Hebrews
- ☐ Tempted as we were: 2.5–18
- ☐ Greater than Moses: 3.1–19
- ☐ Great high priest: 4.14–5.10
- ☐ The better agreement: 8.1–13
- ☐ No more sacrifice: 10.1–18
- ☐ Faith makes us sure: 11.1–40
- ☐ Eyes on Jesus: 12.1–13

James

James, the brother of Jesus, was the leader of the early Church in Jerusalem. He writes to tell early Christians how to live.

> 'My friends, what good is it to say you have faith, when you don't do anything to show that you really do have faith? Can that kind of faith save you?'
> James 2.14

Who & When

The author is generally agreed to be James, the brother of Jesus. Some experts date the letter from the late 60s AD, but it may date from much earlier.

James challenges us to express our faith in practical and loving ways. It champions the **rights of the poor**, criticises **snobs and bigots**, urges us to **control our tongues**. It doesn't say that **actions** are a substitute for **faith**; it says that if our faith doesn't result in practical, loving deeds then it's not real.

This emphasis on actions has led some writers to criticise James for not being 'Christian' enough. However, the letter contains more quotes from Christ than all the other New Testament letters put together.

The Sights: James
- ☐ Trials: 1.1–18
- ☐ Look after the poor: 2.1–13
- ☐ Faith and works: 2.14–26
- ☐ Control your tongue: 3.1–18
- ☐ Why do you fight?: 4.1–5.6

1 Peter

Peter writes to encourage those who are **suffering**.

Who & When

Some experts argue that Peter did not write this letter, claiming that the Greek is too good and the situation described in the book did not exist until after Peter's death. Supporters of Peter's authorship argue that he was helped in the writing by Silvanus (Silas) and that the situation could easily reflect the persecution under Nero when Peter was still alive. If Peter wrote it, it was probably composed some time between 62 and 64 AD.

It was tough being a Christian in the days of the early Church. Follow Jesus and you were very often ostracised, mocked, expelled from your family or work, or even killed. Peter's view is that our suffering is a prelude to glory. He urges people not to lose faith, but to remember they are a special, holy people. Their suffereing will bring rewards on the day when Christ returns. In the meantime, they are called to love to one another and to use their God-given gifts wisely.

'But you are God's chosen and special people. You are a group of royal priests and a holy nation. God has brought you out of darkness into his marvellous light. Now you must tell all the wonderful things that he has done.'
1 Peter 2.9

The Sights: 1 Peter
☐ Hope: 1.1–12
☐ God's people: 1.13–2.17
☐ Don't be surprised: 3.12–19

2 Peter

False teachers were corrupting the true message of God, so the letter urges Christians to stick to their task.

Who & When

2 Peter has generated a lot of argument over its authenticity. The style is different to that of 1 Peter, and much of the letter simply rehashes the letter of Jude. Also, the early church itself didn't set much store by this letter, with no reference to it until the third century AD. Those who argue for the traditional authorship claim that Peter used a secretary to help shape it and that he 'borrowed' from Jude's letter because it said what he wanted to say. The jury is still out...

The letter also contains memorable descriptions of the day of the Lord's return, and practical instructions for living: keep to the real faith and put it into practice; look for understanding, self-control and patience; and wrap everything in love.

'We have everything we need to live a life that pleases God. It was all given to us by God's own power, when we learnt that he had invited us to share in his wonderful goodness.'
2 Peter 1.3

The Sights: 2 Peter
☐ All we need: 1.1–15
☐ Christ's glory: 1.16–21
☐ The Lord's return: 3.1–17

1 John

John writes to combat false teaching and call for pure lives.

Who & When

The author is not mentioned in the book, but the early Church believed that John the Apostle wrote this letter. It was most likely written between 85–95AD, probably after the gospel was written.

The early Church had to counter the teachings of the Gnostics—a group of people who had changed the message of the Bible in several key ways. John exposes these false teachers and their lack of morality. He assures his readers that they have been saved. John had seen Christ, had known Christ, so he knows that Jesus wasn't some kind of spirit being, but a real man and a real God.

> 'When we obey God, we are sure that we know him. But if we claim to know him and don't obey him, we are lying and the truth isn't in our hearts.'
> 1 John 2.3–4

The Sights: 1 John
- ☐ Life and Light: 1.1–2.6
- ☐ Not the world: 2.7–17
- ☐ How he loves us!: 3.1–24
- ☐ God is love: 4.1–21
- ☐ Be sure: 5.1–21

2 John

In 2 John, the Apostle is writing to a 'special lady and her children' to warn her of false teaching.

Who & When

Probably written by John the Apostle, around 85–95AD.

In the early Church the gospel was spread by travelling evangelists, who would stay in the homes of followers. But, John argues, if they are teaching rubbish, then they should be evicted. Christ was fully human and anything otherwise is a lie.

> 'Love means that we do what God tells us. And from the beginning he told you to love him.'
> 2John 6

The Sights: 2 John
- ☐ Defend the faith: 1.1–9
- ☐ Senseless!: 1:10–16
- ☐ Keep building: 1.17–25

The church of St John at Ephesus marks the traditional site of the Saint's grave. Although now disused, if it were rebuilt on its original scale this church would be the seventh largest in the world.

3 John

John criticises Diotrephes, a false leader, and urges true Christians to keep to the truth.

Who & When

Probably written by John the Apostle, around 85–95AD.

> 'Nothing brings me greater happiness than to hear that my children are obeying the truth.'
> 3 John 4

John writes to a follower called Gaius, encouraging him to keep faithful and promising that he will come to sort out the split in the church, a split caused by the gossip of someone called Diotrephes. He urges Gaius to keep supporting and welcoming those who speak the truth.

The Sights: 3 John
☐ Greetings: 1–4
☐ Work together: 5–12
☐ I'll be there soon: 13–14

Jude

The letter of Jude was written to encourage Christians to stay strong in the faith and to reject false teaching.

Who & When

The book is traditionally ascribed to Jude, brother of James and Jesus [Mt 13.55; Mk 6.3], but the authorship is a matter of a lot of discussion, with some experts arguing that it was written by an anonymous author. Similarly, debate rages as to the date. It could be as early as 65AD, or as late as 80AD.

> 'Dear friends, keep building on the foundation of your most holy faith, as the Holy Spirit helps you to pray. And keep in step with God's love, as you wait for our Lord Jesus Christ to show how kind he is by giving you eternal life.'
> Jude 20–21

From the very earliest times there have been question marks about this book, particularly because of its quotations from the 'apocrypha'—writings that were not seen as scriptural books. Also it is very similar to 2 Peter. Whatever the case, the problem it addresses was a very real one for the church at the time: the problem of false teaching and failing leadership.

It doesn't take a genius to work out or guess at some of the unusual activities that the false teachers were introducing. Jude says that 'They abuse anything they do not understand.' They are more like animals. There is an emphasis on the dirtiness, the almost physical manifestation of their sin which indicates that they were abusing their authority by luring others into sexual acts, a sad feature of cults and false teaching throughout the ages.

The Sights: Jude
☐ Defend the faith: 3–7
☐ Dreamers: 8–16
☐ Warnings: 17–25

Revelation

John is a prisoner on the isle of Patmos. There he sees a vision, and is told to write it down.

'Yes, God will make his home among his people. He will wipe all tears from their eyes, and there will be no more death, suffering, crying or pain. These things of the past are gone for ever.'
Revelation
21.3–4

Who & When

As early as 140AD Justin Martyr attributed Revelation to 'a certain man, whose name was John, one of the Apostles of Christ'. (However some experts argue that it is a different John altogether, known as John the Elder.) The book was probably written around 95AD. The early tradition states that John was in exile on a small, rocky island called Patmos, where he had been sent during the reign of the emperor Domitian (81–96AD). Again, very early tradition records that John was 90 years old when he received the vision.

Initially Rome, the great Imperial power, didn't take much notice of Christianity and saw it largely as another strange Jewish sect. By the time Revelation was written, the situation had changed. After about 60AD the Roman authorities viewed Christianity as something to be suppressed.

So, the setting for Revelation is a time of persecution—probably that of the Emperor Domition. In the face of this, Revelation's message is simple: Christ wins. The book gives a vision of the future, in which Christ is triumphant.

Oceans of ink and forests of paper have been spent trying to 'decode' this difficult book. It's full of secret messages which would no doubt have been understood by the first Christians, but which present even today's experts with a number of problems. So we should beware any literal interpretations. Revelation is not a timetable. It's a vision. The events may lead on from one another and they may appear exactly as described. Or the pictures may point to a different, but no less true, reality.

The Sights

☐ The vision: 1.1–20
☐ Letters to churches: 2.1–3.22
☐ Worship: 4.1–5.14
☐ All nations: 7.9–17
☐ Woman and beasts: 12.1–13.18
☐ Fall of Babylon: 18.1–19.10
☐ Satan's downfall: 19.11–20.10
☐ New heaven and earth: 20.11–22.5
☐ Christ will return: 22.6–21

In the meantime, there is a lot in Revelation that speaks to us now. Jesus, through John, addresses the churches of the day, and the messages he gives them are as much about the need for Christians to stand against idolatry, sin and oppression as they are about the future of the planet.

Explorer's Notes—Part 4
The Life of Jesus

The boots behind some replica first-century tools in Nazareth

Jesus

He was born into a poor family. Soon after his birth the family became refugees, fleeing for their lives and returning a few years later. Little is known of his upbringing. He knew from an early age who his real father was, but for some fifteen years he followed his human father's trade, working as a carpenter and builder in Galilee.

When he was about thirty, he was baptised by his cousin John and, after overcoming the devil in the wilderness, he began teaching the people. Mainly he worked in Galilee, teaching with natural authority, answering the most difficult questions and telling life-changing stories. He healed the sick, raised the dead, cast out demons and miraculously provided food and drink. He controlled the weather and walked on water.

He had, in short, the power of God. He forgave sins and used one of God's sacred names to describe himself. Some of his closest disciples saw him talking with Moses and Elijah.

Soon, they realised he was the Messiah, the one to rescue God's people. Except, he didn't act much like it. Far from driving out the Romans, Jesus told people to love their enemies. He preached forgiveness and peace. He spent time with tax collectors, the poor, the outcasts. He called the priests and religious leaders hypocrites and liars. He threw the corrupt moneychangers out of the Temple.

Stung by his criticism and appalled by his apparent blasphemy, the authorities closed in. After a final meal with his disciples, one of his friends betrayed him, and he was arrested. He was tried and beaten and condemned. There were no charges against him, but they still nailed him to a cross, where he died.

Three days later, strange rumours began...

His followers claimed that he had risen from the dead. Guards had been posted, but his tomb was empty. People started to see him on roads, in rooms, by the lakeside, in the cemetery. The news of his resurrection spread like wildfire. They thought they'd killed him—but he was more alive than ever.

The Family of Jesus

Several New Testament passages mention Jesus' family [Mk 3:31–32, 6:3, Mt 13.55–56, Gal 1:19]. His brothers were called James and Joses (i.e. Joseph), Judas and Simon. They appear not to have believed in Jesus during his lifetime [Jn 2.12, 7.3, 5, 10], but after his death and resurrection his family played an important role in the church. They were with the disciples after his death [Acts 1:14]. He appeared to James [1Cor 15.7], who then became the leader of the church in Jerusalem. According to ancient tradition, after James was martyred his brother Simon succeeded him in the role. He, in turn, was succeeded by Symeon, Jesus' cousin and son of Clopas, who, according to yet another early tradition, was Joseph's brother.

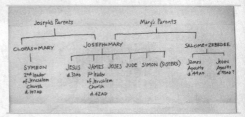

Jesus the Carpenter

The gospels only record in detail the last three years or so of Jesus' life. Before that, he spent some fifteen years as a 'carpenter' [Mk 6:3] in an insignificant Galilean village. In fact, he was more of a builder, used to working with wood and stone.

Nazareth was only a small village, so he would probably have found work in nearby Sepphoris, where Herod Antipas was building a magnificent city. Certainly Jesus drew on his experiences, and his parables abound with stories of men for hire, of references to wood and stone and to the everyday life of an ordinary craftsman or labourer.

A recreation of a first-century carpenter's shop in Nazareth. This is the kind of place where Jesus would have worked for fifteen years.

The Sea of Galilee

Also known as Sea of Chinnereth (Num 34.11), Sea of Chinneroth (Josh 12.3), Sea of Tiberius (Jn 21.1), and Lake Gennesaret (Lk 5.1).

A large, freshwater lake, fed by the river Jordan. Fish from Lake Galilee was famous throughout the Roman empire. It was quite a heavily populated area, the settlements surrounding the lake forming a belt of fishing towns and villages. The lake's position—in the Jordan valley and surrounded by hills—means that it is subject to sudden storms and winds.

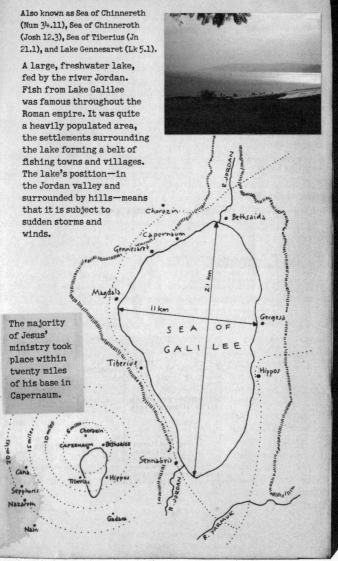

The majority of Jesus' ministry took place within twenty miles of his base in Capernaum.

Capernaum

The town of Capernaum formed the base of Jesus' operations in Galilee. It was a busy port on the main road from Damascus. Since the border between the regions of Galilee and Gaulanitis ran along the river Jordan, the town also had a Roman garrison and a customs post. Even so, it was not a big town, with probably only 1500–2000 inhabitants.

Excavations have revealed a fourth century AD synagogue and also an octagonal church from around 450AD. This church was built over an earlier house church, leading some archaeologists to believe that this was the traditional location of Peter's house.

Jesus' home was in Capernaum. He may have stayed with others, or he might have had his own house [Mk 2.1, 15].

The remains of the synagogue in Chorazin. Most of the buildings in the area were made out of this very dark, black basalt stone.

Magdala

Probably the home town of Mary, hence Mary Magdalene. The area was known as Magadan. Jesus went there after the feeding of the 4000 [Mt 15.39]

Bethsaida

The name comes from the Aramaic words for 'house of fishing'. The home town of Philip, Andrew and Peter.

Chorazin

A town in the hills, four kilometres north of Capernaum. Along with Bethsaida, it was criticised by Jesus for its failure to recognise his authority and repent [Mt 11.21; Lk 10.13].

Hippos was one of the ten cities of the Decapolis—cities allied together to protect trade routes. Hippos was situated on the flat top of a hill, overlooking Galilee and reached by a winding path. It may well have been the inspiration for Jesus' 'city on a hill' which cannot be hidden (Mt 5.14).

Jesus' Jerusalem

In John's gospel, Jesus visited Jerusalem several times, but the synoptics focus on his visit in the final week of his life, when he entered in triumph and confronted the authorities.

It was an action-packed week, and a lot of it centred around the **Temple**. Built by Herod the Great and situated on a great **raised platform** the Temple dominated the city's skyline. Jesus taught on the steps, worshipped in the courtyards, threw the traders out and predicted its destruction. Overlooking the Temple was the **Antonia fortress**, a Roman fortress built so they could keep an eye on their Jewish subjects.

To the south of the city ran the **Hinnom Valley**, where the citizens would chuck their rubbish and burn it. Jesus used it as a synonym for **hell**. To the east was the **Kidron Valley** which ran between the city and the **Mount of Olives**. The road from **Jericho** came through this valley and this was the way in which Jesus would have arrived at the city travelling from **Galilee**.

Also, running north—south within the city was the **Tyropoaen valley**, or 'Valley of the Cheesemakers'. A road ran through this valley, running west of the Temple and up to the Tower Gate at the north-west.

Jesus' journeys on the night of his arrest took him back and forth across the city, and today it is still possible to stand on the Mount of Olives and retrace his steps, using the traditional sites as landmarks.

These Roman steps by the Church of St Peter Galicantu in Jerusalem were probably the steps that Jesus used.

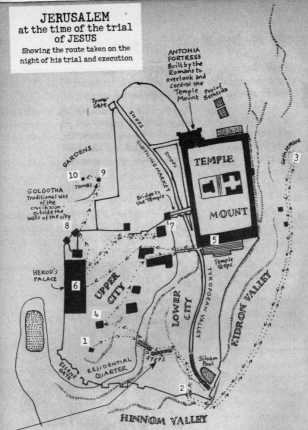

JERUSALEM
at the time of the trial of JESUS

Showing the route taken on the night of his trial and execution

ANTONIA FORTRESS
Built by the Romans to overlook and control the Temple Mount

Pool of Bethesda

Tower Gate

SHOPS

CLOTHING MARKET

SHOPS

GARDENS

TEMPLE

MOUNT

Gethsemane

GOLGOTHA
Traditional site of the crucifixion - outside the walls of the city

Tombs

Bridge to the Temple

Temple Steps

HEROD'S PALACE

UPPER CITY

LOWER CITY

TYROPOEAN VALLEY

KIDRON VALLEY

RESIDENTIAL QUARTER

ESSENE GATE

STEPS

Siloam Pool

HINNOM VALLEY

(1) Thursday 18:00 Last supper begins.

(2) Thursday 21:00 Jesus and the disciples head down into the Lower City, and out through the gate into the Kidron valley.

(3) Thursday 22:30 After praying in the Garden of Gethsemane, he is arrested.

(4) Thursday 23:00 Back in the city Jesus appears before Annas and Caiaphas at the High Priest's residence. He is imprisoned.

(5) Friday 04:30 At daybreak he is rushed across to the Temple for a formal trial before the Sanhedrin.

(6) Friday 05:30-06:00 He appears before Pilate, probably residing in the Palace of Herod the Great.

(7) Friday 07:00 Pilate sends him across to see Herod Antipas, probably in the Palace of the Hasmoneans.

(8) Friday 08:30 He is returned to Pilate who offers his freedom to the crowd in front of the palace. They choose Barabbas. Jesus is beaten.

(9) Friday 09:00 Jesus carries his cross to Golgotha where he is crucified.

(10) Friday 15:00 Jesus dies. A short time later he is buried in a nearby tomb.

Jesus the Teacher

Jesus spent a lot of his time **teaching**. He taught in synagogues, in fields, in a boat, on the side of a hill, in houses—wherever the opportunity afforded itself.

It was always said that Jesus taught '**with authority**'. A lot of the **scribes** and **rabbis** of his time backed up their arguments with masses of references and quotations from other teachers. Jesus occasionally quoted from the **Scriptures**, or referred to figures like Jonah, but mostly he just spoke, simply and powerfully.

Not that his teaching was just about making pronouncements; it was also about asking and answering **questions**, about debate and **discussion**. He also told lots of **stories**. In fact, he never taught without using parables. He made **cryptic statements** or told **difficult stories** and did not explain them. Some people found it demanding, but Jesus wanted people to think about what he said.

Jesus was not interested in making clever points or just winning the argument. He wanted people to actually change the way they behaved. He wanted to change lives.

Jesus the Jew

Jesus was **Jewish**. In fact, he wasn't actually called Jesus—Jesus is the Greek version of his Hebrew name, **Joshua**. He was really Joshua ben Joseph— **Joshua the son of Joseph** [John 1.45]. Joshua was a very common name in Israel; it's as if the son of God was called Dave or Joe.

We should never forget the Jewishness of Jesus. He was raised in a Jewish home, and circumcised as a boy; he was part of God's chosen people. God had promised **Abraham** that a great blessing would come through his descendants, and Jesus is the fulfilment of that promise.

Jesus was brought up knowing Jewish law and tradition. He was called '**Rabbi**' by some of his followers, which means teacher. He knew the **Jewish scriptures** inside out. So much so that he managed to sum up the entire lot in a few words [Mt 22.37–40].

Because he was a Jew, he knew what he was saying. When he forgave people their sins, when he called himself '**I Am**', he knew, as a Jew, he was claiming to be God.

Jesus the Miracle Worker

People came to see Jesus because he performed miracles.

By miracles, we mean God taking an active part in creation in a special way. Miracles are things of wonder, divine surprises which cannot be explained in any other way, other than to say God is at work. They are also displays of God's power. He is the only one who could do these things. His is the power to heal, to create, to destroy.

The gospels describe some thirty-six miracles, but they also make clear that he performed a lot more [Jn 20.30–31]. These miracles fall into several different types.

Jesus **healed people**; he gave them back their sight, helped them to walk, cured their leprosy (which was a horrifically contagious disease) and even put back an ear that had been sliced off. He **raised the dead**; we have three accounts of Jesus bringing people back to life [Mk 5.21–43; Lk 7.11–17; Jn 11.1–53]. He **controlled nature**, from killing trees to changing the weather [Mt 21.19–21; Matt 8.23–27]. He **provided for people**, changing water into wine, multiplying loaves and fishes and giving huge catches of fish [Jn 2.1–11; Matt 14.13–21; Luke 5.1–11]. He **threw out evil spirits** from people [Mt 8.16]. He knew things that other people thought were hidden and secret [Jn 2.23–25].

To ignore Jesus' miracle working is to ignore something that is at the very core of his work. The miracles demonstrated who he was: the son of God.

People came to see him because he did miracles, and they stayed to listen. Which is not to say that he did these things for show. In fact, he tended to do things very simply and quickly, and he refused to 'perform' for people.

The sights: Miracles

☐ The works of the one true God: Deut 4.32–40
☐ The blind army: 2 Kings 6.8–23
☐ Remember his miracles and wonders: 1 Chr 16.7–36
☐ 'You alone work miracles': Psa 77.11–20
☐ False miracles: Mt 7.21–23
☐ The fish and the bread: Mt 15.13–21
☐ The demons and the pigs: Lk 8.26–39
☐ The walking dead: Jn 11.1–46
☐ You will do greater things: Jn 14.8–14
☐ The man at the door: Acts 3.1–26
☐ The open jail: Acts 16.16–40

Jesus the King

Perhaps Jesus' most persistent theme in his speaking and teaching was the '**Kingdom of God**'. The gospels mention the Kingdom over eighty times and almost two-thirds of Jesus' parables take it as their subject. It was a kingdom that, to some extent, had already come—Jesus told his disciples to go out and tell people that the kingdom was at hand. But it was also a future kingdom. So perhaps the message that Jesus was giving was 'the kingdom is here, and it's growing all the time.'

All kingdoms need a **king**, of course, and that person is Jesus. His supporters recognised his kingship [Jn 1.49] and several of his stories liken him to a king in judgement [Mt 18.23–35; 22.1–14; 25.31–46].

Jesus' claims to be a king formed one of the main planks of the case for his execution. His opponents accused him of claiming to be **king of the Jews**. Pilate even hung the phrase 'King of the Jews' above him [Jn 19.19].

Jesus never denied he was a king, but he made it clear his kingdom was **not of this world** [Jn 18.33–38]. Indeed, he was careful to distance his kingdom from the kingdoms of the world. In a society that was hyper-sensitive to potential revolutionaries, Jesus taught people to pay their taxes and to make a clear distinction between the powers of the earth and the one power that really matters [Mk 12.13–17].

His kingdom was a kingdom of the oppressed, the outcast, the dispossessed, the desperate—all those who, as citizens, would usually be at the bottom of the pile in any earthly realm. In Jesus' kingdom, the poor were wealthy and enemies were friends. In the kingdom of God, servants were masters and only those who lost their lives would truly live [Mt 10.39, 16.25-26, 23.11]. He was a king, he never denied his kingship; but it was a kingship that was completely different to any that had previously been known.

Explorer's Notes—Part 5
Maps and Places

The boots by a Roman street
sign on a pavement in Ephesus.
The sign means 'this way to the
brothel'.

The Ancient Middle East and Abraham's journey

The **Hittites** came from what is now Turkey, and invaded northern Syria and Lebanon, where they established a series of city states. Solomon had Hittite wives (1 Kings 11.1) and David had an affair (and later married) Bathsheba, wife of Uriah the Hittite (2 Sam 11). Eventually the Hittites were absorbed by the Assyrians and Babylonians.

The **Phoenicians** were sea-traders who travelled throughout the Mediterranean, trading in wood, pottery and purple cloth (the name 'Phoenician' comes from a Greek word meaning 'purple dye'). The Israelites generally had good relations with the Phoenicians. There was a colony of Phoenician merchants living outside Jerusalem (Zeph 1.11). One Phoenician king, Hiram of Tyre, supplied materials and craftsmanship for the Temple (1 Kings 5).

The **Philistines** were a maritime race, who produced fine pottery and art and even had metalworking before the Israelites. They were the only neighbours of Israel who were not defeated by the judges. Philistia as a power declined after the reign of David. They were eventually defeated by the Babylonians.

Supposedly the descendants of Esau, The **Edomites** were tough people who lived in a mountainous land. Conquered and almost wiped out by David, they remained foes of Israel, and defeated Judah during the reign of Ahaz (2 Chr 28.17). They were eventually conquered by the Assyrians and the Babylonians.

The **Midianites** were nomads and travellers who lived in the desert regions. Moses went to Midian after fleeing from Egypt, working for **Jethro**, a Midianite priest (Ex 2). It was while in Midian that Moses met God in the burning bush. After much conflict, Gideon defeated the Midianites (Judg 6).

Troy

Hattush

HITTITES

TAURUS

Tarsus

Ugarit

Ham

Syr

THE GREAT SEA

Sidon

Tyre

PHOENICIA

Damas

3

PHILISTIA

CANAAN

Rabbi

Jerusalem

5

MOAB

Memphis

EDOM

4

EGYPT

SINAI

MIDIAN

RED SEA

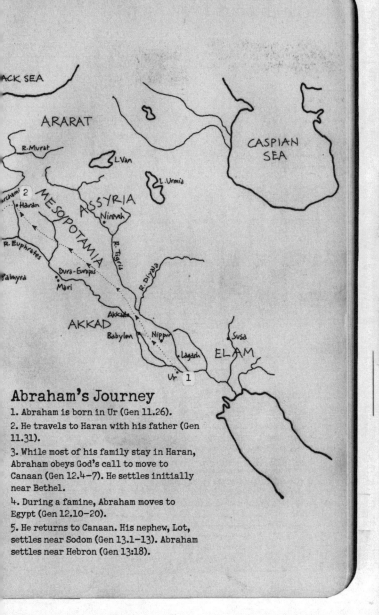

Abraham's Journey

1. Abraham is born in Ur (Gen 11.26).

2. He travels to Haran with his father (Gen 11.31).

3. While most of his family stay in Haran, Abraham obeys God's call to move to Canaan (Gen 12.4–7). He settles initially near Bethel.

4. During a famine, Abraham moves to Egypt (Gen 12.10–20).

5. He returns to Canaan. His nephew, Lot, settles near Sodom (Gen 13.1–13). Abraham settles near Hebron (Gen 13:18).

The Exodus from Egypt

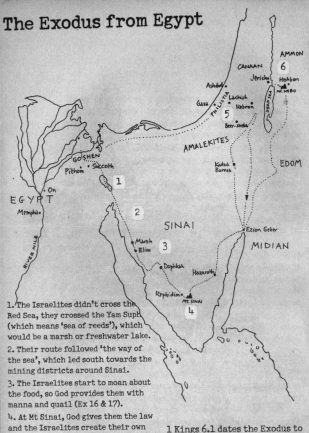

1. The Israelites didn't cross the Red Sea, they crossed the Yam Suph (which means 'sea of reeds'), which would be a marsh or freshwater lake.

2. Their route followed 'the way of the sea', which led south towards the mining districts around Sinai.

3. The Israelites start to moan about the food, so God provides them with manna and quail (Ex 16 & 17).

4. At Mt Sinai, God gives them the law and the Israelites create their own God in the shape of a calf.

5. Only eleven days after leaving Sinai, the Israelites reach Hebron. Moses sends spies into Canaan, but when they report back the people decide not to invade. This lack of faith means that they spend the next forty years wandering in the wilderness.

6. At Mount Nebo, Moses sees the Promised Land but he does not get to enter it. The Israelites eventually cross the Jordan to Jericho.

1 Kings 6.1 dates the Exodus to 480 years before the fourth year of Solomon's reign, which would make it 1446BC. But this may be a symbolic figure—most experts place it between 1300–1200BC. The mention of the city of Rameses (Ex 1.11) has led some to argue for a later date, to fit in with the Pharaoh Rameses II who ruled around 1290BC.

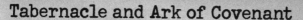

Tabernacle and Ark of Covenant

The inner tent was made of embroidered linen [Ex 26.1-6] covered with layers of goat hair [Ex 26.7-13]

The only thing in the most holy place was the Ark of the Covenant, containing the stones on which the Ten Commandments were written

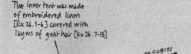

The outer tent was made of waterproof leather [Ex 26.14]

70 CUBITS

10 CUBITS

10 CUBITS

30 CUBITS

The tabernacle was a huge tent — a kind of flat-pack temple. Inside, a curtain divided the space into two 'rooms' — the 'holy place' and the 'most holy place' [Ex 26.31-35]. Only the high priest could enter the most holy place.

The holy place contained a table (on which was the sacred bread), a lampstand representing the glory of the Lord, and an altar where the high priest burnt incense.

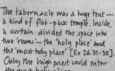
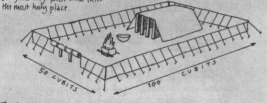

50 CUBITS

100 CUBITS

The tabernacle was situated in a large, fenced area. Along with the tabernacle itself, the area contained an altar on which offerings were burned and a huge bronze basin in which the priests could wash themselves before entering the tent.

The Ark of the Covenant was a box made of gold-covered wood. It contained the tablets of stone on which God had written the Ten Commandments. It stood in the Most Holy Place in the tabernacle, and later at Bethel (Judg 20.27), then Shiloh (1 Sam 1.3) and eventually in the Temple in Jerusalem. Its fate is unknown. It was probably lost during the Babylonian invasion of Jerusalem in 587BC.

The lid, or mercy seat, was made of gold and had sculptures of two angels with their wings outstretched.

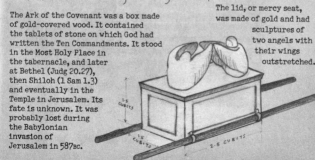

1.5 CUBITS

1.5 CUBITS

2.5 CUBITS

Distribution of Canaan among the Tribes of Israel

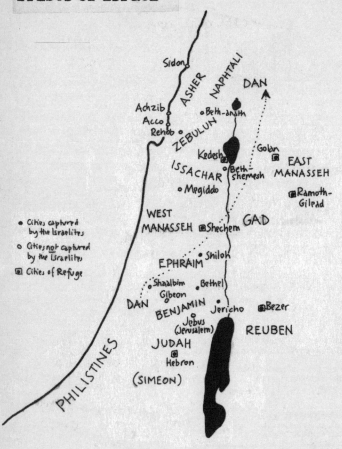

Sidon

ASHER

NAPHTALI

DAN

Achzib

Acco

Rehob

• Beth-anath

ZEBULUN

Kedesh

Golan

ISSACHAR

Beth-shemesh

EAST MANASSEH

• Megiddo

• Ramoth-Gilead

WEST MANASSEH

Shechem

GAD

EPHRAIM

Shiloh

• Cities captured by the Israelites

○ Cities not captured by the Israelites

▣ Cities of Refuge

• Shaalbim

Gibeon

• Bethel

DAN

BENJAMIN

Jericho

▣ Bezer

Jebus (Jerusalem)

REUBEN

JUDAH

▣ Hebron

(SIMEON)

PHILISTINES

The Twelve Tribes

Jacob's twelve sons became the ancestors of the twelve tribes of Israel. There are different lists of the 12 tribes in different parts of the Bible [Gen 35:23–26; Ex 1:2–5; Num 1:20–43; 1 Chr 2:2; Rev 7:5–8].

Most experts agree the 12 tribes to be **Simeon, Levi, Judah, Issachar, Zebulun, Benjamin, Dan, Naphtali, Gad, Asher, Ephraim** and **Manasseh**. Of the original 12 sons, Reuben lost his rights as firstborn because he slept with Bilhah, one of his father's concubines [Gen 35:22; 49:3–4]. His place was given to Joseph's sons **Ephraim** and **Manasseh** [Gen 48:5–6].

The Levites were assigned to serve at the Temple [Josh 14:3]. They were given 48 towns throughout the land, but no actual territory. Among the towns they owned were the six cities of refuge.

The tribe of Dan originally had territory in the south of Canaan, but, after attacks from the Philistines, they migrated to the north [Josh 19.47].

The Israelites were supposed to completely conquer the land, but they failed to finish the job. the result was that there were Caananites lign among them in cities such as Megiddo, Gibeon and Jebus (later Jerusalem). their gods were a continual temptation to the Israelites [Judg 1.21, 27–36].

The Cities of Refuge

When they took over the Promised Land, Joshua set up six cities of refuge (Josh 20).

These were cities which provided a haven for someone guilty of accidental killing. The idea was that if you were accidentally responsible for the death of someone, you could make your way to the nearest city of refuge and, once there, you would be safe from retribution by the friends and kinsfolk of the victim (Josh 20.3-4).

In the cities of refuge a trial would take place. If it was proven that the killing was not accidental and that it was premeditated, the offender was returned to his home town for execution. If the verdict was 'not guilty' the accused still could not go back home but had to stay in the city of refuge—a kind of exile. If they left the city, then the victim's family could take revenge.

The six cities were located to allow easy access for all inhabitants of Israel. Golan, Ramoth-gilead, and Bezer were east of the Jordan; Kedesh, Hebron and Shechem were on the west bank.

Israel of David and Solomon

Under David and his son, Solomon, Israel reached the zenith of its power and influence. David expanded the territory in a series of successful wars, conquering Ammon (2 Sam 10.1-14), Edom (2 Sam 8.13-14), Moab (2 Sam 8.2) and parts of Syria (2 Sam 8.3-8; 10.15-19).

Solomon was not a military leader, but relied on diplomacy and highly profitable commercial and trade ventures.

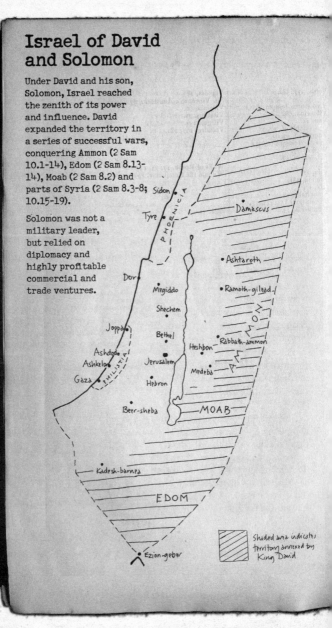

Sidon

Tyre

PHOENICIA

Damascus

Ashtaroth

Dor

Megiddo

Ramoth-gilead

Shechem

Joppa

Bethel

Heshbon

Rabbath-ammon

Ashdod

Jerusalem

Ashkelon

Medeba

Gaza

PHILISTIA

Hebron

Beer-sheba

MOAB

Kadesh-barnea

EDOM

Ezion-geber

Shaded area indicates territory annexed by King David

Solomon's Temple

King David made **Jerusalem** the capital of Israel and brought the **Ark of the Covenant** into the city. He captured the city by sending his troops up through underground water tunnels (2 Sam 5.6-12). David wanted to build a **temple**, but the work was completed by his son, **Solomon**. It was a magnificent building, but still basically followed the same shape as the **Tabernacle** with a main room and a smaller inner sanctuary.

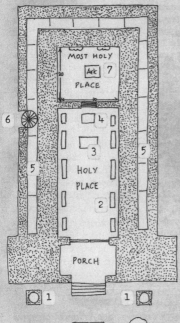

The layout of the Temple is not exactly known. Its description is drawn in 1 Kings 6-7

1. Outside the Temple were two huge, bronze, free-standing, richly-ornamented pillars, called Jachin and Boaz (1 Kings 7.15-22).

2. Along each wall of the Holy Place were tables for candlesticks.

3. A table for the shewbread.

4. An incense altar.

5. The sides of the Temple housed storerooms and chambers for the Priests.

6. There was probably some kind of spiral staircase to the upper floors.

7. The Most Holy place contained the Ark of the Covenant and two angels, made of olive wood and covered with gold (1 Kings 6.23-28).

In the Temple courtyard was the large basin for ritual purification, a huge main altar and ten smaller basins on moveable stands (1 Kings 7.23-39).

Israel and Judah
The Disunited Kingdom

There had long been tension between the northern and southern parts of David's kingdom. The northern tribes had always found it harder to accept kings and leaders like **David** and **Solomon**, who came from the **tribe of Judah**. Even under David's rule, the northern tribes rebelled twice. But the split came about in a strange way.

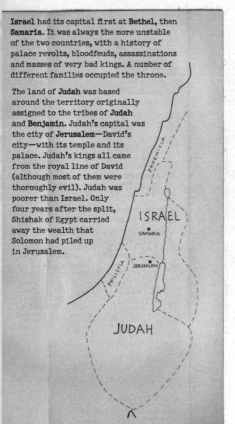

Israel had its capital first at **Bethel**, then **Samaria**. It was always the more unstable of the two countries, with a history of palace revolts, bloodfeuds, assassinations and masses of very bad kings. A number of different families occupied the throne.

The land of **Judah** was based around the territory originally assigned to the tribes of **Judah** and **Benjamin**. Judah's capital was the city of **Jerusalem**—David's city—with its temple and its palace. Judah's kings all came from the royal line of David (although most of them were thoroughly evil). Judah was poorer than Israel. Only four years after the split, Shishak of Egypt carried away the wealth that Solomon had piled up in Jerusalem.

One of Solomon's greatest triumphs was also the cause of the kingdom's ruin. When he built the **Temple**, Solomon treated some of the tribes more harshly than the others. He imposed **unjust taxes** and used some Israelites as **forced labour**. People resented these injustices, not to mention the extravagance of his reign, so when his son **Rehoboam** took over, they wanted assurances that things would change.

Rehoboam refused to reassure them. He told them that he'd be even harder on them than his father was. Immediately, the **ten northern tribes** split away from the **two southern tribes**.

The **northern kingdom** retained the name of Israel. And the **southern kingdom** called itself **Judah**, after the biggest tribe.

Elijah and Elisha

1. Elijah is born in Tishbeh.

2. Elijah stays with a widow and her son in Zarephath, Phoenicia, where he performs miracles (1 Kings 17).

3. Elijah wins a contest with the priests of Baal at Carmel (1 Kings 18).

4. Somewhere in Israel, Elijah finds Elisha and apoints him as his successor (1 Kings 19).

5. Elijah is taken up to be with God (2 Kings 2.11).

6. Elisha raises a child from the dead (2 Kings 4).

7. Elisha tells Hazael that he will be king of Syria (2 Kings 8).

8. King Ahab of Israel is killed in battle. Jehu is appointed king by a prophet sent by Elisha (2 Kings 9).

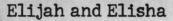

Moab was ruled by Israel, but rebelled during the reign of King Jehoram (2 Kings 3).

Edom was ruled by Judah, but rebelled (2 Kings 8.16-24).

Nineveh and Assyria

One of the most powerful empires in history, Assyria was noted for its wealth, military might, brutality and cruelty.

The Assyrian emperor Shalmaneser V invaded Israel, destroyed the city of Samaria and took the Israelites away to Nineveh. It was the end of the northern kingdom of Israel.

Assyria also attacked Judah and laid siege to Jerusalem. However, God miraculously intervened and the siege was lifted (2 Kings 19).

Prophets like Zephaniah and Nahum predicted the end of Assyria and, in 612BC, an alliance of the Babylonians and the Medes attacked Nineveh, the capital, tore down the walls and flooded the city (2 Kings 19.36). The once mighty empire was gone and it's greatest city was a huge, ruined pond.

Assyria today

The remains of Nineveh can be found near modern Mosul in Iraq. It was discovered in 1847 by a young British explorer Austen Henry Layard. He discovered the palace of Sennacherib, which contained a sculpture depicting Sennacherib's own account of his siege of Jerusalem and the capture of cities like Lachish (2 Kings 18.13–14). Many of these objects are in London's British Museum.

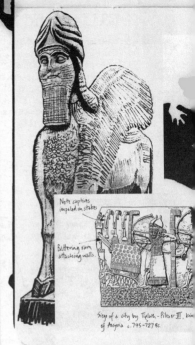

Note captives impaled on stakes

Battering ram attacking walls.

Siege of a city by Tiglath-Pileser III, king of Assyria c.745–727 BC

Israel had been paying tribute money to Assyria for a long time—the **Black Obelisk** in the British Museum shows **Jehu** bringing his tribute money to Shalmaneser III around 841BC. But it was not until around a century later that it actually invaded. The first invasion was led by King **Tiglath-Pileser**, but King Menahem of Israel bought the Assyrians off with 34,000kg of silver [2 Kings 15.19–20]. Tiglath-Pileser returned in the reign of King **Pekah**, capturing several cities [2 Kings 16.29].

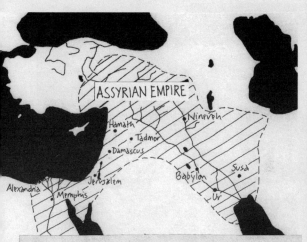

ASSYRIAN EMPIRE

Hamath · Nineveh
· Tadmor
· Damascus
Alexandria Jerusalem Babylon · Susa
· Memphis Ur

Assyria, though primarily known as a military power, also had its cultured side. Its craftsmen were particularly skilled in producing carving and relief work (like the huge winged creatures sketched on the left). Ashurbanipal (669–627BC) amassed a huge library at Nineveh. The emperors even created the world's first botanical parks and zoos around the capital cities.

When Pekah, in alliance with **Syria**, invaded Judah, King **Ahaz** of Judah called on the Assyrians for help. Tiglath-Pileser defeated Syria and Israel but forced Judah to pay tribute. Ahaz was a fan of Assyria anyway; he even copied their religion [2 Kings 16.10–18]. The end for Israel came under King **Hoshea** who stopped paying the tribute money. The Assyrians invaded, destroyed the cities and took, according to Assyrian records, 27,290 Israelites to Assyria.

The Assyrians replaced the Israelites with foreign settlers, many of whom settled in Samaria, the region between Israel and Judah. These settlers developed their own version of Judaism, built their own temple on Mount Gerazim and eventually became the Samaritans that we meet in the New Testament. The Jews viewed the Samaritans as half-breeds, and hated them with a passion that was to last for centuries.

The Babylonian Empire

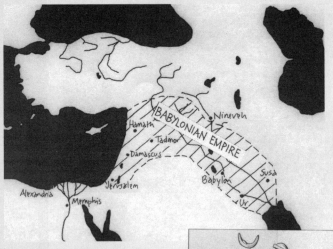

The **Babylonian empire** reached its height during the reign of **Nebuchadnezzar** who reigned from 605–561BC. He expanded the empire through Syria and Palestine to the Egyptian border. He defeated the Egyptians at the battle of Carchemish in 605BC, establishing Babylon as the major power (Jer 46.2). When Judah revolted against the Babylonians, Nebuchadnezzar simply destroyed the capital and took the people into captivity (Ezk 29.17).

They were taken to **Babylon**—a massive city with walls so thick that you could drive chariots around them. The walls were tiled with blue enamelled bricks, and surrounded by a moat channelled from the mighty River Euphrates.

The captive Jews would have been confronted by magnificent buildings, including temples and towers at almost every corner. In the centre of the city stood the huge central ziggurat, or temple tower, of Bel (Dan 4.30). There were also the hanging gardens, built, according to legend, to cheer up Nebuchadnezzar's wife Amyitis, Princess of the Medes.

'Sin', the Babylonian moon

An Assyrian depiction of the Hanging Gardens of Babylon

☐ Restored Ishtar Gate of Babylon is in the Vorderasiastisches Museum in Berlin.
☐ Glazed blue bricks from Babylon can be seen in the British Museum.

Persia

First there were the **Assyrians**, then there were the **Babylonians**, then there were the **Persians**. Under the leadership of **Cyrus the Great**, the Persian empire swept away the Babylonians in 539BC. The capital of the Persian empire was at **Susa**, noted for its luxury and elegance and the work of the jewellers and gold-smiths. This luxury is reflected in the book of **Esther** where the action takes place in one of the royal palaces built by **Darius**.

The Persians had a **liberal religious policy**. Cyrus allowed the Jews to return to Judah and authorised the rebuilding of the **Temple**. He also returned the religious objects that the Baby-lonians had looted. He declared that he would not destroy Babylon or its culture and wrote this down on a clay cylinder, which can be seen in the British Museum.

Cyrus' son, **Cambyses II**, continued the expansion of the empire, but it reached its greatest extent under **Darius I**, who invaded Thrace in Europe. He was stopped from conquering Greece at the battle of Marathon. This first Persian empire (there were others later) was the most powerful empire the world had seen up to that date. It had a sophisticated system of local government, a road-building programme and even a network of spies known as 'the King's Eyes and Ears'. The state religion was Zoroastrianism. The Magi who came to Je-sus' birth were probably Persian Zoroastrians.

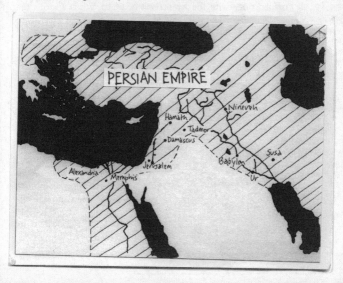

Roman Empire

The Roman empire was huge, stretching from Spain and the British Isles in the west, to Syria in the east. Within this empire, the nation of Israel had become the province of 'Palaestina' or 'Palestine'. It was divided into a series of administrative regions such as **Galilee**, **Judaea** and **Samaria**, which the Romans parcelled out to local rulers. **Herod the Great** controlled Judaea, and several more areas, for thirty-three years. On his death, his territory was split between three of his sons. **Archelaus** ruled Judaea, Samaria and Idumaea; **Antipas** ruled Galilee; and **Philip** ruled several regions north-east of Galilee. They were **tetrarchs**—the Roman word for a ruler of any part of a province.

The Romans brought in a **stable currency**, built **roads** to carry their troops, and encouraged **trade** and economic expansion. Communication was easy, with one main language spoken throughout the empire—**koine**, or **common Greek**. Travel was easy as well, people in the first century Roman empire probably travelled more than at any time until the nineteenth century. This meant that ideas could travel fast.

Jews were given religious freedom and exemption from military service but, even so, Roman rule was evident. As well as imposing punitive taxes, the Romans appointed the High Priest. This resentment boiled over—catastrophically as it turned out—with the **Jewish revolt** of 66AD. When Florus, the last Roman procurator, helped himself to a load of silver from the Temple, the people rioted, wiping out the small Roman garrison in Jerusalem. Cestius Gallus, the Roman Governor, sent in a larger force and the Jewish insurgents routed them as well. Rome did not tolerate such a loss, and Nero sent in Vespasian, one of his best generals, with 60,000 heavily armed

THE ROMAN EMPIRE

troops. They slaughtered thousands in Galilee then moved on to Jerusalem. After besieging the city, they broke through the walls and engaged in an orgy of destruction, culminating in the complete destruction of the Temple and the removal of its treasures to Rome.

Roman Palestine

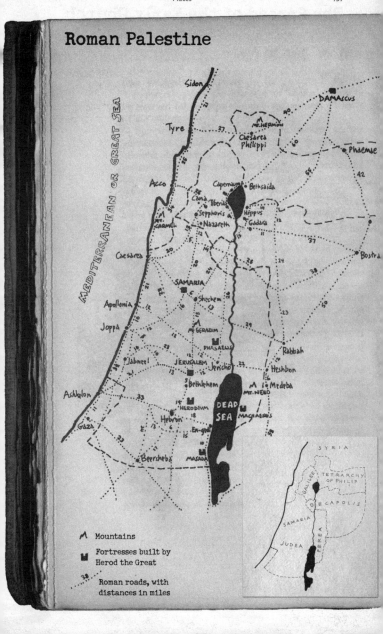

MEDITERRANEAN OR GREAT SEA

Sidon

Tyre

DAMASCUS

MT.HERMON

Caesarea Philippi

Phaeme

Acco

Capernaum   Bethsaida

Cana   Tiberias

Sepphoris   Hippus

CARMEL   Nazareth   Gadara

Caesarea

Bostra

SAMARIA

Shechem

Apollonia

Joppa

GERAZIM

PHASAELIS

Rabbah

Jabneel   JERUSALEM   Jericho

Heshbon

Bethlehem   Medeba

Ashkelon   MT. NEBO

HERODIUM   DEAD SEA   MACHAERUS

Gaza   Hebron

En-gedi

Beersheba   MASADA

⋀ Mountains

▮ Fortresses built by
Herod the Great

⋯²⁸ Roman roads, with
distances in miles

SYRIA

TETRARCHY OF PHILIP

GALILEE   DECAPOLIS

SAMARIA   PEREA

JUDEA

The Spread of the Early Church

The early church spread rapidly. Within ten years of Jesus' death, the church had spread to Antioch and Tarsus (where Paul was). Another ten years took it to Greece and before 60AD it had reached Rome and the heart of the empire. It was very much an urban religion; it flourished in towns and cities, where people could meet to learn, pray and support one another.

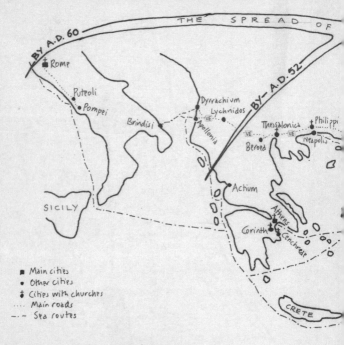

■ Main cities
● Other cities
✝ Cities with churches
···· Main roads
—·— Sea routes

During the winter season, from mid-November to early March, shipping was hazardous, but at other times it was fast—with a good wind you could make up to one hundred miles in a day. The best you could manage on a horse was about twenty miles and on foot perhaps fifteen. Grain ships travelled regularly from Alexandria across to ports like Myra, Patara and Miletus and then west to Rome. It was on one of these ships that Paul and Luke were shipwrecked.

The key to the spread of Christianity was the Roman road network. The roads meant that evangelists like Paul and Barnabas could travel relatively easily from place to place, and where they couldn't travel, they could send letters. Two routes that Paul used in particular were the Common Route from Ephesus to Antioch, and the Via Egnatia across Greece.

CR The common route (koiné hodos) ran from Ephesus, past Trailes and up the Maeander Valley to Laodicea, Antioch in Pisidia, Iconium, then down to Tarsus, from where you could go south to Antioch or continue east to Zeugma on the River Euphrates.

VE The Via Egnatia ran from the Adriatic coast to Lychnidos, across the mountains to Heraclea, then down to Thessalonica and on to Philippi. From there the traveller could take a boat from Neapolis to Troas, or follow the land route to Byzantium.

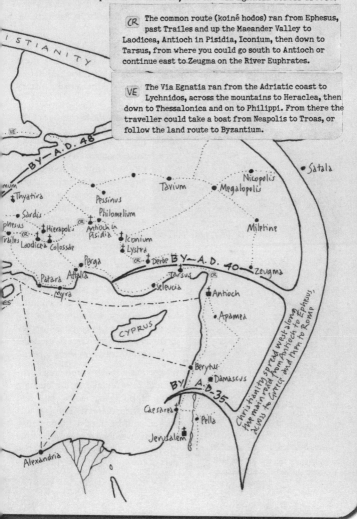

World of Acts—Major Cities

Antioch on the Orontes, or Syrian Antioch, was the capital of the Roman province of Syria and the third largest city in the empire. Christianity spread there quickly, not only among the large Jewish population, but also among gentiles, which is why Barnabas was sent to check on the church. In Antioch the term 'Christians' was first coined.

Athens was a city with a long, long history. Home of great dramatists, poets and thinkers, it was one of the three great university cities (along with Tarsus and Alexandria). Although Rome was by far the more powerful city, Athens had a history and culture that was unique.

The aqueduct at Caesarea Maritime.

Caesarea Maritime was one of the most splendid cities in Palestine. A pet project of Herod the Great, the city had a magnificent artificial harbour, a large waterside palace complex, a theatre and a stadium. Because of all this, Roman governors preferred to spend time in Caesarea, rather than Jerusalem.

Corinth was one of the biggest cities in Greece, with a population of some 250,000 people. It was a wealthy, cosmopolitan city with a reputation for debauchery and immorality. Indeed, such was the emphasis on sex in the city that the Greeks used the word 'corinthianise' as slang for sex.

Ephesus was a major commercial centre and port located at the meeting point of both the major land and sea routes to the east. The city was packed with impressive monuments, the biggest of which was the Temple of Artemis—one of the seven wonders of the world.

Ephesus—looking down the colonnaded street towards the main market place.

Philippi was one of the key cities of northern Greece. Situated on the Via Egnatia—the great Roman road from Rome to the East—it was a Roman colony; that is, it was filled with retired Roman soldiers. It was, in fact, a little slab of Rome set down in Greece.

Thessalonica was the capital of Macedonia, and an important trading and commercial centre. In 146BC it became the capital of the Roman province of Macedonia. Many religious cults flourished in the city—perhaps this interest in religion is one reason why Paul's preaching aroused such a response [Acts 17.4].

Rome was the centre of the Roman empire, and home to the emperor. Famed for its many buildings, including temples and palaces, it was the most influential city in the world. A population of over one million people lived in multi-storey tenements, while the aristocracy spent money, drawn from across the empire, on monuments and estates. It was a city of spectacle, from the scale of its buildings to the barabaric 'entertainments', such as gladiator fights in the amphitheatres such as the Colosseum.

Tarsus was a large city in Roman times, housing some half a million inhabitants. It was close to the coast and only fifty kilometres from the Cilician Gates—a famous pass through the Taurus mountains. That meant a lot of traffic and trade.

The remains of the forum in Rome. Containing many temples and public buildings, the forum was the centre of civic and economic life. Through it ran the **Via Sacra** which was the route taken by victorious Roman generals during their triumphal processions. Such triumphs might also be commemorated by arches (such as the **Arch of Septimus Severus** which can be seen above).

Paul's First Missionary Journey

Paul's missionary journeys

It has been estimated that, during his missionary journeys, Paul travelled over 10,000 miles. For much of the time he travelled on foot, along the Roman roads, from city to city. Usually, when he arrived at the city, he went first to the Jewish districts. Jews had spread throughout the Roman Empire and there were synagogues in virtually every major city. Once in the city, however, he spoke to Jew and Gentile alike. His missionary journeys increased in scope each time. On the first, he went into Galatia, before returning to Jerusalem. The second and third journeys took him much further, across into Greece and maybe even as far as Illyricum—modern day Croatia (Rom 15.19). His final journey took him to Rome, where he probably ended his life. (One early tradition even suggests he went as far as Spain, but there is no proof of this.)

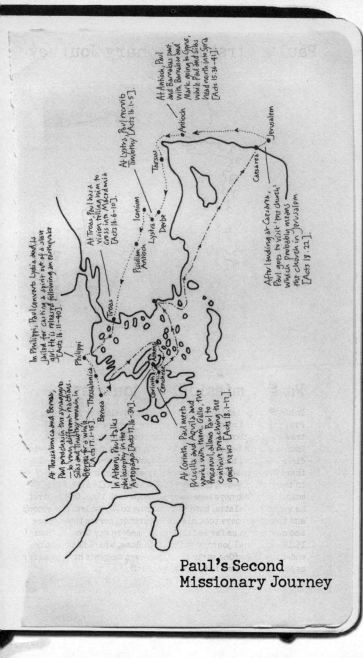

At Antioch, Paul and Barnabas part, with John Mark going to Cyprus, while Paul and Silas head north into Syria [Acts 15:36-41].

At Lystra, Paul recruits Timothy [Acts 16:1-5].

At Troas, Paul has a vision telling him to cross into Macedonia [Acts 16:6-10].

In Philippi, Paul converts Lydia and is jailed for casting a spirit out of a slave girl. He is released following an earthquake [Acts 16:11-40].

At Thessalonica and Berea, Paul preaches in the synagogue — to win different reactions. Silas and Timothy remain in Berea for a while [Acts 17:1-15].

In Athens, Paul talks philosophy in the Areopagus [Acts 17:16-34].

At Corinth, Paul meets Priscilla and Aquila and works with them. Gallio, the proconsul, allows Paul to continue preaching the good news [Acts 18:1-17].

After landing at Caesarea, Paul goes to visit 'the church,' which probably means the church in Jerusalem [Acts 18:22].

Jerusalem

Antioch

Tarsus

Caesarea

Pisidian Antioch

Iconium

Lystra

Derbe

Troas

Philippi

Thessalonica

Berea

Athens

Corinth

Cenchrea

Paul's Second Missionary Journey

The theatre at Miletus. From this port, Paul set sail for the last time to Jerusalem.

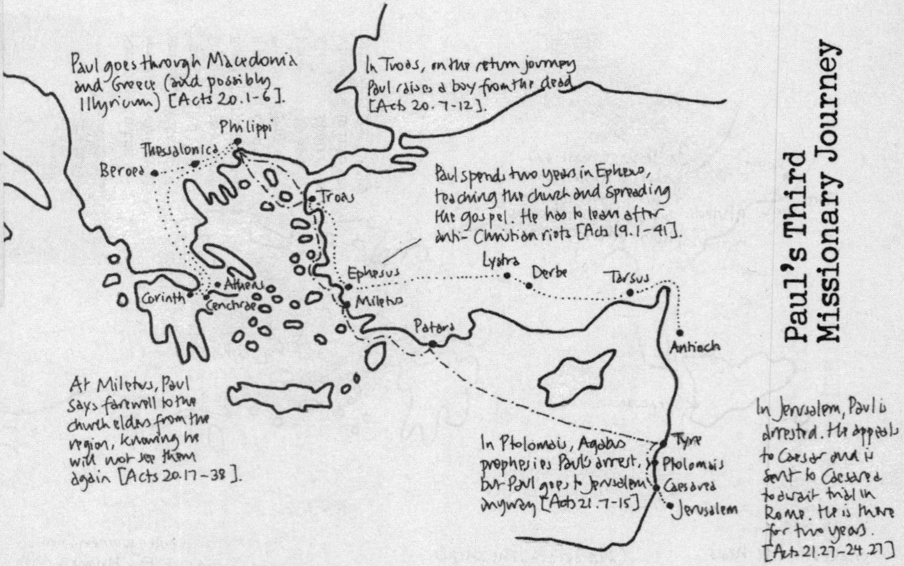

At Miletus, Paul says farewell to the church elders from the region, knowing he with not see them again [Acts 20:17-38].

Paul goes through Macedonia and Greece (and possibly Illyricum) [Acts 20:1-2].

In Troas, on the return journey Paul raises a boy from the dead [Acts 20:7-12].

Paul spends two years in Ephesus, teaching the church and spreading the gospel. He has to leave after anti-Christian riots [Acts 19:1-41].

In Ptolemais, Agabus prophesies Paul's arrest. At Ptolemais Paul goes to Jerusalem anyway [Acts 21:7-15].

In Jerusalem, Paul is arrested. He appeals to Caesar and is sent to Caesarea to await trial in Rome. He is there for two years. [Acts 21:27-24:27]

Paul's Third Missionary Journey

(map labels: Berea, Thessalonica, Philippi, Corinth, Athens, Cenchrea, Troas, Ephesus, Miletus, Patara, Lystra, Derbe, Tarsus, Antioch, Tyre, Ptolemais, Caesarea, Jerusalem)

Paul's Journey to Rome

Sometime in the spring of 60AD, Paul arrived in Italy. Accompanied by Luke, he was met by Roman Christians at a place called the Three Taverns and proceeded to Rome along the Appian Way which leads into the city from the south.

At Myra, Paul is transferred to an Alexandrian cargo ship taking Egyptian wheat to Rome [Acts 27.1-6].

After a difficult journey, the ship arrives at Fair Havens in Crete. Despite Paul's advice, they decide to set sail again [Acts 27.7-12].

Once at sea, the ship is caught in a terrible storm. After 14 days adrift, they are shipwrecked off Malta - but all 276 passengers survive [Acts 27.13-44].

In Malta, Paul survives a potentially fatal snake bite. He heals many on the island [Acts 28.1-10].

In Italy, Christians come out from Rome to greet Paul. Once in the city, he is put under house arrest [Acts 28.11-31].

Sidon

Caesarea

Myra

Cnidus

CRETE

Fair Havens

Syracuse

MALTA

Rome

Three Taverns Puteoli

Herod's Temple

Solomon's Temple was destroyed by the Babylonians in 587BC. When the exiles returned, they rebuilt the Temple on a smaller scale, which is how it remained for some 400 years, until it was massively redeveloped by **Herod the Great**.

Work began in 20BC. A massive building on a vast, raised platform, it dominated the skyline of Jerusalem. Although the Temple itself was completed in eighteen months, work on the surrounding site and buildings carried on for decades, with work finally completed in 64AD.

In the end, it only stood for six years, before it was completely destroyed by the Romans in 70AD, following a Jewish uprising. There was never a temple in Israel again.

The only part of the original Temple still visible is the Western, or Wailing, Wall. These massive, Herodian stones were originally the base of the Temple Mount. Today, Jews come from all around the world to pray at the only remnant of their long-lost temple.

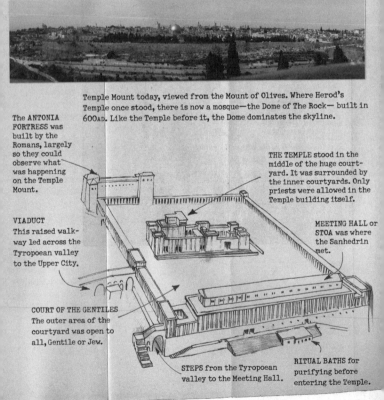

Temple Mount today, viewed from the Mount of Olives. Where Herod's Temple once stood, there is now a mosque—the Dome of The Rock— built in 600AD. Like the Temple before it, the Dome dominates the skyline.

The **ANTONIA FORTRESS** was built by the Romans, largely so they could observe what was happening on the Temple Mount.

VIADUCT
This raised walkway led across the Tyropoean valley to the Upper City.

THE TEMPLE stood in the middle of the huge courtyard. It was surrounded by the inner courtyards. Only priests were allowed in the Temple building itself.

MEETING HALL or **STOA** was where the Sanhedrin met.

COURT OF THE GENTILES
The outer area of the courtyard was open to all, Gentile or Jew.

STEPS from the Tyropoean valley to the Meeting Hall.

RITUAL BATHS for purifying before entering the Temple.

Explorer's Notes—Part 6
People (and other beings)

The boots on top of a Corinthian pillar.

Who's Who: Old Testament

Aaron was the brother of Moses. He acted as Moses' spokesman and second-in-command. When the Israelites left Egypt, Aaron was appointed the first High Priest. Although specifically chosen by God [Num 17.1–13], he made a dubious success of the role. He went along with the creation of the golden calf, criticised Moses (although his sister was punished, he got away with it [Num 12.1–16]) and, like Moses, never got to the Promised Land. His two sons died as a result of not obeying the Lord's commands precisely [Lev 10.1–3].

Abdon judged Israel for eight years [Judg 12.13–15].

Abel was Adam and Eve's second son. He was murdered by his brother Cain when God preferred Abel's sacrifice [Gen 4; Heb 11.4; Matt 23.35; 1 John 3.12].

Abner led Saul's army [1 Sam 14.50]. When Saul died, he declared Saul's son, Ish-Bosheth, king [2 Sam 2.8], but his army was defeated by David. While retreating he killed Asahel, Joab's brother, in self-defence [2 Sam 2.12–32]. Later he quarrelled with Ish-Bosheth and swapped to David's side. Joab murdered him in revenge for killing Asahel [2 Sam 3.6–27].

Absalom was David's third son. Handsome, strong and hungry for power [2 Sam 14.25–26], when his sister was raped by Amnon, he waited two years, then invited Amnon to a banquet and murdered him. After a brief period in exile he returned to the court, but soon proclaimed himself king and declared war on his father. He was defeated by the king's army and, while fleeing, caught his head in the branches of an oak tree. As he hung there, helpless, he was executed by Joab. He was buried in a nearby pit [2 Sam 18.9–17].

Adam was the first man. The Hebrew word *adam* (it means 'of the ground' or 'from the red earth') is also used in the Old Testament as a general noun for 'mankind'. He was told to look after the garden in Eden, but disobeyed God by eating the fruit of the tree of the knowledge of good and evil. He was banished from the garden with his partner Eve.

The Sights: Adam
- ☐ Happy birthday: Gen 2.7–22
- ☐ Disobedience: Gen 3.1–8
- ☐ Excuses, excuses: Gen 3.9–24
- ☐ Adam's children: Gen 4.1–19; 5.1–5
- ☐ Adam and Christ: Rom 5.12–21

Amasa was the captain of Absalom's forces when he rebelled against David. David eventually made him commmander of his own army in place of Joab [2 Sam 11.13]. Joab treacherously killed Amasa [2 Sam 20:8–10].

Amnon was a son of King David. He raped his half-sister Tamar as she tended to him during a fake illness. He was later murdered in revenge by his half-brother Absalom [2 Sam 13.1–29].

Amos was a farmer from Tekoa, just south of Jerusalem. He raised sheep and goats [Am 7.14] and grew fig trees. He prophesied during the reign of Jeroboam II (c. 786–746BC)—a time of great corruption.

Angels are God's messengers and servants (the word angel comes from the Greek word for messenger). Angels also perform actions on behalf of God: they were active in the destruction of Sodom [Gen 19]; they brought food to Elijah [1 Kings 19.5–7]; and they even gave military assistance [2 Kings 19]. They are created beings, capable of moral judgment (after all, some of them chose to rebel against God). Their usual depiction as chubby-cheeked cherubs with wings is a hang-over from Greek and Roman myth. While angels can look just like humans, they can also appear as dazzling creatures of light, and generally they strike terror into the hearts of those who see them.

The Sights: Angels
- [ ] At Sodom: Gen 19.1–29
- [ ] An angel leads Israel: Ex 23.20–23
- [ ] An angelic army: 2 Kings 6.8–23
- [ ] Gabriel talks to Mary: Lk 1.26–38
- [ ] Angel jailbreak: Acts 5.17–24
- [ ] Angels bring judgment: Mt 13.47–50
- [ ] Announces God's plans: Rev 10.1–11

The **Angel of the Lord** is a being closely identified with God, so closely that at times he seems a direct extension of God's personality. He is God's representative, his 'spokes-angel' [Gen 16.7; Ex 3.2]. At other times he is distinguished from God [2 Sam 26.16]. In the New Testament, he is specifically identified as **Gabriel**.

Asher's name means happy [Gen 30:13]. The tribe of Asher was given land in north west Canaan, by the Mediterranean.

Balaam was a prophet who was ordered by Balak, the King of Moab, to curse the Israelites. His donkey, however, warned him off and Balaam blessed them instead. Later he persuaded the Midianite women to infiltrate the Israelites and seduce them into worshipping Baal [Num 31.16, Jude 11; 2 Pet 2:15]. He was killed in battle.

Barak's name means 'lightning'. His victory over the Canaanites led to peace in Israel for forty years [Judg 4–5].

Bathsheba was the wife of Uriah the Hittite, a commander in David's army. David committed adultery with her [2 Sam 11], then tried to cover up the crime by having Uriah killed [2 Sam 11.6ff]. She married David and, after the death of their first child [2 Sam 12.14ff], gave birth to three more sons, including Solomon [2 Sam 5.14; 1 Chr 3.5].

Belshazzar was the grandson of Nebuchadnezzar. During a drunken orgy held in 539BC, the fingers of a man's hand wrote his doom on the wall [Dan 5]. The Babylonian empire crumbled and fell to the Persians and Belshazzar was killed. It was the end of the Babylonian empire.

Benjamin was Jacob's youngest son. His mother Rachel died giving birth to him. The tribe that came from him had territory between Judah and Ephraim [Josh 11:18ff]. They fought a civil war with the other tribes [Judg 19–20].

Boaz was a rich man living in Bethlehem when his relative Naomi returned. He was an honourable, caring man who recognised the goodness of Ruth and married her [Ruth 2–4].

Cain was the eldest son of Adam and Eve. He was a farmer who murdered his brother Abel, when God chose Abel's sacrifice instead of his [Gen 4].

Cyrus was the first great ruler of the Persian empire. He conquered the Medes and then the Babylonians [Dan 5.1–30], entering Babylon on 29 October 539BC. He freed the captives in Babylon, including the people from Judah, whom he allowed to return to Judah and rebuild the Temple [2 Chr 36.22–23; Ezra 1.1–6]. Isaiah calls him the Lord's 'anointed' [Isa 45.1].

Dan was Jacob's fifth son. The Danites were given lands between Judah and the sea. When invaded by the Philistines, the tribe moved north [Josh 19:47; Judg 18:1–29].

Daniel (also known as Belteshazzar [Dan 1.7]) was probably only about fourteen when he was taken captive to Babylon. Possibly he came from the royal family, which is why he was taken to serve in the Babylonian royal palace. There, with his friends, he decided to live according to God's law. He ate a vegetarian diet and despite the anxieties of his teachers looked good on it [Dan 1.8–16]. His God-given wisdom helped him to interpret the

King's dreams [Dan 2], and understand some mystical writing on the wall of a banquet house [Dan 5]. When he refused to pray to the new Emperor, Darius, he was thrown into the lion's den, but survived because God protected him [Dan 6]. He had a succession of visions to do with the future.

Darius I (Hytaspes) was a Persian emperor who allowed the Jews to return to Jerusalem to repair the Temple and rebuild the city walls [Ezra 4.5, 24; 5.5–7; 6.1–15; Hag 1.1; 2.1, 10, 18; Zech 1.1, 7; 7.1]. His forces were defeated by the Greeks at the battle of Marathon in 490BC.

Darius the Mede is a mysterious figure. He only appears in Daniel [Dan 5.31; 6.1, 6, 9, 25, 28; 1.1; 11.1]. Some experts believe him to be Gubaru, a Persian army officer under Cyrus.

David is celebrated as Israel's greatest king. The son of Jesse, grandson of Ruth and Boaz, he was a shepherd boy who was chosen by God to replace Saul [1 Sam 16.1–13]. He showed his courage from an early age, by fighting lions to protect his sheep [1 Sam 17.34–37]. When no-one else would volunteer, David fought and killed Goliath [1 Sam 17]. He went on to become a great military leader, before Saul's increasingly paranoid behaviour forced him to flee. After Saul's death he reigned for seven years at Hebron, then captured the city of Jerusalem and made it his capital. He brought the Ark of the Covenant into the city and planned a glorious temple to the Lord [2 Sam 6]. Under his rule, Israel's borders spread to their furthest ever extent.

Then it all went wrong. He committed adultery with Bathsheba, tried to cover it up with lies and ended up committing murder [2 Sam 11]. Confronted with the truth by the prophet Nathan, he confessed his sins. God forgave him, but he had to live

The Sights: David

- ☐ Samuel anoints David: 1 Sam 16.1–13
- ☐ v. Goliath: 1 Sam 17.1–54
- ☐ Saul becomes jealous of David: 1 Sam 18.6–30
- ☐ Jonathan helps David: 1 Sam 20.1–42
- ☐ David spares Saul's life: 1 Sam 24.1–22
- ☐ David mourns Saul's death: 2 Sam 1.1–2.7
- ☐ The Ark comes to Jerusalem: 2 Sam 6.1–23
- ☐ The Lord's promise to David: 2 Sam 7.1–29
- ☐ David and Bathsheba: 2 Sam 11.1–27
- ☐ Nathan confronts David: 2 Sam 12.1–25
- ☐ Rape of Tamar: 2 Sam 13.1–38
- ☐ Absalom's rebellion: 2 Sam 14.25–15.22
- ☐ Death of Absalom: 2 Sam 18.7–19.8
- ☐ Death of David: 1 Kings 1.1–4; 2.1–12

with the consequences. After that, things were never quite the same. His favouritism towards his eldest son caused murder and rebellion within the family, who rose against David and behaved appallingly towards each other.

Despite his actions, David truly loved God. God made a covenant with David to 'establish the throne of his kingdom forever' [2 Sam 7]. Which is why the Messiah was to come from his line—from the house of David.

Deborah was a prophet, wise woman and leader in Israel. Her 'office' was under a palm tree, where she settled disputes and dispensed advice. She told Barak to raise an army and fight the Canaanites. When the Canaanites were defeated, Deborah sang a famous song in celebration [Judg 4.1–24; 5.1–31].

Ehud was a left-handed assassin from the tribe of Benjamin. He killed the king of Moab, and led the people against the Moabites. The assasination was particularly gory: Eglon was so obese that when Ehud plunged the sword in, the fat covered over the hilt and he couldn't get it out again [Judg 3.15–30].

Eli lived at Shiloh next to the tabernacle [1 Sam 1–4; 14.3; 1 Kings 2.27]. As a young boy, Samuel came to live with him. When the Philistines captured the Ark of the Covenant he fell off his seat in shock and broke his neck [1 Sam 4.10–18].

Elijah was the first great prophet of the divided kingdoms. He came from Tishbe (which was probably in Israel) and his name means 'the Lord is my God', which sums up his message. With his rough garments and wild appearance, he was a living reminder of the primitive, authentic faith they had thrown aside.

Elijah presented the people of Israel with a stark choice: serve God or serve Baal. By doing so he made himself very unpopular, especially with King Ahab and his wife Jezebel, who was responsible for much of the popularity of Baal worship.

Elijah demonstrated God's power through a series of miracles including the raising of the widow's son at Zarephath (the first recorded instance of

The Sights: Elijah
- Elijah predicts the drought: 1 Kings 17.1–7
- Elijah helps the widow: 1 Kings 17.8–24
- Elijah fights the prophets of Baal: 1 Kings 18.1–46
- Elijah meets God in the wilderness: 1 Kings 19.1–18
- Elijah appoints a successor: 1 Kings 19.19–21
- Elijah condemns king Ahaziah: 2 Kings 1.1–18
- Elijah is taken away by God: 2 Kings 2.1–18

the raising of the dead in Scripture [1 Kings 17.7–24] and his victory over the prophets of Baal at Carmel [1 Kings 18].

Elijah's presence was an indication of God's presence. When he goes to live in the ravine at Kerith, it is a sign that God himself has left Israel. Many of his miracles take place outside Israel—a sign that God's favour is resting on other nations. In the end, Elijah didn't die: God came to collect him.

Elisha was a farmer's son who was chosen as Elijah's successor [1 Kings 19.19–21]. His acts were similar—and even greater—than Elijah's . He provided a widow with a miraculous supply of oil [2 Kings 4.1–7]; he brought back a boy from the dead [2 Kings 4.8–37]; in anticipation of Jesus, he provided for one hundred people using twenty loaves and some grain [2 Kings 4.42–44]. He even took the entire Syrian army into captivity [2 Kings 6.8–23].

Elon judged Israel for ten years [Judg 12.11–12].

Enoch was the father of Methuselah [Gen 5.21–22; Luke 3.37]. He went to be with God, without actually dying.

Ephraim was Joseph's youngest son, but even so he was given the preferential blessing by his grandfather Jacob [Gen 48.1–22]. The Ephraimites had land in the central hill country of Canaan. Jeroboam I, the first king of the northern kingdom of Israel was an Ephraimite [1 Kings 11.26], which is why the northern kingdom is sometimes called Ephraim.

Esau is also known as **Edom** [Gen 36.1]. His name means 'hairy', referring to Esau's abundant red hair. He was the son of Isaac and slightly older than his twin brother Jacob. He became a hunter, a red-headed, hot-tempered man of action who gave away his birthright because he fancied a bowl of stew [Gen 25.30–34]. Later, tricked out of his father's blessing by his scheming brother, he vowed to kill Jacob, forcing him to flee [Gen 27]. Many years later, Jacob returned to Canaan and Esau greets him joyfully. Even without his father's blessing, he prospered [Gen 33.4]. He moved to the hill country, where he became the ancestor of the Edomites.

The Sights: Elisha

☐ Elisha is appointed: 1 Kings 19.19–21
☐ Elisha and Elijah: 2 Kings 2.1–18
☐ Some miracles: 2 Kings 4.1–44
☐ Naaman healed: 2 Kings 5.1–27
☐ Elisha stops an army: 2 Kings 6.8–23
☐ Elisha visits Syria: 2 Kings 8.7–15
☐ The death of Elisha: 2 Kings 13.14–21

Esther lived in exile with many other Jews in Persia in the fifth century BC. She won a kind of beauty contest for a new queen and was instrumental in defeating a plot to kill all the Jews in Persia.

Eve was created to be Adam's partner. Her name sounds like the Hebrew word for 'living'. She gave in to temptation and persuaded Adam to do the same. Like him, she was banished from the garden [Gen 2; 2 Cor 11.3; 1 Tim 2.13].

Ezekiel was in his mid-twenties and training to be a priest when, in 598BC, the Babylonians invaded Judah for a second time and took him away to captivity—along with around 10,000 of the most prominent leaders, soldiers, and craftsmen [2 Kings 24.14]. Ezekiel settled in his own house in a village near the Chebar river in Babylonia [Ezekiel 3.15, 24]. He prophesied for at least twenty-two years, probably receiving the call the be a prophet when he was about thirty. Through his sometimes extreme prophecies, God explained to the people of Israel why he had allowed the captivity to happen, and also how one day the land of Israel would be restored.

Ezra was an exiled Jew in Persia where he was a kind of 'Minister for Jewish Affairs'. He returned to Jerusalem around 458BC with orders from King Artaxerxes I to restore observance of the Jewish law. He brought along with him a large number of fellow exiles as well as valuable gifts for the Temple. He tried to deal with the problem of mixed marriages and led a revival in Jerusalem among those who had been living there. He may well have returned to Persia after this, since he was only sent on a temporary mission, but he returned later with Nehemiah and he led a public reading of the law of God which, again, led to revival among the hard-pressed residents of Jerusalem.

The **Fallen Angels** are a group of angels who, led by **Lucifer**, rebelled against God and were cast out of heaven [Mt 25.41; Re 12.9; Lk 10.18]. Sometimes these fallen angels—or demons—attack or possess human beings. These are the spirits that are cast out by Jesus, such as those cast into the pigs [Lk 8.26–39]. Sometimes they tempt people or accuse them or attack them in other ways. They fight against the forces of good, but will one day be totally defeated.

Gabriel—see '**Angel of the Lord**'.

Gad was Jacob's seventh son [Gen 30:9–11]. The Gadites were warlike shepherds who had pastures east of the Jordan.

Gideon lived in Ophrah near Mt Gerizim. His name means 'hewer' or 'feller' and, indeed, he was called to chop down the Midianites. Unsure of the call at first, it took several 'tests' for him to really believe God. With God's help he routed the enemy with a force of only three hundred and brought peace to the land. Gideon was asked to become King, but refused, believing that only the Lord should rule Israel. However, he took home the gold that he had won and made it into statues, which he later worshipped. He had, apparently, 71 sons, 69 of whom were killed by his eldest boy [Judg 8.30].

> **The Sights: Gideon**
> ☐ Gideon is called: Judg 6.1–32
> ☐ Gideon defeats the Midianites: Judg 6.33–7.22
> ☐ Gideon refuses to be king: Judg 8.22–35

Habakkuk probably wrote between 605 and 587BC, during the reign of the Judean king Jehoiakim [Hab 1–3].

Hagar was an Egyptian slave in the household of Abraham. She became the mother of Abraham's first child, because his wife Sarah couldn't conceive. Inevitably, the wife and the servant fell out and, although pregnant, Hagar was driven out. God met her and promised that her son, Ishmael, would be the father of many descendants. Hagar returned, but a few years later, when Sarah had a child, Hagar was expelled again. Alone in the desert, Hagar crawled away to leave her child to die, but God rescued them and renewed his promise. Her son Ishmael became the father of the Ishmaelites and it is part of Islamic theology that all Arabs are descended from Ishmael.

> **The Sights: Hagar**
> ☐ Hagar sees God: Gen 16.1–16
> ☐ God's promise to Ishmael: Gen. 17.17–27
> ☐ God rescues Hagar: Gen 21.9–21
> ☐ The descendants of Ishmael: Gen. 25.7–17

Haggai was a prophet who lived just after the Israelites returned from captivity in Babylon. A contemporary of Zechariah [Hag 1.1, Zech 1.1], his prophecies are all carefully dated from 520BC [Hag 1.1; 2.1,10].

Hosea's name means 'salvation'. He was born during the reign of Jeroboam II (c. 786–746). He married a temple prostitute to represent the relationship between God and Israel [Hos 1.2–11].

Ibzan was the tenth judge of Israel. He was a native of Bethlehem and ruled for seven years [Judg 12.8–10].

Isaac was the son promised to Abraham when he and his wife were in their old age. He was almost sacrificed by his father, but was saved when God substituted a ram. He married Rebekah, a relative from Mesopotamia, who in answer to prayer gave birth to twins: Esau and Jacob. Jacob tricked his ageing father into handing over the blessing, an action that led to antagonism between Rebekah and Isaac.

Isaiah lived during a time of turmoil and decline. The monarchy was corrupt, the people were worshipping idols, the Assyrians were threatening invasion and there were different factions within the court. He was a brave, courageous man who spoke out for God even when his life was at stake. Many of his prophecies contain beautiful pictures of a future, restored world, where people will live in peace and where the love of God will be evident. He also spoke of a Messiah, a suffering servant who would bring salvation to the world. Along with the book of Isaiah, he also wrote a history of the reigns of Uzziah and Hezekiah [2 Chr 26.22; 32.32].

Ish-bosheth was Saul's fourth son. After Saul's death he was crowned at Mahanaim [1 Sam 2.8ff], but he reigned for just two years, because he was defeated by David. He was eventually murdered by some of his own army captains. His death ended the short, unhappy dynasty of Saul.

Issachar was the ninth son of Jacob [Gen 30:17–18; 35:23]. His descendants formed the tribe of Issachar.

Jacob was the son of Isaac, twin brother of Esau, father of twelve famous sons and a few daughters. His name means 'he grasps the heel', which is an ancient way of saying 'he tricks'. Indeed, he tricked his brother out of his birthright and his blessing and had to flee for his life. On his journey, he dreamt of a ladder between earth and heaven with angels ascending and descending. God spoke to him, repeating the promise to his grandfather, Abraham [Gen 28.10–22]. Jacob then went to stay with his Uncle Laban, who tricked him into marrying the wrong woman. The trickster was tricked.

Eventually he escaped Laban and returned home. Lonely and isolated, he wrestled with a mysterious, powerful stranger

in the night. Jacob held onto him, demanding a blessing. Following this he was given
a new name—**Israel**—a name which means
'he struggles with God'. After being recon-
ciled with Esau, he journeyed to Shechem,
where his daughter Dinah was raped and
two of his sons, Simeon and Levi, took revenge by slaughtering the men of the city
[Gen 34.1–31]. He then went to Bethel, where
his final son, Benjamin, was born. Rachel
died during childbirth.

> **The Sights: Jacob**
> ☐ The birth of the twins: Gen 25.19-26
> ☐ He swaps stew for birthright: Gen 25.27-34
> ☐ He steals Esau's blessing: Gen 27.1-45
> ☐ Jacob's ladder: Gen 28.10-22
> ☐ Jacob's wives: Gen 29.1-35
> ☐ Jacob tricks Laban: Gen 30.25-43
> ☐ Jacob goes home: Gen 32.1-21
> ☐ Jacob fights God: Gen 32.22-32
> ☐ Together with Esau again: Gen 33.1-20
> ☐ Final years in Egypt: Gen 46.1-4; Gen 48.8-21

Jacob ended his life in Egypt, where his
son Joseph was second in command. On
his deathbed he adopted the two sons of
Joseph and pronounced a special blessing over them, preferring the younger
son over the elder (just as he had been
preferred over his elder brother Esau). The twelve tribes who
were to descend from his children took on his name, Israel,
and also his character—a people who struggle with God.

Jair was a judge for twenty years [Judg 10:3–5].

Jephthah was the eighth judge of Israel [Judg 10:6–12.7; 1 Sam 12.11;
Heb 11.32]. The son of a prostitute, he and his men were asked
to lead the fight against the Ammonites. Jephthah agreed and
made a vow that if he was successful he would sacrifice to God
the first thing he saw when he returned home. He defeated
the Ammonites and returned home to be met by his daughter.
Tragically, he kept his word and sacrificed her.

Jeremiah was the son of a priest called Hilkiah, from Anathoth [Jer 1.1]. He started young and was a prophet for around
fifty years. He had many enemies and was frequently beaten,
abused and humiliated. The King even ritually burnt a scroll
of his prophecies. Jeremiah responded by dictating the whole
thing again—and adding a lot of new material [Jer 36]. He
never married and had few friends he could trust. After the
destruction of Jerusalem, Jeremiah remained behind in what
remained of the country.

Jethro was the father-in-law of Moses. He was a Midianite
priest. He advised Moses on the organisation of the Israelites
[18:17–27].

Joab was David's enforcer, a hard, tough soldier who dispatched his enemies with a cold-blooded brutality. As a reward for being the first to enter the fortress on Mt Zion when Jerusalem was assaulted, he was appointed commander of David's forces. He carefully took revenge on his enemies, and it was Joab who put Uriah the Hittite right where he was certain to be killed [1 Sam 11.6–27]. When Absalom rebelled against David, Joab led David's army against the rebels and killed Absalom when the prince was helpless before him. He sternly told David not to grieve [1 Sam 11.1–8]. On his deathbed, David ordered that Joab should pay for his murders and, at the orders of Solomon, this hard man was killed as he clung to the altar in the tabernacle [2 Sam 2.5–6, 28–34].

Joel's name means 'Yahweh is God'. He was the son of Pethuel and probably wrote during the reign of Joash (837–800BC).

Jonah was a successful prophet in Israel [2 Kings 14.25] when God commanded him to go to Nineveh and call on the Assyrians to repent. Jonah, thinking this likely to be a suicide mission, headed in the opposite direction [Jon 1]. God took him to Nineveh via a large fish. When he got there he preached his message and the city repented.

Jonathan was Saul's eldest son and David's closest friend. A brave warrior, he won important victories over the Ammonites [1 Sam 13.2] and the Philistines [1 Sam 14.1–14]. His friendship with David was close, loyal and, given that he knew David would be king, unselfish. He helped David escape from the wrath of Saul and refused to take part in Saul's war against David. He died with his father, battling the Philistines on Mt Gilboa [1 Sam 31.2].

Joseph was Jacob's favourite son. Jacob gave him a magnificent coat (which may imply that he was appointing him leader of his sons). Angered by this, his brothers faked his murder and sold him into slavery. He ended in Egypt, where, after being wrongly imprisoned for assault, God helped him interpret Pharoah's dreams, leading to his appointment as governor of Egypt. He saved Egypt from famine. Because of the famine, Joseph's brothers went to Egypt to get food. Joseph revealed his true identity, and the whole family settled in Egypt. Joseph was the father of the two northern tribes of Manasseh and Ephraim. His bones were buried in Canaan.

Joshua was Moses' personal assistant and succeeded Moses as leader of Israel. Moses gave him the name Joshua, meaning 'the Lord saves' [Ex 17:9] (the Greek version of this name is 'Jesus'). He left Egypt with the exodus and was the only other person allowed on the mountain when Moses encountered God [Ex 24.13–14]. He also stood guard outside the tent when Moses was meeting God [Ex 33.11]. As one of the twelve spies who entered Canaan, only he and Caleb believed that the Israelites could conquer the land. God rewarded him for his faith: while the rest of his generation were not allowed to enter the Promised Land, Joshua led the Israelites into Canaan. He destroyed Jericho [Josh 6:17] and divided Canaan among the twelve tribes [Josh 13:6–7; 14:1; 19:51]. He was 75 when he took over command and he died aged 110.

> **The Sights**
> ☐ Joshua and others explore Canaan: Num 13.1–33
> ☐ Joshua's faith: Num 14.1–38
> ☐ Joshua is appointed leader: Num 27.12–23
> ☐ God's promise to Joshua: Josh 1.1–9
> ☐ Joshua leads the people across the river: Josh 3.7–4.14
> ☐ Joshua leads the capture of Jericho: Josh 5.13–6.27
> ☐ Joshua's final message: Josh 24.1–31

Judah was the fourth son of Jacob and seems to have been the leader of his brothers. It was Judah who persuaded his brothers to sell Joseph rather than kill him [Gen 37.26–7]; and later it was Judah who tried to negotiate with Joseph in Egypt [Gen 44.16–18]. Judah left his brothers for some time to live among the Canaanites, where he slept with his widowed daughter-in-law Tamar, who is disguised as a prostitute [Gen 38.1–30]. Through his son Perez, Judah was an ancestor of both David [Ruth 4.18–22] and Jesus [Mt 1.3–16]. The tribe decended from him lived in the south of Israel, and, after the split, the southern country took the name of Judah.

Levi was Jacob's third son [Gen 29:34; 35:23]. He was the ancestor of the priestly tribe of the Levites.

Lot was Abraham's nephew. He journeyed with his uncle to Canaan, where, given first choice, he chose to settle in the fertile Jordan valley. Later he moved to the evil city of Sodom [Gen 13.13]. He then had to be rescued twice: once by Abraham [Gen 14.11–16] and then by God when Sodom was destroyed. He seems to have been infected by the depravity of Sodom, given his willingess to sacrifice his daughters [Gen 11.8], his inability to control his sons-in-law [Gen 11.14] and his indecision about leaving the city [Gen 11.15–16]. His wife was turned to salt when she looked back at Sodom's destruction. His daughters, scared that they wouldn't have children, got him drunk and slept with him. Their children became the fathers of the Moabites and Ammonites. Despite all this, the New Testament describes him as a 'good man' who 'lived right' [2 Pet 2.7].

Lucifer is also known as **Satan** or the **Devil**. He was thrown out of heaven after a failed rebellion against God.

Malachi wrote after the return from exile, and after Haggai and Zechariah. His name means 'my messenger'.

Manasseh was Joseph's oldest son. Half the tribe descended from him stayed east of the river of Jordan; the rest had land in Canaan [Josh 17:1–10].

Melchizedek was the priest and king of Salem (i.e. Jerusalem) [Gen 14.17–24]. In Hebrew, his name means 'king of righteousness'. Abraham gave him 'a tenth of everything'. Hebrews uses Melchizedek as a forerunner of Jesus [Heb 5–7].

Micah came from Moresheth [Mic 1.1; Jer 26.18] and he prophesied in the late 700s BC. He predicted the fall of Samaria, and events in Hezekiah's reign [2 Kings 18.13–16].

Miriam was the sister of Moses and Aaron. She looked after Moses as a baby and, after passing through the Red Sea, she gave a famous, and very ancient, song of praise and victory [Ex 15:20–21]. She criticized Moses for his marriage to a Cushite woman and was punished by the Lord with leprosy [Num 12:1, 9; Deut 24:9]. (She was restored after a week.) She died at Kadesh and was buried there [20:1].

Moses is one of the great figures of the Bible. Despite physical frailties, he became a mighty leader. He led the Israelites to the very edge of the Promised Land. As a baby, his parents set him afloat on the Nile to avoid Pharoah's cull of the Israelites. Adopted by an Egyptian princess, he was raised in the royal household. Later, after realising his true origins, he killed a guard who was beating a Hebrew slave. He fled from Egypt and spent years in the desert, working as a shepherd. There he met God, in the form of a burning bush, and received the order to free the Israelites. Helped by his brother Aaron, he led the people out of Egypt. He spoke to God on their behalf and received from God the law by which his people were supposed to live. He never made it into the Promised Land. Or perhaps he did, for in the New Testament, Jesus meets two figures on the mount of transfiguration—Elijah and Moses.

> **The Sights: Moses**
> ☐ The birth and the boat trip: Ex 2.1-10
> ☐ Murder and escape: Ex 2.11-25
> ☐ The Burning Bush: Ex 3.1-22
> ☐ Moses' Anxieties: Ex 4.1-17
> ☐ The first few plagues: Ex 5.1-5; 7.1-25
> ☐ The final disaster and the Passover: Ex 11.1-12.30
> ☐ Escape from Egypt: Ex 12.31-41
> ☐ The Red Sea: Ex 14
> ☐ Food from heaven: Ex 16
> ☐ The Ten Commandments: Ex 19.1-20.21
> ☐ The Golden Calf: Ex 32
> ☐ The Israelites Fail: Deut 1.1-40
> ☐ Moses Is Punished: Num 20.1-13
> ☐ The last days of Moses: Deut 31.1-13; 34.1-8

Nahum is the shortened form of Nehemiah. He wrote between 663 and 612BC and predicted the fall of Nineveh.

Naphtali was the second son of Bilhah, Rachel's handmaid. The tribe descended from him lived in the north, west of the Sea of Galilee.

Nathan was a prophet to King David. He was consulted over the building of the Temple [2 Sam 7; 1 Chr 17] and convicted David of adultery by telling the king a story [2 Sam 12.1–25]. Nathan was instrumental in securing the succession of Solomon [1 Kings 1.8–53]. He was also a writer [1 Chr 21.29, 2 Chr 1.29] and even arranged the music for the Temple [2 Chr 21.25].

Nebuchadnezzar (also called Nebuchadrezzar) was one of the great emperors of Babylon, ruling from 605 to 562BC. He conquered Judah and took the people into the 70-year Babylonian captivity. According to Daniel, the king went mad for a time [Dan 4]. He was succeeded by his son Evil-Merodach.

Nehemiah lived in the Persian city of Susa, where he worked as the king's cup-bearer, ensuring that the wine was not poisoned. Depressed by the news from Jerusalem, he asked for permission to go and repair the city's walls. In Jerusalem Nehemiah restarted the rebuilding programme despite local opposition and plots against his life. Before returning to Persia, he encouraged the people to recommit themselves to God. Back in Persia, he heard that some of the abuses he had put down had reappeared, so he returned to Jerusalem to sort things out.

Noah was a righteous person [Gen 6.9], which is why God asked him to build the ark and restart creation. After it was over God promised never to send another such flood, and confirmed it with a rainbow [8.21–22; 1.9–17]. God commanded Noah and his family to multiply and fill the earth. Noah also invented wine [Gen 9.20–27]. He had three sons—Ham, Shem and Japheth.

Obadiah name means 'servant of Yahweh'. He prophesied the destruction of Edom.

Othniel was the first of the Judges. He saved Israel from the king of Mesopotamia [Judg 3.8–11], leading to forty years of peace.

Rahab was a Jericho prostitute who hid two of the spies from Israel and helped them escape. Her actions made her a heroine for the Israelites and she is one of only four women to be mentioned in the family tree of Jesus. The New Testament praises her faith [Heb 11.31] and her good works [Jas 2.25]. According to Matthew, she was the mother of Boaz, the husband of Ruth, and, therefore, the great-grandmother of King David [Ruth 4:18–21; Matt 1:5].

Rebekah was the wife of Isaac, mother of Esau and Jacob. Greatly loved by Isaac, she had to wait many years for children, after which God gave her the twins Esau and Jacob. Her favouritism for Jacob led to disaster when he tricked the blind, aged Isaac and had to flee for his life. She never saw her favourite son again. She died in Canaan and was buried in the family grave in the field of Machpelah, near Mamre in Canaan [Gen 24, 27.42–46, 49.29–32].

Reuben was the eldest son of Jacob [Gen 29:32]. He committed incest, and lost his place as head of the tribes [Gen 35:22]. His descendants, the Reubenites, were a warlike people [1 Chr 5.1–19].

Ruth was a Moabitess who lived in the days of the Judges [Ruth 1.1]. Her loyalty to her mother-in-law was rewarded when she married Boaz. Even though a Gentile, she becomes part of the geneaology of Christ [Mt 1.5].

Samson was a Nazirite who followed a strict set of rules. He was granted superhuman strength, provided he never cut his hair. His strength enabled him to achieve great victories over the Philistines, but his love of women almost led to his capture when he slept with prostitutes in Gaza. His infatuation with Delilah proved fatal. She coaxed his secret out of him and, while he was sleeping, cut his hair. Samson was captured. The Philistines bought him out for entertainment at a banquet, but mistakenly let his hair grow back. Mustering his strength, he pulled down a pillar holding up the roof, killing himself and about 3,000 of the enemy.

Samuel was the last of the judges [1 Sam 7.6, 15–17] and the first of the prophets [1 Sam 3.20]. His mother dedicated him to the Lord at an early age and sent him to serve in the shrine at Shiloh. He became the chief prophet of Israel [1 Sa 7.13–17]. Samuel wanted to appoint his sons as judges to succeed him, but the people complained that they were corrupt and demanded a king. Although Samuel was not in favour, he anointed first Saul and then David. After his death, Saul called up his ghost—much to the dead prophet's annoyance.

Sarah was the wife of Abraham. She journeyed with him from Ur to Canaan [Gen 11.29–31]. She was actually his half-sister [Gen 20.12], a relationship that she used as a disguise later on when Abraham stayed in Egypt and Gerar [Gen 12.10–20; 20.1–18]. She persuaded Abraham to have a child by her servant Hagar and then later drove Hagar away. Eventually God gave Sarah a son, Isaac [Gen 17.15–27; 21.1–3]. She died at Hebron and was buried in the family tomb [Gen 23.1–2].

Saul was the first king of Israel. He was selected by Samuel, but his headstrong nature, emotional fragility and continual disobedience to the Lord meant that, just two years after he had become King, Samuel told him the Lord had a replacement ready. That replacement was David. Saul became obsessed with the popularity of his rival. He tried to kill David, and fought a civil war against him. When the Philistines attacked, Saul visited a witch to try to speak to the deceased of Samuel. In the end, he and his sons died on the slopes of Mount Gilboa, killed by the Philistines.

> **The Sights: Saul**
> ☐ Saul is chosen:
>   1 Sam 9.1–10.8
> ☐ Early successes:
>   1 Sam 11.1–15
> ☐ Saul disobeys God:
>   1 Sam 15.1–35
> ☐ Saul tries to kill
>   David: 1 Sam 18.6–11
> ☐ Saul talks to
>   Samuel's ghost:
>   1 Sam 28.1–25
> ☐ The death of Saul:
>   1 Sam 31.1–13

Seth was the third son of Adam and Eve. His name means 'substitute' indicating that he replaced the murdered Abel. It is from Seth that Abraham, the Patriarchs and, ultimately Jesus, was descended. [Gen 4.25–26; 5.1–8; Luke 3.38]

Shalmaneser V, the son of Tiglath-Pileser, ruled from 726–722BC [2 Kings 17.3–5; 18.9–11]. When Hoshea, king of Israel, decided not to pay tribute to Assyria and instead try to ally with Egypt, Shalmaneser attacked. Although he died during the siege of Samaria, his successor, Sargon II, finished the job, destroying the city and taking the nation of Israel into an exile from which they never returned.

Shamgar was a judge who killed six hundred Philistines [Judg 3.31].

Simeon was the second son of Jacob. He and Levi massacred the Shechemites after the rape of Dinah [Gen 29:33]. His descendants—the Simeonites—lived in the very south of Canaan.

The Sights: Solomon
☐ Solomon Becomes King:
  1 Kings 2.13–46
☐ The wisdom of Solomon:
  - 1 Kings 3.1–28
☐ Solomon's Reputation:
  1 Kings 4.29–34
☐ The building of the
  Temple: 1 Kings 6.1–38
☐ The opening of the Temple:
  1 Kings 8.1–66
☐ The Queen of Sheba: 1
  Kings 10.1–29
☐ The foolishness of
  Solomon: 1 Kings 11.1–43

Solomon was the son of David and Bathsheba. After succeeding his father as king of Israel, God offered to grant him one request; so Solomon asked for wisdom [1Kings 4.29]. His wisdom helped him to solve individual disputes as well as the bigger problems facing his nation. Under his leadership, the United Kingdom of Israel prospered [1Kings 4.20–27]. He built the Temple in Jerusalem (not to mention a huge palace). However, he married around a thousand women, some of whom led him astray and he ended up building shrines to gods such as Molech and Chemosh [1Kings 11.7]. Also, in building the Temple, he used the northern tribes as forced labour and charged them high taxes, a fact that was to lead to a split in the kingdom after his death.

Tamar was the daughter of David and sister of Absalom. She was raped by her half-brother Amnon [2 Sam 13.1–33], causing Absalom to kill Amnon in revenge.

Tiglath-Pileser took over the Assyrian throne in 745BC and became one of the greatest Assyrian emperors, reigning until 727BC. When Ahaz was king of Judah he called on Tiglath-Pileser for help against King Pekah of Israel and Rezin of Syria [2 Kings 16.5–8]. Tiglath-Pileser captured Damascus, deported the people, executed Rezin and took the inhabitants of a number of Israelite cities into exile in Assyria.

Tola was a member of the tribe of Issachar. He judged Israel for twenty-three years [Judg 10:1–2].

Xerxes or Ahasuerus was king of Persia who reigned from 486–465BC and who features in the book of Esther.

Zebulun was Jacob's tenth son [Gen 30:19–20]. The tribe that descended from him had land between Galilee and the Mediterranean. Christ was active there, fulfilling a prophecy in Isaiah [Isa 9:1–2; Mt 4:12–16].

Zechariah was one of a line of priests [Neh 12.4,16; Zech 1.1]. He returned to Jerusalem under King Zerubbabel and was a contemporary of Haggai.

Zephaniah was a distant relative of the kings of Judah [Zeph 1.1]. He prophesied during the reign of King Josiah, before the religious reformation that began around 640BC.

All the Kings of Judah

Rehoboam [1 Kings 12.1–24; 14.21–31; 2 Chr 10–12] set up shrines to Asherah and allowed temple prostitutes.

Abijam/Abijah [1 Kings 15.1–8; 2 Chr 13.1–22] Kings calls him Abijam, Chronicles calls him Abijah. A mix of good and bad king.

Asa [1 Kings 15.9–24; 2 Chr 14.1–16.14] cleared out some evil practices and restored the Temple. But Hanani accused him of not trusting the Lord [2 Chr 16.1–10].

Jehoshaphat [1 Kings 22.41–50; 2 Chr 17.1–21.1] toured the country convincing people to turn back to God [2 Chr 19.4].

Jehoram [2 Kings 8.16–4; 2 Chr 21.2–20] ruled at the same time as his father Jehoshaphat, possibly because his father was ill.

Ahaziah [2 Kings 8.25–9; 2 Chr 22.1–6] was a bad king who was killed by Jehu, King of Israel.

Queen **Athaliah** [2 Kings 11.1–21; 2 Chr 22.10–23.21] murdered the rest of the family and took over [2 Kings 10.12–14]. However Joash, her baby grandson, was hidden away and six years later, Jehoiada the high priest arranged a coup. Athaliah heard people celebrating, went to investigate and was killed [2 Kings 11.13–16].

Joash [2 Kings 12.1–21; 2 Chr 24.1–16] was a good king, but when Jehoida dies, Joash worshipped Astarte. He was assassinated.

Amaziah [2 Kings 14.1–22; 2 Chr 25.1–24] started well, then grew arrogant, turned against God and he, too, was assassinated.

Azariah/Uzziah [2 Kings 15.7; 2 Chr 26.1–23] was a good king who loved farming [2 Chr 26.10], reorganised the army and developed new weapons. But he tried to take on the role of a priest, and was punished with leprosy.

Jotham [2 Kings 15.32–8; 2 Chr 27.1–9] obeyed the Lord, but didn't destroy all the evil shrines.

Ahaz [2 Kings 16.1–20; 2 Chr 28.1–27] was probably the worst king of the lot. He worshipped at pagan shrines and even sacrificed his own son [2 Kings 16.2–4].

Hezekiah [2 Kings 18.1–20.21; Is 37.1–39.8; 2 Chr 32.24–33] was one of the best kings. Hezekiah trusted the Lord and when the Assyrians invaded, prayed to God, who destroyed the Assyrian army.

Manasseh [2 Kings 21.1–18; 2 Chr 33.1–20] worshipped 'Astarte and the stars in heaven' [2 Kings 21.3]. He even practised witchcraft and sorcery.

Amon [2 Kings 21.19–26; 2 Chr 33.21–5] continued his father Manasseh's wicked ways. He reigned for just two years before being assassinated by his officials.

Josiah [2 Kings 22.1–30; 2 Chr 34.29–36.1] was a good king. When the Book of God's Law (probably Deuteronomy) was discovered during temple renovations, Josiah promised to obey its commands [2 Kings 23.2]. But the Lord was still angry and Josiah died at Megiddo in a battle against Egypt.

Jehoahaz [2 Kings 23.31–4; 2 Chr 36.2–4] was Josiah's son. With no real military power, he was captured by Pharaoh Neco.

Jehoiakim [2 Kings 23.35–24.7; 2 Chr 36.5–8] was Jehoahaz's brother. He had his name changed to Jehoiakim. He rebelled against the Babylonians, conveniently dying before the Babylonians took their revenge.

Jehoiachin [2 Kings 24.8–17; 25.27–30; 2 Chr 36.9–10; Jer 52.31–4] served only three months before surrendering to the Babylonians. He was taken to Babylon along with most of his people.

Zedekiah [2 Kings 24.18–25.21; 2 Chr 36.17–21; Jer 52.3–30] rebelled against Babylon. After months of suffering, Jerusalem was taken, and the king was captured, tried, and had to watch his sons being killed. It was the last thing he saw, because Nebuchadnezzar had him blinded.

Gedaliah [2 Kings 25.22–26; Jer 40.7–9; 41.1–3] was appointed to govern what was left of the country. He was assassinated.

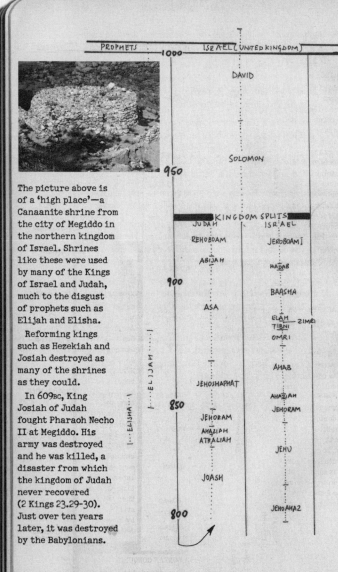

The picture above is of a 'high place'—a Canaanite shrine from the city of Megiddo in the northern kingdom of Israel. Shrines like these were used by many of the Kings of Israel and Judah, much to the disgust of prophets such as Elijah and Elisha.

Reforming kings such as Hezekiah and Josiah destroyed as many of the shrines as they could.

In 609BC, King Josiah of Judah fought Pharaoh Necho II at Megiddo. His army was destroyed and he was killed, a disaster from which the kingdom of Judah never recovered (2 Kings 23.29-30). Just over ten years later, it was destroyed by the Babylonians.

The timeline labels (as drawn on the chart):

PROPHETS — 1000 — ISRAEL (UNITED KINGDOM)

DAVID

950 — SOLOMON

KINGDOM SPLITS
JUDAH | ISRAEL

REHOBOAM — JEROBOAM I
ABIJAH — NADAB
900 — BAASHA
ASA — ELAH — ZIMRI / TIBNI / OMRI
JEHOSHAPHAT — AHAB
850 — AHAZIAH / JEHORAM
JEHORAM —
AHAZIAH —
ATHALIAH — JEHU
JOASH
800 — JEHOAHAZ

[...ELIJAH...]
[...ELISHA...]

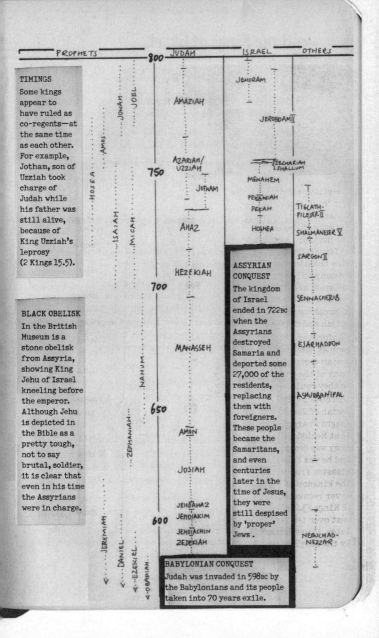

PROPHETS | 800 | JUDAH | ISRAEL | OTHERS

TIMINGS
Some kings appear to have ruled as co-regents—at the same time as each other. For example, Jotham, son of Uzziah took charge of Judah while his father was still alive, because of King Uzziah's leprosy (2 Kings 15.5).

BLACK OBELISK
In the British Museum is a stone obelisk from Assyria, showing King Jehu of Israel kneeling before the emperor. Although Jehu is depicted in the Bible as a pretty tough, not to say brutal, soldier, it is clear that even in his time the Assyrians were in charge.

ASSYRIAN CONQUEST
The kingdom of Israel ended in 722BC when the Assyrians destroyed Samaria and deported some 27,000 of the residents, replacing them with foreigners. These people became the Samaritans, and even centuries later in the time of Jesus, they were still despised by 'proper' Jews.

BABYLONIAN CONQUEST
Judah was invaded in 598BC by the Babylonians and its people taken into 70 years exile.

Prophets: HOSEA · AMOS · JONAH · JOEL · ISAIAH · MICAH · NAHUM · ZEPHANIAH · JEREMIAH · DANIEL · EZEKIEL · OBADIAH

Judah: AMAZIAH · AZARIAH/UZZIAH · JOTHAM · AHAZ · HEZEKIAH · MANASSEH · AMON · JOSIAH · JEHOAHAZ · JEHOIAKIM · JEHOIACHIN · ZEDEKIAH

Israel: JEHORAM · JEROBOAM II · ZECHARIAH/SHALLUM · MENAHEM · PEKAHIAH · PEKAH · HOSHEA

Others: TIGLATH-PILESER III · SHALMANESER V · SARGON II · SENNACHERIB · ESARHADDON · ASHURBANIPAL · NEBUCHAD-NEZZAR

All the Kings of Israel

Jeroboam [1 Kings 12.25–14.20] did not obey God. He set up shrines to rival Jerusalem.

Nadab [1 Kings 15.25–32] reigned for just two years, but in that time managed to kill all the rest of his family. He was assassinated.

Baasha [1 Kings 15.33–16.7] was a soldier who, after killing Nadab, carried on a long conflict with Judah and its king, Asa.

Elah [1 Kings 16.8–14] was the son of Baasha who reigned for two years before he was killed while drunk at the home of his prime minister.

Zimri [1 Kings 16.15–20] assassinated Elah and then, a week later, besieged by Omri, killed himself by setting fire to the palace [1 Kings 16.18].

Omri [2 Kings 16.21–8] took over from Zimri, and established the city of Samaria as his capital.

Ahab [1 Kings 16.29–22.40] was always plagued by the activities of the great prophet Elijah. He was an evil man who, along with his wife Jezebel, organised Baal worship, persecuted true followers and killed prophets. He came to a sticky end, bleeding to death after a battle. His chariot was washed with a whore's bath water, and the dogs licked away his blood.

Ahaziah [1 Kings 22.51–3; 2Kings 1.1–18] was the son of Ahab and as bad as his dad.

Joram [2 Kings 3.1–27] was another son of Ahab's and not much improvement.

Jehu [2 Kings 9.1–10.35] was an army officer who killed not only Joram, but also Ahaziah, King of Judah. Then he killed Jezebel, took Samaria, and removed the rest of Ahab's family. He wiped out the prophets of Baal by inviting them to a sacrifice. They filed into the Temple and the guards killed them.

Jehoahaz [2 Kings 13.1–9] was bad man and an even worse military commander. His army was decimated by the Syrians.

Jehoash [2 Kings 13.10–19] was weak and ineffective. He defeated the Syrians and recaptured the territory they had taken, although that was a deathbed gift from Elisha.

Jeroboam II [2 Kings 14.23–9] oversaw a time of prosperity and military success, as well as a time of hypocrisy and wealthy cynicism. The prophets Amos and Hosea offer a true perspective on this reign.

Zechariah [2 Kings 15.8–12] ruled for only six months before he was assassinated by...

Shallum [2 Kings 15.13–16], who ruled for just one month before he was killed by...

Menahem [2 Kings 15.17–22], a violent, bloody murderer who even attacked pregnant women.

Pekahiah [2 Kings 5.23–26] was bad king who was assassinated. His killer was one of his officials, a man called...

Pekah [2 Kings 15.27–31], who ruled for twenty years, but was eventually attacked by the Assyrians. They took over huge portions of Israel and took many of the inhabitants into captivity. In the end he was assassinated by...

Hoshea [2 Kings 17.1–41], who rebelled against the Assyrians. The result was that the kingdom of Israel was wiped out, and all the inhabitants were carted away into captivity in Assyria.

Who's Who: New Testament

APOSTLES & DISCIPLES

The twelve close followers of Jesus are called the disciples, or apostles.

Disciples were people who followed a particular teacher and learned from him. After the Resurrection, the twelve disciples of Jesus were called apostles, which comes from the Greek word for 'one who is sent'. No longer learners, they are now representatives of Jesus.

They were a mixed bag of individuals. Often afraid and frequently baffled, they were genuinely committed to Jesus. Ultimately, this group of ordinary individuals was to change the world.

There are minor differences about the names. The accounts agree on eleven of them: Simon Peter, Andrew, James, John, Philip, Bartholomew, Thomas, Matthew, James, son of Alphaeus, Simon the Zealot and Judas Iscariot. However, Matthew and Mark have Thaddeus, while Luke lists Judas, son of James. These were probably the same person—Thaddeus was his nickname (Mt 10.2–4; Mk 3.16–19; Luke 6.13–16). John doesn't give a list, but he does mention a 'Nathanael', who was probably the same as Bartholomew.

Agabus was a prophet who saw the famine that was to cover the Roman world [Acts 11.27–30]. He was probably the same prophet who, years later, went to Caesarea to warn Paul that he would be imprisoned if he went to Jerusalem [Acts 21.10–11].

Agrippa II (the Bible calls him 'Agrippa' [Acts 25 and 26]) was the last Herodian king. He lived in Caesarea and witnessed the destruction of his country after the futile rebellion of 66–70AD. He died in 100AD.

Andrew lived in Bethsaida. He brought his brother Peter to see Jesus. According to tradition, after Jesus' ascension he preached in Scythia and was crucified on an X-shaped cross, now called a St Andrew's cross.

Annas was a high priest, appointed by Quirinius in 6AD when he was thirty-seven. In 15AD, he was deposed by Valerius Gratus, the governor of Judea. He was father-in-law of Caiaphas [Jn 18.13] and at least three of his sons were appointed high priests in turn. Although he was not technically a high priest when Jesus was tried, he still played a big part in the trial [John 18.13].

Apollos was a Jew from Alexandria. He was a disciple of John the Baptist, but was later told about Jesus by Aquila and Priscilla [Acts 18.24–26]. He debated with the Jews in Corinth [Acts 18.27–28]. He was a major teacher in the early Church and an 'Apollos' faction appeared in the Corinthian church [1 Cor 3.4]. Despite this, Paul and Apollos were friends. Paul asked Apollos to go back to Corinth [Acts 16.12], and suggested he take Titus to help him [Tit 3.13]. Some experts believe that Apollos wrote the letter to the Hebrews.

Aquila (see **Priscilla**).

Archelaus inherited all his father Herod's bad characteristics, without any of his abilities [Mt 2.22–23]. He was ruler of Samaria, Judaea and Idumea, but his rule was disastrous and he was eventually exiled to Vienne in Gaul.

Barnabas (whose real name is Joseph [Acts 4.36] was a Levite, born in Cyprus, who was an early convert to Christianity. He sold some property and gave the money to the early Church [Ac 4.36]. The apostles called him Barnabas, which means 'son of encouragement'. When Paul became a Christian, Barnabas was his 'champion'. Later, when he went to Antioch at the request of the Apostles, he called in Paul to help [Acts 11.22–25]. He became one of Paul's travelling companions but they fell out, first because Barnabas seems to have supported Peter [Gal 2.13], and then because Paul refused to take Barnabas's cousin Mark on his second journey. Barnabas went with Mark to Cyprus, and Paul to Asia Minor [Acts 15.36–41].

> **The Sights: Barnabas**
> ☐ Barnabas sells a field: Acts 4.32–37
> ☐ Barnabas speaks up for Saul: Acts 9.26–31
> ☐ In Antioch: Acts 11.19–30
> ☐ Travels with Saul: Acts 13.1–12
> ☐ Worshipped then attacked: Acts 14.8–20
> ☐ At Jerusalem: Acts 15.1–35
> ☐ The split with Paul: Acts 15.36–41

Luke describes Barnabas as 'a good man of great faith, and he was filled with the Holy Spirit'. Even though he and Paul fell out, whenever Paul mentions Barnabas it is with affection and thankfulness. Some early writers believed that Barnabas was the author of Hebrews.

Bartholomew was probably the same as the Nathanael mentioned by John.

Caiaphas held the office of High Priest from 18–36AD. He played a major part in the death of Jesus, declaring that it would be better for one man to die than for the nation to perish [Jn 11.49–50]. After his arrest, Jesus was sent to Caiaphas's house in the Upper City of Jerusalem. His family tomb was discovered in Jerusalem in 1990.

Epaphras is the shortened form of the name Epaphroditus. He was part of the church at Colossae, possibly its founder and leader. He appears to have been in prison with Paul, either voluntarily, or because he, too, had been arrested.

Felix's name means 'happy', but there was nothing cheerful about him. As Procurator of Judea, a Roman historian said of him that 'he revelled in cruelty and lust, and wielded the power of a king with the mind of a slave'. He appears in the Bible in Acts when Paul appears before him [Acts 23.24–25.14]. He imprisoned Paul for two years, maybe because he was hoping for a bribe. He was succeeded by Festus.

Gallio is an important figure in the history of the early Church. When the Jews brought Paul before him, they argued that Paul was offending against the Roman religion and therefore against Rome itself [Acts 18.12–17]. Gallio rejected their argument. His decision effectively allowed the early Church to spread throughout Asia.

Herod Agrippa (the 'Herod' in Acts 12) was the grandson of Herod the Great. When Philip the Tetrarch died, he took over his realm. Through subtle plotting and close friendship with the Roman emperors Caligula and Claudius, he managed to add Galilee and the rest of Judea. He was responsible for the death of James the Apostle, whom he had killed to keep the Jews happy. He also imprisoned Peter [Acts 12.2–4]. Acts describes how Agrippa died after being called a god [Acts 12.20–23].

Herod Antipas was a cunning, astute ruler whom Jesus called a 'fox' [Luke 13.32]. He ruled Judea until 39AD. On a trip to Rome he met Herodias, the wife of his half-brother Philip (not the Tetrarch). He brought her back with him to Palestine as his wife, provoking the rage of John the Baptist. Antipas had John executed [Mk 6.14–29] in the Machaerus prison. It was a turning point in the fox's life. Caligula deposed him, on the basis of accusations of treason from his nephew Herod Agrippa I.

Herod the Great was, strangely, not Jewish. He was an Idumaean and for thirty-four years he governed a people who looked down on him. After coming to the throne with the support of the Romans, he did whatever it took to show his gratitude. The city of Samaria was renamed Sebaste (the Greek rendering of Augustus), he created a port called 'Caesarea' on the Mediterranean coast and he established Roman-style games at Jerusalem. He undertook building works worthy of a great Roman ruler. In 20BC he began to build his great temple, which took forty-six years to complete [John 2.20]. He was a tough, brutal ruler—he had his wife Mariamne killed, as well as her two sons, Alexander and Aristobulus, although it has to be said that this was largely as a result of plots by his sister

Salome. There is no historic confirmation of the murder of the children in Bethlehem outside the Bible, but it is in keeping with his character.

After his death, his kingdom was split between three of his sons—Archelaus, Herod Antipas and Philip.

James was the brother of John, and cousin of Jesus. He was a Galilean fisherman who was one of the three in Jesus' inner circle. He died in 44AD when he was beheaded by Herod Agrippa. He was the first of the disciples to be martyred.

James, the son of Alphaeus, is sometimes called 'James the less' or 'James the younger'. Levi is also described as 'the son of Alphaeus' [Mk 2.14], so he and James may have been brothers.

James was the brother of Jesus [Mk 6.3; Matt 13.55; 27.56]. He seems to have disbelieved Jesus' mission at first [John 7.2–5] and then become a Christian when the risen Lord appeared to him [1 Cor 15.3–8]. After this, he became the leader of the Church in Jerusalem and a major figure in the expanding early Church. He was married [1 Cor 9.5]. As the leader of the Jewish Christians he had the tricky task of balancing the views of those who believed that Christians should follow Jewish traditions and customs. According to an early historian, his adherence to the Jewish laws earned him the title 'James the Just'. The letter that he wrote reflects his character, with its emphasis on practical action. He was stoned to death in 61AD, during a Jewish uprising.

Jesus (see pp.132–140).

John was a fisherman, the brother of James and probably the cousin of Jesus (his mother was Salome and Mary was his aunt [Mt 27.56; Mk 16.1; Jn 19.25]). They lived in Galilee, probably at Bethsaida [Mark 1.19–20]. John met Jesus when he was with the disciples of John the Baptist [John 1.35]. Jesus called him and his brother 'sons of Thunder' indicating, perhaps, a fiery temper. He was one of Jesus' inner circle of followers, along with James and Peter. He saw the events of Jesus' trial, since he apparently knew the High Priest [John 18.16]. At his death, Jesus asked John to take care of his mother.

The Sights: John

☐ John joins Jesus: Mk 1.16–20
☐ Not kings, but slaves: Mk 10.35–45
☐ A new responsibility: Jn 19.25–27
☐ Running to the tomb: Jn 20.1–10
☐ So many books: Jn 21.20–25
☐ Healing the lame: Acts 3.1–10
☐ Arrest: Acts 4.1–22
☐ Love one another: 1 Jn 3.11–24
☐ Truth and love: 2John
☐ A vision on an island: Rev 1.1–20
☐ Tell them all: Rev 22.6–21

After the resurrection he was with Peter, then he fades from the scene. Early tradition has it that he went to Ephesus, where he lived to old age. It was probably there that he wrote his gospel and the letters that bear his name. During the persecution of Christians under the Roman emperor Domitian, he may have been the John sent to the tiny isle of Patmos, where he saw the visions which later became the book of Revelation.

The church of St John in Ephesus, built on the traditional site of the apostle's grave. Now derelict, in its time it was one of the biggest churches in the world.

John the Baptist lived in the Judean wilderness where he called people to repent of their sins and be baptised. His first public appearance is dated by Luke to around 26 or 27AD [Lk 3.1–2]. He had disciples whom he trained in prayer [Lk 11.1] and fasting [Mt 1.14]. John was one of the first people to recognise who Jesus really was [Mt 3.14]. He accused Herod Antipas of incest for marrying his half-brother's wife. Herod imprisoned John and had the prophet beheaded (albeit reluctantly) [Mk 6.17–29]. John's disciples remained loyal to him; they cared for his body after his death, and twenty years later there were still disciples of his, such as Apollos [Acts 11.1–7].

Joseph was Mary's husband and the 'adoptive' father of Jesus. A carpenter and builder [Mt 13.55], he lived in Nazareth [Luke 2.4] and came from the line of King David. He taught Jesus his trade [Mk 6.3]. He may have been alive after Jesus' ministry began, but he seems to have died before the crucifixion, because Jesus asked John to care for his mother [John 11.26–27].

Judas was an apostle, probably the same as the Thaddeus listed by Matthew. Perhaps Matthew called him this to distinguish him from Judas Iscariot.

Judas Iscariot probably came from Kerioth in southern Judah. Always the odd one out of the apostles, he looked after the money;

indeed, money seems to have exercised a big influence over him. He argued that perfume used to anoint Jesus should have been sold and the money given to the poor. He betrayed Jesus for thirty pieces of silver, but later, filled with remorse, he returned the blood money he'd taken and went out and committed suicide. [Mt 27.3–5; Acts 1.18]

Jude was one of Jesus' brothers [Mt 13.55]; his proper name was Judas. The letter of Jude is attributed to him. Like his brothers, he did not believe in Jesus at first [Jn 7.5], only becoming a follower after the Resurrection [Acts 1.14].

Lazarus lived in Bethany, a village near Jerusalem, with his sisters Martha and Mary. He became sick and died, but after some delay, Jesus raised him from death [Jn 11.1–12.19].

Luke was a doctor from Antioch in Syria. The only non-Jewish writer in the New Testament, he wrote a history of Jesus and also a history of the early Church. Like all good historians, he 'made a careful study of all that happened' [Luke 1.1–4]. He joined with Paul and accompanied him on several of his missionary journeys.

Mark—or to give him his full name, John Mark—lived in Jerusalem and was related to Barnabas [Col 4.10]. His mother Mary's house was a meeting place for the early Church. He may have been the young man who ran away when Jesus was arrested [Mk14.51]. He joined Paul and Barnabas at Antioch, but later returned home, which caused a row between Paul and Barnabas. Mark then travelled with Barnabas to Cyprus. The row appears to have been healed, because Mark joined Paul in Rome [Col 4.10] and Paul sent him on missions. Mark also worked with Peter, who viewed him as a 'son' [1 Pet 5.13]. An early tradition records that Mark worked as Peter's translator and wrote his gospel from Peter's account. One early manuscript gives Mark's nickname as *kolobodaktylos*, or 'stumpy fingered'.

> **The Sights: Mark**
> ☐ Was Mark the mystery streaker?:
>   Mk 14.50–52
> ☐ The church at Mark's home: Acts 12.6–19
> ☐ An argument: Acts 15.36–41
> ☐ Friend of Paul: 2 Tim 4.11; Col 4.10; Philem 1.23–25
> ☐ 'Son' of Peter: 1 Pet 5.12–14

Martha's name means 'mistress' in Aramaic. She was the sister of Lazarus and Mary. They may have lived in Galilee before moving to Bethany—Luke talks of Jesus visiting the home of a 'Martha' [Lk 10:38]. She knew Jesus well enough to complain to him about his delay in coming to Lazarus's aid [Jn 11.1–3, 21].

Mary of Bethany was the sister of Lazarus and Martha [Jn 11.1]. She was more interested in listening to Jesus than providing dinner [Lk 10:42]. A week before his death, in the house of Simon the Leper [Mk 14.3], she anointed Jesus' feet with ointment and wiped it away with her hair [Jn 12.3], an act which Jesus predicted would always be remembered [Mt 26.6–13; Mk 14.3–9, Jn 12.7–8].

Mary Magdalene was one of Jesus' closest followers. She probably came from Magdala in Galilee. Jesus cast seven demons out of her [Mark 16.9; Luke 8.2]. She was the first person to meet the risen Jesus. (Although she thought he was the gardener.)

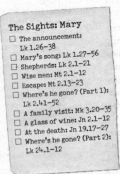

The Sights: Mary
☐ The announcement:
   Lk 1.26–38
☐ Mary's song: Lk 1.27–56
☐ Shepherds: Lk 2.1–21
☐ Wise men: Mt 2.1–12
☐ Escape: Mt 2.13–23
☐ Where's he gone? (Part 1):
   Lk 2.41–52
☐ A family visit: Mk 3.20–35
☐ A glass of wine: Jn 2.1–12
☐ At the death: Jn 19.17–27
☐ Where's he gone? (Part 2):
   Lk 24.1–12

Mary, Mother of Jesus, was probably only fourteen when she gave birth to Jesus. Her real name is Miriam (Mary is the Greek version). She came from a poor family, but one descended from King David's line [Rom 1.3; Acts 2.30; 2 Tim 2.8]. Later in life, she appears to have had doubts about his mission [Mark 3.21], but she was there at the end, standing by the cross when he died. She was also among the first to know of his resurrection, after she visited the tomb. She is known as 'the Virgin Mary' because Jesus was born by the Holy Spirit. After Jesus' birth she seems to have had more children.

Matthew (also known as Levi) was a tax collector who lived in Capernaum near Galilee. As a Jew working for the Roman government he was the object of hate and distrust. When he joined Jesus, he invited his former colleagues to meet Jesus at a meal at his house [Mt 5.29–32]. His background in writing and record-keeping was put to good use in writing a gospel which is primarily aimed at the Jews.

Matthias was the replacement for Judas Iscariot and was chosen by lots [Acts 1.23–26]. Nothing more is known about him.

Onesimus's name means 'useful', which was probably a common nickname for a slave. He had stolen from his master Philemon, and run away to Rome. While there, he became a Christian and was persuaded to return home. Paul wrote to Philemon to ask for mercy. Onesimus left Rome with Tychicus, probably carrying letters to the Ephesian and Colossian churches.

Paul was originally called Saul. He was born to Jewish parents in the city of Tarsus, a place famous for its manufacture of goats' hair cloth. Here he learnt his trade of tentmaking, probably from his parents' business [Acts 18.3].

Paul was a Roman citizen by birth, implying that his parents possessed some wealth and position. He was a Pharisee [Acts 23.6], and when young studied in Jerusalem under the Rabbi Gamaliel [Acts 22.3]. Fanatical about his religion [Gal 1.14], he coordinated an anti-Christian campaign which included the murder of Stephen and the arrest of Christians in Jerusalem and elsewhere [Acts 8.3].

Then he went to Damascus and, on the way, had a life-changing vision of Jesus, who gave him the task of taking the good news to the Gentiles. After some time recovering, he caused so much trouble in Damascus that he had to be smuggled out of the city [Acts 9.1–22]. He then went to Jerusalem, where Barnabas stood up for him amidst a great deal of suspicion.

> **The Sights: Paul**
> ☐ Conversion: Acts 9. 1–31
> ☐ Saul, Barnabas and Antioch: Acts 11.19–30
> ☐ On the way: Acts 13.1–12
> ☐ Paul v Jerusalem: Acts 15.1–35
> ☐ Missionary life: Acts 17.16–34
> ☐ Arrest: Acts 21.17–36
> ☐ The defence: Acts 26.1–32
> ☐ Shipwreck!: Acts 27.1–44
> ☐ House arrest in Rome: Acts 28.16–31
> ☐ Jews and Gentiles: Rom 3.1–31
> ☐ Sin and the Spirit: Rom 7.7–8.17
> ☐ Love: 1 Cor 13
> ☐ Mission: Ephesians 3
> ☐ Ending the race: 2 Tim 4.1–22

After that he returned to Tarsus for a period of eight to ten years. Little is known of his activities, but he probably preached and taught in his home city [Gal 1.23]. Eventually Barnabas invited Paul to Antioch, and for the next twenty years, Paul travelled throughout the Mediterranean area, taking the gospel to Jew and Gentile alike, preaching, teaching, and founding churches.

In the end, he was arrested by the authorities in Jerusalem. As a Roman citizen he was allowed to be tried in Rome, so he was shipped there, where he spent some time under house arrest. He may have been released, but then re-arrested when a new wave of Christian persecution broke out. Tradition states that he was executed in Rome sometime around 67AD.

A second century document describes Paul as 'a man small of stature, with a bald head and crooked legs, in a good state of body, with eyebrows meeting and nose somewhat hooked, full of friendliness: for now he appears like man and now he has the face of an angel'. Perhaps this is reflected in his change of name. In Hebrew, Saul means 'asked for' while his Roman equivalent *Paulos* means 'little'.

Bronze statue of Peter from St Peter's in Rome. The church is built over the traditional site of Peter's grave. Centuries of pilgrims touching his right foot have worn the surface smooth.

The Sights: Peter

☐ Fishers of men: Lk 5.1–11
☐ Walking on water: Mt 14.22–32
☐ Rocky: Mt 16.13–20
☐ Think before you speak: Mt 8.31–38
☐ Denial: Mt 26.31–35; 69–75
☐ Running to the tomb: Jn 20.1–10
☐ Restoration: Jn 21.1–19
☐ Pentecost and preaching: Acts 2.1–42
☐ Healing the lame: Acts 3.1–26
☐ Arrest: Acts 4.1–31
☐ Peter and Cornelius: Acts 10.1–48
☐ Peter on trial: Acts 12.1–19
☐ Suffering and leadership: 1 Pet 4.12–5.11
☐ How we should live: 2 Peter 1.1–15

Peter was known as **Simon**, or in Hebrew 'Symeon' [Acts 15.14]. Jesus called him **Cephas** or the 'rock' [John 1.42]. The Greek word for rock is Petra, from which we get Peter. He was married [Mark 1.30] and was a fisherman from Bethsaida. He lived in Capernaum, where he was in business with Andrew, James and John. After giving them a miraculous catch of fish, Jesus called Peter to be a 'fisher of men'.

He was the most prominent disciple, their natural spokesman and one of the inner core of the three or four intimate apostles of Jesus. Enthusiastic and committed, it was Peter who tried to walk on water, who drew out his sword and charged at Jesus' arrest, who first called Jesus the Messiah. But when Jesus was being tried, Peter denied ever having known him.

After the Holy Spirit came at Pentecost, he preached a sermon that led to 3,000 people being converted. He healed the sick and was the first of the disciples to recognise that the Gentiles had a part to play in the church [Acts 15.6–11, 14]. (Although he later argued with Paul about it [Gal 2.11–21].) He and his wife travelled widely [1 Cor 1.5, Gal 2.9]. Tradition says that Peter went to Rome where he was put to death in Nero's persecutions around 64AD.

Philemon was a Christian who had a church in his home, probably in Colossae. He was married to Apphia and probably had a son called Archippus. His slave, Onesimus, had run away, and Paul wrote to ask for mercy.

Philip's home was in Bethsaida. He may have been a fisherman, since the village was a well-known fishing village. He brought Nathanael to Jesus [Jn 1.43]. The tradition is that, after the resurrection, he taught in Asia Minor.

Philip the Tetrarch was a son of Herod the Great. He married Salome, daughter of Herodias and his own niece. He was probably the best of Herod's three ruling sons, but that's not saying very much.

Pilate was the representative of imperial Rome in Palestine for ten years, from 26–36AD. Governing Palestine took a mixture of strength and subtlety. Pilate had one but not the other. He offended the Jews by bringing the Roman standards into Jerusalem. He hung shields inscribed with the names of Roman deities in the Temple. His usual headquarters were in Caesarea, but at the time of Jesus' trial he was in Jerusalem, presumably because it was passover and he wanted to keep an eye on the place. His career ended some six years later when he put down with too much force a rebellion in Samaria. After compaints, Pilate was recalled to Rome. He lost political support in the capital and, according to the historian Eusebius, he committed suicide.

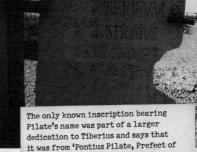

The only known inscription bearing Pilate's name was part of a larger dedication to Tiberius and says that it was from 'Pontius Pilate, Prefect of Judea.' This replica is at Caesarea where the original—now in the Jerusalem Museum—was found.

Priscilla and **Aquila** were Jewish Christians. They lived in Rome, but were expelled when Claudius expelled the Jews around 49–50AD. They were tentmakers like Paul, and he met them first in Corinth [Acts 18.2]. They later went to Ephesus [Acts 18.24–26] where they taught Apollos, and then later still they were in Rome [Rom 16.3], where they had a church in their house [1 Cor 16.19]. The church of S. Prisca in Rome is built on the traditional site of their house (Priscilla is the diminutive of the Roman name Prisca [Rom 16.3]). Aquila came from Pontus, a region in northern Asia Minor on the south shore of the Black Sea. Since Priscilla is often listed before her husband [Acts 18.18–19, 26; Rom 16.3; 2 Tim 4.19], she may have come from a higher social class.

Silas was a member of the church in Jerusalem [Acts 15.22, 32]. Like Paul he was a Roman citizen [Acts 16.38]. With Paul and Barnabas, he was commissioned to deliver the letter from the Jewish council to the church at Antioch [Acts 15.22–23]. Later he accompanied Paul to Philippi and then Corinth [Acts 18.5].

Simon was an apostle and a Zealot, a political group that was actively opposed to Roman occupation.

Stephen was one of seven Christians appointed to look after practical matters in the early Church in Jerusalem, including the distribution of food to the poor [Acts 6.1–6]. He was a significant figure who performed signs and wonders, and debated with the Jews in the synagogue. Accused of blasphemy, he was stoned to death while Saul looked on. His death triggered an outburst of persecution of the early Church [Acts 7.57–8.3].

Thomas was also known as Didymus, which is Greek for 'twin'. He did not believe the rest of the apostles when they said they'd seen the risen Jesus, which is why he's known as 'doubting Thomas'. The moment he saw the risen Jesus, all doubts disappeared. According to tradition he went east to Persia and even as far as India.

The Sights

☐ Paul meets Timothy:
Acts 16.1–3
☐ 'Like a son': 1 Cor 4.14–17;
Phil 2.19–24
☐ In Thessalonica: 1 Th 3.1–6
☐ In Ephesus: 1 Tim 1.1–20
☐ 'You belong to God':
1 Tim 6.11–21
☐ Do not be ashamed:
2 Tim 1.1–14
☐ Last instructions:
2 Tim 3.10–17

Timothy was a native of Lystra. His father was Greek and his mother, Eunice, a Jew [Acts 16.1; 2 Tim 1.5]. He was probably a convert of Paul's first missionary journey. He became an assistant to Paul, an evangelist and church leader. Shy and occasionally fearful, he was also extremely loyal [1Corinthians 16.10–11; 2 Tim 1.7] and often ill [1 Tim 5.23]. To Paul, Timothy was like a son. He supported Paul in prison and later may even have become a prisoner himself [Heb 13.23]. Probably he became a church leader in Ephesus [1 Tim 1.3], where he received letters from Paul on how to run his church.

Titus was a convert of Paul and accompanied him on many journeys. He was a Greek Gentile, who went with Paul to Jerusalem. Paul argued that, as a Gentile, he should not have to be circumcised. Paul later sent Titus to Corinth to help with the problems and collect money for Christians in Jerusalem. He then went on to run the church in Crete [Tit 1.4–5].

Explorer's Notes—Part 7
History and Real Life

The boots in front of a
Roman toilet (gents)

Arms and Warfare

There's a lot of warfare in the Bible. Sometimes it was **open warfare**, where two armies meet on a battlefield; sometimes it was a **siege**, where one army attacks a fortified city. There were also many surprise attacks (Joshua was good at these [Josh 6]).

Even while wandering in the desert, the Israelites had some sort of military force. But there was no official, standing army until after the first king.

Saul had a band of 3,000 [1 Sam 13.2]. David had around 600 core troops, as well as a large army of which 24,000 were on duty each month. According to the Law, you could be released from military service if you had just built a house, got engaged, planted a vineyard or were just a bit scared [Deut 20.5–8]. Which gives most people a get out, really.

Swords were usually hung round the waist and were the size of a large dagger. There were **spears** and **bows** and some fighters were experts in using the **sling**, which could throw a stone as large as an orange with a lot of accuracy. (And the big advantage of slings is there's always a lot of ammo lying around.)

Helmets were originally made of leather and then later of bronze or iron. **Breastplates** were generally pieces of metal sewn onto shirts. King Uzziah was the first king to issue helmets to his troops [2 Chr 26.14]. Most **shields** were small, but important soldiers would have a large shield, carried by a shield-bearer.

Chariots didn't come into common use in Israel until after Solomon's time. They were lightweight carts pulled by one or two horses.

Big armies, such as the Assyrian, also had sophisticated **siege engines** and **battering rams**. These needed a huge amount of manpower to move them, but once in position they could prove devastatingly effective.

Books, Letters and Writing

The standard writing material was **papyrus**, made from the stalk of marsh reeds. If you couldn't afford papyrus, you could write on broken shards of pottery called *ostraka*. There was also **parchment**—made of animal skin—and wax tablets, which were good for taking notes, since the wax could be smoothed out and reused. Earlier civilisations such as the Assyrians wrote on clay tablets which were then left to harden. Most documents were either single sheets, or sheets sewn together to make a scroll.

Pens were made out of sharpened reeds. Ink was made out of soot mixed with gum or vinegar; or sepia—the ink from a cuttlefish. If you were writing an important manuscript you might mix some wormwood (a bitter herb) into your ink which would stop the mice from eating the document!

The Library of Celsus at Ephesus had a capacity of more than 12,000 scrolls. Scrolls were kept in cupboards in niches on the walls.

There were many **libraries** throughout the world. The most famous—such as that at Alexandria—had hundreds of thousands of scrolls. Private citizens, if they had enough money, would also collect their own libraries—one rich Roman was said to have a personal library of 62,000 manuscripts.

Books—and long documents—were written by dictation. There were expert scribes and secretaries who could write quickly and fluently.

Letters were very common. There was an Imperial postal service, but this was restricted to official business. If you wanted to send a private letter you had to send someone to deliver it personally or find someone who was heading that way and would take it for you. Paul usually had his letters carried by specific, trusted people. Letters from important or notable people were copied and preserved; indeed, such people wrote knowing that their letters would be kept.

Circumcision

Circumcision is a **ritual operation** which removes all, or part, of the foreskin from the male penis. The practice dates back to very early times and has been practised by many cultures, including African, South American, Australian and Native American. Generally it is used as a **rite of passage,** to mark the transition from being a boy to being a man.

For the Jews, however, it was not to do with becoming a man, or even belonging to a tribe: it was to do with **belonging to God**. It was part of his **covenant** with Abraham that God ordered all Jewish sons to be circumcised. The Jews circumcised their babies on the **eighth day** after their birth as a physical sign of the covenant between God and his people. God says that any male not circumcised 'hasn't kept his promise to me and cannot be one of my people' [Gen 17.14].

Much later in Bible history, however, many Jews started to believe that circumcision was enough on it's own; that as long as they were circumcised, they were holy, they were OK. This attitude was criticised by prophets such as **Jeremiah**, who said to the people, 'Your bodies are circumcised, but your hearts are unchanged' [Jer 9.26].

Later still, in New Testament times, the issue became the cause of conflict between Jewish and Greek Christians. Some Jewish Christians argued that everyone should be circumcised. Peter, and later Paul, fought this, arguing that Christians were justified by faith in Christ and did not need the physical act of circumcision [Rom 4.9–13].

Cities and Towns

Unlike modern towns and cities (at least in the western world) cities in the Bible were **cramped** and **confined**.

The first requirement was **defence**, which is why many cities were built on a hill. They couldn't spread out, they had to be surrounded by a wall. The earliest **walls** were mud brick, but later towns and cities had stone walls with observation towers. The outside of the wall was often covered with chalk in order to make it too slippery to climb.

If you have walls, you need **gates**. The gates were the busiest parts of the city, where the streets were wider and where everyone was coming and going. Gates often housed markets (such as the Fish Gate in Jerusalem) and prophets often delivered their announcements at the gates [1 Kings 21.10; Acts 7.58]. The gates were closed every night, and secured with iron bars. Streets were not paved, except in the richest cities.

Cities usually had a **citadel** or **palace** which was the main administrative centre, where the king or governor lived. They also had **market areas** and even **industrial zones**, where 'smelly' industries such as cloth-dying or leather-tanning were put.

If you were well-off, you lived on the western side of the city, or on the higher ground, where the ventilation was better. Poorer homes were generally crammed into the lower regions of the city.

There was no indoor plumbing, of course. All water had to be carried in large clay jars or drawn from a well. Some sophisticated cities like Jerusalem had water tunnels, aqueducts and pools. In Roman times water might even be distributed throughout the city through clay pipes.

The Graeco-Roman cities, such as those visited by Paul, usually had a similar plan, with a **colonnaded main street** with shops along each side, an **agora** or marketplace where news could be shared, and often an **acropolis**, a hill where the main temple was.

The main agora at Perge. This would have been the hub of city life, a bustling marketplace, lined with shops and teeming with gossip.

Clothes

Clothes in Bible times were valuable. Cloth took time to weave
and sewing was laborious hard work. So, people tended to
keep their clothes simple.

In the Old Testament people generally wore a **loin cloth**, and
then a simple **tunic** tied at the waist with a belt. Everyone wore
open **leather sandals** on their feet.

Whereas today clothes are often designed to reveal the
shape of the body, or to accentuate a person's appearance or
sexuality, things were totally different in Bible times. Women
generally wore **veils** over their faces and covered their hair.
Only prostitutes wore revealing garments.

Clothes took a lot of work and were therefore valuable.
Joseph's 'coat of many colours' attracted his brother's envy
because it was a highly valuable gift, not only because it was
brightly coloured. Sometimes these fine displays of clothing
attract criticism. Isaiah criticises the finery of the women of his
time, contrasting that with the poverty of people around them
[Isa 3.18–23]. Ezekiel likens Israel to a beautifully and expensively
dressed young woman who then, unfortunately, behaves like a
hooker. [Ezk 16.10–14].

In New Testament times, both men and women wore a
tight-fitting, ankle-length tunic. This was tied at the waist with
a belt. The **belt** would also have a purse or bag for money hanging from it. Over this, they wore a **cloak**. The Jewish cloak had
tassels attached to the four corners. Paul had a thick winter
cloak to which he was particularly attached (possibly he had
made it himself out of goatshair, the same material he used for
tent-making [2Tim 4.13]).

The Pharisees wore impressive white linen tunics with dyed
blue edges. (They really did look like whitewashed tombs [Mt
23.27].)

Crucifixion

Described by Cicero as a 'cruel and frightful sentence', **cruci-fixion** was reserved for the **lowest criminals**—robbers, bandits and rebels. The Romans used it on a mass scale—Hadrian is said to have had five hundred rebels crucified on one day.

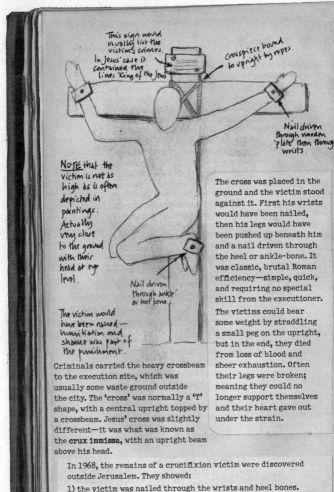

This sign would visually list the victim's crimes. In Jesus' case it contained the lines 'King of the Jews'.

Crosspiece bound to upright by ropes.

Nail driven through wooden 'plate' then through wrists.

NOTE that the victim is not as high as is often depicted in paintings. Actually very close to the ground with their head at eye level.

Nail driven through ankle or heel bone.

The victim would have been naked—humiliation and shame was part of the punishment.

The cross was placed in the ground and the victim stood against it. First his wrists would have been nailed, then his legs would have been pushed up beneath him and a nail driven through the heel or ankle-bone. It was classic, brutal Roman efficiency—simple, quick, and requiring no special skill from the executioner.

The victims could bear some weight by straddling a small peg on the upright, but in the end, they died from loss of blood and sheer exhaustion. Often their legs were broken; meaning they could no longer support themselves and their heart gave out under the strain.

Criminals carried the heavy crossbeam to the execution site, which was usually some waste ground outside the city. The 'cross' was normally a 'T' shape, with a central upright topped by a crossbeam. Jesus' cross was slightly different—it was what was known as the **crux immissa**, with an upright beam above his head.

In 1968, the remains of a crucifixion victim were discovered outside Jerusalem. They showed:

1) the victim was nailed through the wrists and heel bones.

2) The nail had first been nailed through a piece of wood as a guide.

3) The legs had been broken to hasten death.

Early Church

For the early Christians 'church' meant people. The word 'church' comes from the Greek word *ecclesia*, which means 'a gathering of people at the call of a herald'. So, the first Christians saw themselves as people who were responding to a call.

The early Church didn't have special buildings. They met in **houses** and, in the early years at least, Jewish converts still went to **synagogue**. Paul mentions several 'house churches', including those run by **Priscilla** and **Aquila** [Rom 16.5], **Nympha** [Col 4.15] and **Philemon** [Phil 2]. From very early times **Peter's house** at Capernaum was a focus for worship, and sometime in the first century one room was enlarged to allow more people to meet there (see opposite). Since they met in houses these churches were probably not more than 20–30 strong. Many of these houses were eventually turned into church buildings

They probably met every day of the week, at least in the early days. They celebrated the **Lord's Supper** on the first day of the week [1Cor 16.2]. Their church services included **prophecies**, **teaching**, **singing** and **reading** from Scriptures. Sometimes a collection was taken up for those in need.

All believers were thought of as part of the priesthood [1Pet 2.5,9], but there was a leadership structure. At the top were the **apostles** because they had known Jesus. **Jesus' family** also had a prominent position in the early Church, particularly his brother James who was the leader in Jerusalem and presided over a council of elders.

At the local level there were **elders**, who were probably the strategic and spiritual leaders of the local church. Along with the elders there were **deacons**, from the Greek word for 'servant'. These people may have had a more practical role in the running of their church.

The first followers of Jesus were known by different names. According to the Bible, they were first called '**Christians**' at Antioch [Ac 11.26]. They were also known as Ebionites (which meant 'the poor' and later referred to a particular Christian-Jewish sect), Nazarenes [Ac 24.5] and people of 'the way'.

Peter's House in Capernaum

From very early times this was a place where Christians gathered in Capernaum. Later the house was converted into a bigger space for worship, and in the 5th century a church was built on the site.

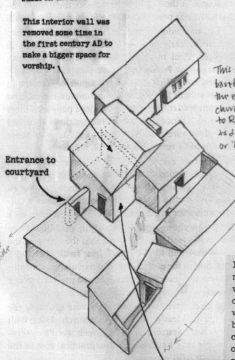

This interior wall was removed some time in the first century AD to make a bigger space for worship.

Entrance to courtyard

This style of church – based in a house – was the earliest setting for churches from Palestine to Rome. It is known as DOMUS ECCLESIA or 'house church'.

Today, millions of Christians still meet and worship in houses.

the lakeside

In Rome, Christians met in houses, warehouses and over shops. Later, when Christianity became accepted, churches were built over these original sites.

Today you can still see the original floor of Peter's house, enclosed within the walls of the 5th century octagonal church.

Education

In Old Testament times, what little education there was took place in the **home**, with the parents as tutors, but by the time of Jesus things had changed. There were **schools** in every town, and boys were expected to attend by the age of five or six. (Girls didn't receive a formal education but were educated at home by their mothers.)

The 'school' took place in the **synagogue** or in the open air, with the local rabbi as the teacher. After learning to read and write, Jewish boys would learn the **Hebrew scriptures**, starting with Leviticus and then moving on to the Pentateuch and the prophets and the rest of the books. After the age of ten they would study the traditional law, or **Mishna**, and then at fifteen move on to 'higher education' involving theological discussion. So, no room for maths, science, general history or geography—and no P.E. Just a diet of Jewish religion and ritual.

Keen or able scholars could then go on to a kind of university, studying under **renowned teachers**. Paul, for example, studied under a famous rabbi called Gamaliel [Acts 22.3].

In Greece and Rome the education was much broader, with more emphasis on athletics, literature, maths and music. Students might also learn rhetoric—the art of public speaking—and even architecture, philosophy, medicine and astronomy.

In terms of further education, there were **universities** (of a sort) at places like Tarsus, Carthage and Alexandria, as well as travelling lecturers who moved from place to place speaking in lecture halls, such as the lecture hall of Tyrannus in Ephesus [Acts 19.9].

The Gymnasium at Sardis. In Roman and Greek cities, along with sports and athletics, children would also go to the gymnasium for the rest of their lessons.

Families

In Bible times, and especially in Old Testament times, families meant much more than just Mum, Dad and the kids.

In ancient society, the family was a larger **kinship** group, more what we would call an 'extended' family. A Biblical family would include the father, his wife (or wives), their children, various other dependent relatives and even the servants.

The blood-ties between members of the same family were strong, and members of the family had the right to expect protection and provision from their kinsfolk.

A New Testament household would include the slaves and employees of the family, as well as the core 'family' members. Perhaps it is easier to imagine if we think about it in terms of the word **'household'**; that is, those dwelling together under the same roof. The household of Cornelius, for example, included Cornelius and his family, his servants and even some close friends [Acts 10.7, 24].

Both Old Testament and New Testament societies were **patriarchal**; that is, the father was the undisputed head of the household. What he said, went. (Although there are plenty of examples in the Bible of women being able to get their own way.)

The children generally remained under the father's control until they got married. Young children were looked after by their mother, but as soon as the boys were old enough, they started to work alongside their father.

Farming

Olive oil was one of the most versatile and important crops. You could cook with it, use it to dress wounds, put it on your hair, burn it in lamps: it was a staple of every farm.

Farming was one of the main occupations of ancient times. With no shops as we know them, most families kept some **livestock** and grew some **crops**. Even Kings like King Uzziah, got involved [2 Chr 26.10].

The main **livestock** were goats and sheep. The Israelites, because of the restrictions on them in the Law, did not eat pigs. Farmers also had oxen, donkeys and mules to help with ploughing and transport. They also had geese and ducks, but chickens only arrived in the sixth century BC, when they were brought back from the Babylonian captivity.

Basic **arable** crops included wheat and barley. Farmers also grew vegetables such as leeks, onions, cucumbers and melons; fruit trees such as pomegranate, date and fig; olive and nut trees; and herbs such as hyssop, dill, mint and cumin. Walls were often built around fields to keep animals such as goats out.

This plough is the kind used in Biblical times. The two inverted 'V' shaped pieces would have gone over the necks of the oxen. If you wanted straight plowing, you had to keep looking ahead and have equally strong animals under each yoke.

Wine was a basic part of the ancient diet. Then, as today, wine was made by crushing grapes in a press, and letting the juice ferment. According to Genesis, Noah was the first person to make wine [Gen 9.20]. Stone **watchtowers** were often built in the vineyards and farmers often slept in the tower, on constant watch to protect their crop from predators such as birds and foxes.

Festivals

Festivals formed the backbone of the Israelite calendar. There were three main festivals: Passover, Pentecost and Atonement.

Passover (Lev 23.4–5) commemorated God's rescuing of the Israelites from Egypt. It took place over one evening in the first month. Families would eat a special meal of lamb. Passover was followed by the week-long **Festival of Thin Bread** (Lev 23.6–8), which commemorated the speedy exit of the Israelites from Egypt.

Pentecost (or the **Feast of Weeks**) (Lev 23.15–22; Num 28.26–31) celebrated the main harvest and was a time of sacrifice in the Temple. On the first day of the seventh month there was another harvest celebration, the **Festival of Trumpets** (Lev 23.23–25). This was followed by the **Day of Atonement** (Lev 16.1–34; 23.26–32), a day of fasting and repentance, where the people would asking forgiveness for their sins.

Then came **Tabernacles,** or the **Festival of Shelters** (Lev 23.33–44), which lasted for eight days and celebrated Israel's wanderings in the desert. Families would live in a tent for seven days and offer the best fruit from their trees.

Hanukkah or the **Feast of Lights** commemorated the purification of the Temple after the Maccabean revolt. Candles were lit to celebrate the re-lighting of the Temple lamps (1 Macc 4.50–51) or, according to another source, the miracle during the first celebration of the feast when a small amount of oil in the Temple burnt for eight days.

Finally there was **Purim** which commemorated the rescue of the Jews in Persia told in the story of Esther (Esth 9.26–32).

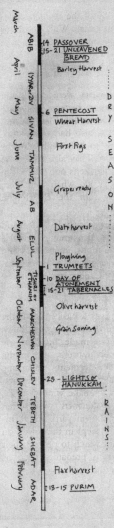

Fishing

Fishing isn't mentioned much in the Old Testament, mainly because the Israelites had limited access to the coast and they hadn't yet developed fishing in other waters. By the time of the New Testament, however, things were different, and the **Sea of Galilee**, especially, was home to a large number of fishing boats.

In Galilee, most fishing was done at **night,** just before dawn. The main way of fishing was by **throwing nets** from the boats. The nets had clay or stone weights along the lower edge, and cork or wood floats along the top. Two teams of men then take hold of each end of the net and start to haul it in. As long as the hauling is continuous the fish will be unable to escape. Jesus compares the **kingdom of heaven** to this type of net [Mt 13.47–48].

Another method of fishing was for a single fisherman to use a **casting net**, which he spun out over the water. As the net fell through the water, it would take on a dome-like shape capturing the fish. The fisherman would draw the net in with a line attached to the centre.

Fishermen also used a **hook and line**—probably Peter used this method to catch the fish on Jesus' instructions [Mt 17.27].

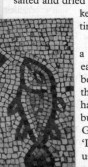

Loaves and fishes. From a mosaic floor at Tabhga, on the shores of Lake Galilee.

In those days, of course, there were no fridges, so fish had to be salted and dried if it was going to be kept for any length of time.

The fish became a **key symbol** for the early Church, partly because so many of the church founders had been fishermen, but also because the Greek word for fish— 'Icthus'—could be used as an acrostic code for Jesus.

Food and Drink

Almost all the family's food was grown and prepared at home. Since preparing meals took a long time, the main meal was in the evening. The basic daily food was **vegetables**, cooked with herbs and eaten with **bread**. Since the common herbs were things like cumin, garlic and onion, food was probably quite spicy. And Jewish food laws meant **no blood** and nothing 'unclean', such as pork or seafood.

Bread was made from wheat or barley flour, mixed with olive oil and yeast to make it rise; then baked on a flat oven floor, or a baking tray over an open fire.

Olive oil was a vital ingredient. You fried food in it, used it as a dressing, and used it in the lamps of the house. You could even use it as an ointment for wounds, or add scents to it to make perfume.

Bread was a staple part of the diet. Here it is being baked in the traditional way, on a metal hood over an open fire.

Meat was generally only for special occasions and mostly boiled. Most people ate **goat** or **mutton**. You could eat doves, or chickens, or, if you were really hungry, fried locusts or grasshoppers.

If you lived near the sea, or Galilee, then **fish** would have been a common part of your diet. Jerusalem had a 'Fish Gate' where fresh and dried fish were sold.

There was a wealth of **vegetables**, including lentils, beans, cucumbers, leeks, onions and garlic, and they were all cheap and filling. **Fruit** included figs, pomegranates and grapes.

Water was common but often unhealthy, so most people drank **wine**, or vinegar mixed with water. Cows, goats and sheep produced **milk**, which was either drunk or used to make butter, cheese and **yoghurt**. Most **cheese** was made from goats' milk.

Typical New Testament food. An earthenware mug of wine, some olives and a sauce made out of olive oil and herbs into which your bread could be dipped (Mk 14.20).

'Great is Artemis of the Ephesians'
(Acts 19.34). A replica of the Temple
statue from Ephesus, where she was
worshiped mainly as a fertility
goddess, and was identified with
Cybele, the eastern mother goddess.

Foreign gods

One of the most serious failings of
the people of Israel was their ad-
diction to **foreign gods**. These were
mainly imported from the nations
surrounding Israel.

In the Old Testament, probably
the best known of these gods is **Baal**
(the name actually means 'lord'), a
Canaanite god who was supposed
to bring rain. (This is why Elijah
challenged the priests of Baal to a
rain-making contest; he wanted to
show how useless Baal was.) There
was also **Asherah**, who seems to
have been a fertility goddess. The
Canaanites set up many 'Asherah
poles', which were local shrines.
Gods were linked to specific topics: you might have a sun god for
heat, a storm god for rain, nature gods
to provide crops and plants; and fertility
gods to help with having babies.

The worship of foreign gods was of-
ten repulsive. Many shrines had **male and female prostitutes** who
would have sex with the followers and give the money to the
shrine priests. Some gods demanded **human sacrifices**, an act
which was forbidden to Israel. But even the Israelites engaged
in the practice—King Ahaz and King Manasseh of Judah sacrificed their own sons to foreign gods [2 Kings 16.3; 21.6]. Jeremiah
accused the people of sacrificing children to Baal [Jer 7.30–33].
They did this outside Jerusalem, in a place known as Slaughter Valley or the **Valley of Hinnom**. Later, Jesus used this location
as a synonym for hell.

In New Testament times, the Romans and Greeks had their
own pantheon of gods, and it was expected that citizens would
join in their festivals and worship. More, the emperor himself
was worshipped. The refusal of Christians and Jews to worship the all-too-human emperor was a cause of widespread
mistrust and persecution.

Funerals

When you died, you had to be **buried**. Not to be buried was a punishment and a scandal [Deut 28.26; I Kings 14.11; Jer 22.19]. That's why Jacob asked his family to ensure he was buried in his family tomb [Gen 49.30; 50.5] and why the people of Jabesh in Gilead risked so much to rescue the body of Saul [1 Sam 31.8–13].

Once the body had decomposed, the bones were put in a box like this, called an ossuary.

Tombs were often made out of **caves** where all the family were buried. Abraham bought the cave of Machpelah for his family, including Sarah, Abraham, Isaac, Rebekah, Leah and Jacob [Gen 49.29–32].

Big tombs usually had a deep tunnel, leading into a square or oval burial chamber. The **opening** was sealed with rocks to stop animals or grave-robbers. Later tombs were often multichambered and cut into rocks, with ledges cut into the walls where the dead were placed.

Cremation was not practised by the Jews or early Christians. In fact, burning was considered shameful and was inflicted as a death penalty for criminals [Lev 20.14; 21.9].

Houses for the dead. Lycian rock tombs at Myra form a necropolis—a city of the dead—where each family has its own 'house' to lie in.

Coffins were rarely used. Instead the body was simply wrapped in a cloth. Later on, after the body had decomposed, the bones were collected and put into a box (called an **ossuary**) which was placed in another area of the same tomb.

Jesus was placed in a Roman-style tomb, which had a burial chamber containing one or more benches where the body would be laid. The more elaborate tombs had a **stone** which rolled in a groove, like a kind of sliding door.

Not that it always worked...

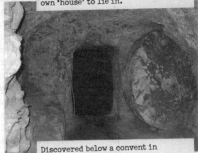

Discovered below a convent in Nazareth, this tomb is typical of the cave tombs used in Biblical times. The bodies would be laid on shelves in the cave and then the huge circular stone rolled across the entrance to seal the tomb and keep out predators.

Gentiles

Gentile was a catch-all term for anyone who wasn't a Jew. They could be Greeks, Romans, Syrians, Egyptians—but if they weren't Jewish, they were Gentiles.

Gentiles could become Jews. Those who did were called **proselytes**. By New Testament times, there appear to have been two forms of proselyte: those who went the whole way and took on all the Jewish practices; and those called **'God-fearers'** who attended synagogue but didn't go much beyond that. The Temple had a special **Court of the Gentiles**, where Gentile worshippers of Israel's God could gather.

Some Jews of Jesus' time used the word 'Gentile' as a term of abuse. After all, the Jews were the **chosen people**, Israel was the holy nation: to be a Gentile was to be second best. To be fair, sometimes the Jews had a point. Many citizens of Roman and Greek cities had standards of behaviour that were scandalous and sinful and that the Jews were absolutely right to shun.

This is part of the reason why the early Church had so much discussion about Gentiles. They didn't act like the Jews. They were part of a **different culture**. So shouldn't they have to become Jews, like the proselytes? The Jewish Christians were not against preaching the gospel to the Gentiles, it's just they thought they should become more Jewish.

In the end, Paul won the day. He argued that Christ had changed the rules; that the law and outward observance had been superseded, that what mattered was **faith in God**, not what clothes you wore or what food you ate.

Gnosticism

One of the biggest problems the early Church had to face was a set of ideas called **'Gnosticism'**. 'Gnostic' comes from the Greek word Gnosis meaning 'secret knowledge'. From this we get the word 'agnostic' for people who just don't know.

The Gnostics claimed that they had **secret knowledge** about Jesus. They believed that God had kept some truth back and only allowed special people to be enlightened.

They also believed that the material world, the stuff all around us, was evil. Some gnostics tried to punish their bodies and to live eating and drinking only a very few things. Others pretended that reality wasn't actually real. So they indulged in all kinds of sin in the belief that somehow it didn't affect them. (This approach is condemned in 1 John.)

If nature was evil, that meant changing their view of Jesus. 'If bodies are bad,' they argued, 'surely God's son wouldn't have used one?' So, the Gnostics claimed that Jesus **wasn't really a human** at all; he was a spirit who sort of rented out a human body and moved out just before the nasty death bit.

Apostles like **Paul** and **John** worked hard to combat these theories. Paul knew that Jesus had been a real man who had died a real death and rose to life again. And he knew that God was for everyone, not just the select few.

By the second and third centuries AD, the gnostics were producing their own **scriptures** in the form of fake gospels. Despite what some novels and films might have you believe, these were almost entirely fabrications (apart from maybe a few fragments in the **Gospel of Thomas**, which may preserve some original statements of Jesus). Forget what you might have read about the church 'suppressing' these books; the early Church ignored them because they were so ridiculously unbelievable.

Harvest

Harvest was vitally important. If food went short, the people would starve. They couldn't just nip down to the supermarket and pick up a packet of imported fish fingers.

The harvest usually took place around **April** and **May**. **Barley** was the first crop to be harvested, followed by **wheat** a few weeks later [Ruth 2.23].

Men would cut the crops with sickles, followed by women who would gather up the cuttings into sheaves. Then people would go through again, doing what was called '**gleaning**', which means collecting the stalks which had been missed. According to the law, gleaning had to be left to the poor; the owners were not to take absolutely everything [Lev 19.9–10]. Because you only had a limited time to get the crops in, it was important to get as many **labourers** as possible; any labourers for hire would gather in the marketplace in anticipation of employment [Mt 20.1–16].

The wheat was taken to the **threshing floor**, where it would be **winnowed** (tossed or thrown in the air), either by hand or with winnowing forks. Threshing floors were wide open spaces which allowed the wind to get in and blow away the straw, while the grains would simply fall to the ground. The wheat would then be sifted to remove any other impurities, put into bags and then either stored or taken to be milled into flour.

For the people of those days, a successful harvest was the most **important economic event** of the year. It was their pay day. So it's significant that the best of their harvest was supposed to be presented to God—a symbolic reminder of who it was who gave them the harvest in the first place.

Houses

The first Israelites lived in **tents**. Each family within the tribe
would have had a big tent which was made from goat skins or
goat hair. (Goatskins have good insulating properties: warm
and dry in winter, relatively cool in summer.)

In the summer, they may have moved to higher ground to
catch what breeze there was, in the winter they would have
used the shelter of the mountains, while avoiding the valley floor in case of flooding. Channels would have been dug
around the edge of the tent for drainage and briars and twigs
laid around to stop animals and snakes entering.

In cities and towns, the **houses** followed a similar pattern.
They were single or double storied houses, with storage and
workrooms on the ground floor and living accommodation
above. Several homes would have been clustered around a
central courtyard, where the food would have been prepared.
Homes had their own **water reservoirs** to collect and store rain-
water. Doors and windows were very small, so the houses were
dark inside. Light would have been provided by oil-lamps,
fuelled by olive oil.

Most homes were **furnished simply** with stools, a table and
beds. When Elijah stayed with the Shunammite widow, his
room contained a table, chair, bed and lamp [2 Kings 4.10]. People
slept on the floor or on a mattress made of animal skins or
reeds. Or they could use their clothes as a mattress and blan-
ket. Richer people had **beds** which could double as couches, on
which people reclined to eat. **Tables** were normally owned by
the rich. Everyone else sat on the floor, with their food laid out
on a sort of picnic mat made out of animal skin or cloth.

In New Testament times, in the big cities frequented by
Paul, the Romans built huge **tenement or apartment blocks** called
insulae. These could be as many as five or six storeys high. The
ground floor often held shops or warehouses, with flats on the
first floor and above. Some **Roman churches** were built over these
warehouses, indicating that early Churches might have met in
the space, or in the rooms over the shops.

Languages

The language of the Old Testament was **Hebrew** (apart from some bits of Daniel and Ezra, which are in Aramaic). After the exile, it was replaced by **Aramaic** in common use, but it continued to be the 'religious language' used in religious ritual and, of course, when reading the Hebrew scriptures.

Aramaic language was used throughout most of the Assyrian and Persian empire. After the restoration of the Jews, Aramaic was adopted as the common language. This was the language that Jesus spoke. Aramaic words that appear in the New Testament include 'Abba' [Mk 14.36] and 'Talitha, koum' [Mk 5.41].

The New Testament is written in what is known as *koine* or 'common' **Greek**. This is the language used by ordinary people throughout the Roman empire, the language used for trade and commerce. Even in Rome most people spoke Greek, with **Latin** being reserved for official use, or used by the upper classes. Paul and the Gospel writers used Greek, because everybody spoke it—it was the language of the ordinary, working man and woman of the time.

Latin only occurs in the New Testament in a handful of places, mostly to do with official terms such as census, Centurion or denarius. However, Latin became widely used in the medieval church and the first translations of the Bible were into Latin.

Part of a Greek text of the Old Testament. This comes from the book of Esther.

Money

In Old Testament times nobody used coins. At first people paid for goods by **bartering** or exchanging them for other goods such as livestock, timber, wine or honey. This was eventually replace by **precious metal**, mainly in the form of **silver**, which was weighed out in units such as shekels, talents, minas, etc. So, for example, Solomon purchased chariots at 600 **shekels** of silver; that is, 6.84kg of silver [1 Kings 10.29]. Jeremiah's field cost him seventeen shekels of silver [Jer 32.9] and Omri bought the hill and city of Samaria for two talents of silver (around 68kg) [1 Kings 16.23–24].

Thus, the shekel, the mina, etc. became the unit of currency. (We have exactly the same system in the UK; we pay in 'pounds', which originally were pound weights of gold or silver.)

Coins came in around the seventh and eighth centuries BC, but they spread slowly to Israel and Judah, perhaps because the coins had images on them and the Jews were opposed to anything with an image on it, because of the Ten Commandments.

By Jesus' time, there were three major currencies available: Jewish, Greek and Roman. The Greek currency was the **drachma**, and the Roman currency, the **denarius**. The denarius was roughly **one day's pay** for a working man.

The Jews still had the **shekel**, which was now an 11.4g coin. The Jews also had smaller currency, notably the **lepton**, a bronze coin that represented the smallest amount of currency. It is this coin that Jesus talks about when he sees the poor widow giving it to the Temple [Luke 21.2].

Musical Instruments

Music plays a huge role in the Bible, and continues to do so in the church today.

The oldest instrument was, of course, the **voice**. Moses and Miriam sang songs of victory when Pharaoh's armies were drowned [Ex 15]. Deborah and Barak sang a song about the death of Sisera [Judg 5]. And, of course, Psalms were sung.

The **Ram's Horn** was mainly used for signalling, to announce events or call people together. It could only do two or three notes, so it wasn't used for melodies. The **trumpet** was a tube of straight metal (bronze or silver) which had a higher pitched sound than the ram's horn, but still only played a couple of notes.

Pipes or **flutes** were made of wood or bone with drilled holes. They were probably more like oboes, with a mouthpiece of one or two reeds. They were sometimes used for sad music, during times of mourning.

Harps came in different shapes and sizes, with strings made of stretched sheepgut. The **Psaltery** was a larger harp, usually with ten or more strings. The **lyre** had a soundbox, so was a cross between a harp and a guitar. There was also a triangular harp with four strings which is sometimes called a 'sackbut'.

Tambourines were either beaten with the bare hand or with sticks. Often they were used by dancers. **Cymbals** were made of copper and there was also the **sistrum**, a kind of rattle, either with metal plates attached to rods, or with beads in an empty gourd.

Persecution

Early **opposition to Christianity** came from the **Jews** rather than from the **Romans**. The Jewish leaders saw Christians as blasphemers who rejected the Law, believed Jesus was the Messiah and even ate unclean food. So they tried to hunt down the Christians, with the death of Stephen starting a wave of persecution [Acts 6.14].

It was a bit like throwing water on a blazing chip-pan: all it did was spread the fire. Forced out of Jerusalem, many Christians spread north, starting up churches as they went. For those who remained, the persecution continued. **James the Apostle** was executed in 44AD by Herod Agrippa. Christians were banned from the synagogues and took to meeting in their own homes.

Initially, the Romans were **tolerant** of Christianity. The Jews asked **Gallio**, the Proconsul in Asia, to act against the Christians, but he refused, allowing Christianity to spread throughout the empire. However, gradually the Romans realised that Christians had a completely different set of values. Christians refused to participate in pagan ceremonies or to worship the Roman emperor. It was even rumoured that they were cannibals who ate flesh and drank blood!

So, when Rome was ravaged by fire in 64AD, **Nero** blamed the Christians. Both **Peter** and **Paul** are believed to have been martyred in Rome during this period. Later centuries saw a policy of **torture**, **mass execution** and the **destruction of church buildings**. Christians were often tied to posts and attacked by wild animals as a form of public entertainment.

It was too late. Christianity had spread too far and become too well established. The Christians' bravery in the face of torture and death only served to promote their cause. The fire was spreading and nothing could put it out.

The Colosseum in Rome. It is believed that many Christians lost their lives here, martyred for their faith and killed simply to provide amusement for the Roman crowds.

Pharisees, Sadducees and Others

The **Pharisees** were the local priesthood. They worked in the **synagogues** and opposed the powers that ran the Temple. The word 'Pharisee' comes from a Hebrew word meaning 'to separate'. They emphasised things like Sabbath-day observance, tithing and ritual cleanliness. Jesus criticised the Pharisees for their hypocrisy, but he had friends who were Pharisees and later, Pharisees were to become Christians [Acts 15.5]. Paul was a Pharisee before he met Jesus.

The **Sadducees** were aristocratic traditionalists who occupied all the most powerful positions in the **Temple** and the **Sanhedrin**. They rejected all religious writings except the Pentateuch (Genesis to Deuteronomy). This meant that they threw out any theories—such as the resurrection of the dead—that were not found in those five books. The Pharisees and the Sadducees hated each other, except on special occasions when they could both agree to hate someone else, such as Jesus.

The law always needed explanation and interpretation. This was the job of the **Scribes**. The Scribes explained and applied the law to special cases, building up a huge database of rules of conduct. Eventually these decisions came to have the same status as the law itself. They are sometimes referred to in the New Testament as '**lawyers**' or '**teachers of law**'.

The **Nazirites** were a special group who took strict vows of purity. They were people who chose to devote their lives to the Lord. Both men and women could be Nazirites. They did not cut their hair, drink alcohol or have contact with dead bodies, not even their parents. This vow could be perpetual, or for a set period.

Then there was a group in the desert called the **Essenes**, who followed a strict rule of ritual purity, common ownership of property and observance of the law. They are, perhaps, most famous for the discovery of the remains of their library—the Dead Sea Scrolls—at the settlement of

This cave at Qumran (known as 'Cave 4') is probably the most famous of the Dead Sea Scroll caves. Some 15,000 fragments from over 200 books—including many Old Testament books—were found here.

Priests

Aaron was the first **High Priest** of Israel (Ex 28–9) and from then on, all priests of Israel were supposed to come from his descendants, assisted by other members of the **tribe of Levi**. Later on, after the kingdom of Israel split in two, the priests of the northern kingdom came from a different tribe, in defiance of God's rules (1Kings 13.34).

Their main job was to offer **sacrifices**. (In fact, this was how they made a living, because they were entitled to a proportion of all the offerings brought to the Temple.) In the early days of Israel they also had some teaching duties, **teaching the Law**. It was not an easy job, at least in the early times. If you didn't obey the instructions exactly, it might mean death (Lev 10). Their service began at the age of twenty-five, and they retired when they were fifty (Num 8.24–6).

Priests wore a special uniform, consisting of a two-piece 'apron' called an **ephod**, and a chestpiece inset with twelve precious stones, representing the twelve tribes of Israel.

The chestpiece had a pocket, directly over the priest's heart, which included the **Urim** and the **Thummim** (Ex 28.30). No one really knows how these worked, but experts think that they were some kind of device such as stones, which were thrown to determine the will of God. A bit like throwing dice.

Only the high priest could enter the **holy of holies**, the sacred inner room in the tabernacle and the Temple, and then only for one day a year—on the **Day of Atonement**.

Priests were supposed to act as the go-betweens between God and the people. Once Jesus arrived on the scene, there was no more need for priests as such. Jesus had no need to offer sacrifices—he was the sacrifice, once and for all (Heb 7.27–8). After Jesus, all Christians are described as a **'royal priesthood'** (1Pet. 2.9).

Slavery

Slavery was taken for granted in the ancient world. Today it is one of the features that we find most shocking, but in those days, slaves were everywhere.

A person could become a slave in one of three ways: by **capture in war** [Num 31.7–9]; by **voluntarily selling themselves into slavery** in order to pay a debt or fine [Lev 25.39]; or by being **born to slave parents** [Ex 21.4]. Once they were enslaved, they were the property of their owner. They could not resign or leave his service.

While slaves could lead harsh, hard lives, many slaves were more like **servants**, trusted and respected members of the family. And Jewish law meant that Hebrew slaves were, or should be, treated fairly. Foreign slaves could be circumcised and become almost a Jew, attending festivals and feasts such as Passover. And, like everyone else, he would not be allowed to work on a Sabbath.

Slaves could gain their freedom in a number of ways [Ex 21.2–27; Lev 25.47–55; Deut 15.12–23]. Relatives or friends could buy them out of service, or the owner might set the slave free. On their freedom, it was expected that the slave would be given a 'leaving gift' of money. They would also take their master's name.

In the Roman world, slaves were more 'things' than people. They could not legally marry, nor could they own any property in their own name. They could be harshly treated and they would have to work whatever hours the owner chose; but they could also be very well treated and, indeed, be given a large amount of responsibility. There were slaves who ran their master's business, and slaves who were highly skilled. (Many doctors were slaves—sort of like the family physician—and it is entirely possible that Luke was an ex-slave who had taken his master's name of Lucius.)

Paul did not argue for an end to slavery—probably because he realised that it they were so woven into the fabric of society that such a request would be impossible. He did, however, argue for **fair treatment** on both sides [Tit 2.9; Col 3.22; 4.1]. More than that, he made the astonishing claim that in Christ there was **no real difference** between slave and free. Society saw it as a massive gulf, but Paul argued that Christ had put everyone on the same level [1Cor 12.13].

Synagogues

When the Jews were exiled in Babylon, there was no temple at which they could worship and gather to make sacrifices. So, thousands of miles away, they developed a more personal, small-scale expression of worship, centred around the reading and discussion of the Scriptures and personal prayer. The Jewish faith could be practised anywhere where there was a **scroll** and someone to read it.

The remains of the fourth century synagogue at Capernaum

On their return to Israel, this new expression of their faith persisted and led to the development of **synagogues**—small, local meeting places, where Jews gathered to worship, pray and study the Scriptures.

The synagogue leader or **rabbi** would stand in the middle of the building, with the people sat on raised benches around him. He would then read a passage, talk about it and answer questions.

Exterior of a typical synagogue of Jesus' time, reconstructed in Nazareth

Often visiting teachers would be invited to choose a passage from the scriptures to talk about. In Luke, Jesus visits the synagogue in his home town of Nazareth and speaks about a passage from Isaiah [Lk 4.16–30].

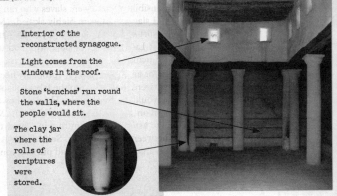

Interior of the reconstructed synagogue.

Light comes from the windows in the roof.

Stone 'benches' run round the walls, where the people would sit.

The clay jar where the rolls of scriptures were stored.

Taxes

The Romans did a lot for the countries they occupied. They built roads and markets, town halls and stadia. They policed the countries and installed law and order. They built baths and aqueducts and all kind of amenities. But all this cost money. And that money had to be raised by **taxes**.

There were various kinds of taxes. In Syria, there was a poll tax, with a direct charge of one per cent of your income. There was a property tax called a *tributum*. There was tax on food, on property, on the sale of slaves, and **customs** had to be paid every time goods crossed a border into different territory. (This was why Matthew had his office in Capernaum—it was a customs and excise operation at the border between the territories of Philip and Herod Antipas [Mt 9.9–13].)

All these taxes had to be collected and this was the job of a Roman official called a **Censor**. It was his task to collect the taxes from a region as cheaply as possible. So he would auction the task, and those bidders who promised to take the least commission got the job.

It was bad enough that these tax collectors—Jews themselves—were collaborating with the occupying forces. What really annoyed the people was the fact that the tax collectors were **ripping them off**. They would add a little bit more to the tax demands; they would cream off a percentage of the tax money for themselves. They would accept **bribes** from rich people to lower their tax demands. They were little more than criminals.

Thus, in Jesus' time, everyone hated the tax collectors. To be a tax collector in the time of Christ was to be completely despised and hated by your friends and neighbours.

Which was why it was so shocking to all those 'virtuous' people that Jesus spent so much time with tax collectors. He talked to them. He went to their houses for parties. He even had an ex-tax collector as part of his gang of followers! It was as if he was saying that anyone could be forgiven.

Temples and Shrines

In ancient times, **temples** were seen as places where a god lived and where his followers would bring offerings. Usually, the Temple contained a **statue of the god**, as well as an **altar** for the offerings. Israel's God was different. He did not need a house in which to dwell and he had no statue. Even so, the Bible lists a number of different shrines, altars and buildings built in his honour, and where he spoke to his people.

The **Tabernacle** was a huge tent which could be packed up and transported from place to place. It was a kind of flat-pack temple, with an altar, priests, candles, tables and an inner room where God could be consulted.

After the Israelites entered Canaan they had a number of **shrines**. They put up the sacred tent at **Shiloh** [Josh 18.1], where it was eventually replaced by a building. Shiloh became a famous shrine, as did **Bethel** [Judg 20.26–7]. These shrines also housed the Ark of the Covenant at various times.

After the Ark of the Covenant was brought into Jerusalem, King David wanted to build a temple to house it. In the end, the work was completed by his son, Solomon. This magnificent building followed the same shape as the Tabernacle.

After Israel split into two kingdoms, the Kings of Israel set up their own version of the Temple in Bethel, to compete with the traditional centre in Jerusalem. This shrine later became the centre of idolatrous worship [Hos 10.15; Jer 48.13]. Later Josiah, the king of Judah, invaded Israel, destroyed the temple at Bethel and killed the priests [2 Kings 23.15–20].

A carving of the Ark of the Covenant, from Capernaum. Here it is depicted on a wagon, presumably during one of its journeys into battle or across Israel.

Transport

For the most part, people **walked**. Only the rich few had **horses** or vehicles drawn by animals. **Chariots** were generally military or government vehicles.

Another reason why so many people walked was that the roads were not good. Even in Roman times, when the road network was pretty sophisticated, roads were still tracks. Road building consisted mainly of moving the big boulders out of the way and filling the holes.

Animals were used for transporting goods or equipment. It was always important to look after your animal, so, wherever possible, people walked alongside their donkey or mule, rather than ride on it. The most common pack animals were **asses** and **donkeys**. Horses were more used for war than for transport. **Camels**, of course, were used by desert tribes and traders making long journeys. Returning to Jerusalem from exile in Babylon, the Jews used 435 camels [Neh 7.69]. David had so many camels that he had to appoint an Arab expert—Ofil the Ishmaelite—to look after them. [1 Chr 27.30].

Mules were like turbo-charged donkeys. They were faster and hardier than donkeys or asses and were often used as steeds for a king to ride [1 Kings 1.44]. **Wagons** were used mainly on the plains, where the going was easier. Again, most travellers walked alongside the wagon, rather than ride in it.

For long distances, sailing was the best way. A **ship** could take you further and faster (and it was cheaper, because you didn't have to hire transport or pay extra for staying at an inn). With a good wind, a ship could make up to one hundred miles in a day. The fastest a horse could travel would be between twenty-five and thirty miles a day; and to do that, you'd have to have a change of horses. The only problem with sea-travel was that it could be very dangerous. Unless there was no choice, ships wouldn't sail during the dangerous winter season, from mid-November until early March. Paul's experiences on the journey to Rome show just how dangerous sailing during this period could be [Acts 27].

Wives, Concubines and Prostitutes

Marriage was very different in Bible times. Most marriages were **arranged** by the parents. Not that love didn't come into it. Rebekah fell in love with Isaac, and Samson chose his bride. (He still asked his parents to arrange things [Judg 14.1–3].)

Engagements were then a matter of drawing up the **contract**. The bride was usually purchased by the groom's family, usually by paying a '**bride-price**', which was supposed to compensate the bride's family for the loss of a useful worker. Brides could also be captured in wars [Deut 21.10–14] or even gained as the result of seduction [Ex 22.16]. Brides were heavily veiled on the wedding day, which is why Jacob could be fooled into marrying the wrong woman [Gen 29.21–28].

If the husband died, in Old Testament times it was customary for widows to marry their dead husband's **nearest living relative**, usually the brother [Deut 25.5–6]. This is the custom behind the story of Ruth [Ruth 4.1–8] and the Sadducees question to Jesus [Lk 20.27–36]. It's also why **Tamar** goes to such great lengths: she is asserting her rights as a woman [Gen 38]. Tamar is one of the few women mentioned in the family tree of Christ [Mt 1.3].

Kings and powerful men might also have concubines. Concubines had legal rights, and their children were regarded as legitimate, but they had less status than a wife. Solomon had 300 concubines along with his 700 wives [1 Kings 11:3].

Then there were prostitutes. In the ancient world there were two main kinds of prostitute. **Temple prostitutes** performed sex as part of their 'worship', or to make money to support the Temples of false gods. These are always condemned in the Bible. '**Ordinary' prostitutes** stood on street corners, or worked in brothels. Generally the Bible disapproves of these as well, although in early times it was less frowned upon. Proverbs, for example, is full of warnings to young men not to get ensnared into this kind of 'trap'.

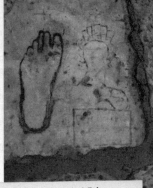

This sign on the pavement at Ephesus shows a foot next to a drawing of a woman. It means 'this way to the brothel.'

Weights and Measures

In the Old Testament, **weights** were based on the **shekel**, which weighed 11.4g. Fifty shekels made one **mina** and sixty minas made one **talent**. So, a talent was 3,000 shekels. By the time of Jesus, **Roman measures** had taken over and the standard measure was the Roman **'pound'**, which weighed 325g or 11.5 oz.

The standard Old Testament **liquid measure** is the **bath** (24 litres) and a **hin** of a bath (6 litres). In the New Testament capacity is measured by a different, mainly Roman, system. The New Testament bath held around 40 litres.

The standard unit of **length** in the Bible was the **cubit**—roughly the length of an arm, from elbow to fingertips. Accordingly, the value of the cubit varied between 45–55 cm. The Old Testament cubit was around 45cm, the New Testament cubit 55cm.

Similarly, the **span** was the distance from the thumb to the little finger—around 22cm. Thus, there were two spans in a cubit. Continuing the 'arm' theme, there was the **palm** (7cm) and the **finger** (1.85cm). There were three palms in a span and four fingers in a palm.

In the New Testament, the Roman system of measurements is more apparent; ships measured depths in **fathoms** (1.8m), and longer distances included the **stadion** (furlong) at 185m and the **milion** (mile) at 1478m.

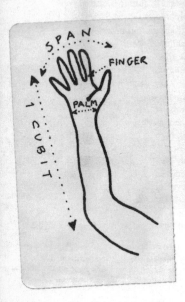

Explorer's Notes—Part 8
Where are they now?

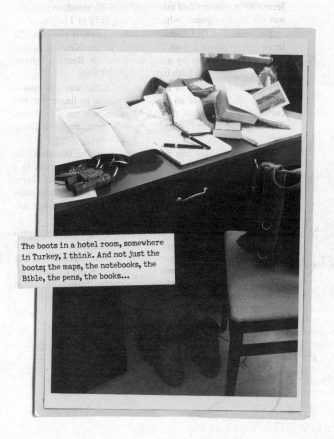

The boots in a hotel room, somewhere in Turkey, I think. And not just the boots; the maps, the notebooks, the Bible, the pens, the books...

Bible lands today

Today, many of the sites talked about in the Bible can still be visited. Israel (pp 240–7), of course, is the obvious place to start, but Turkey (p.248–9), Greece (p.250) and Italy (p.251) all have places with New Testament associations as well.

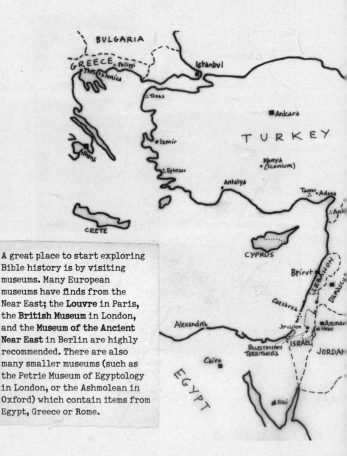

A great place to start exploring Bible history is by visiting museums. Many European museums have finds from the Near East; the **Louvre** in Paris, the **British Museum** in London, and the **Museum of the Ancient Near East** in Berlin are highly recommended. There are also many smaller museums (such as the Petrie Museum of Egyptology in London, or the Ashmolean in Oxford) which contain items from Egypt, Greece or Rome.

Old Testament sites can also be found in Egypt, Syria, Jordan and Lebanon. Some of the most famous Old Testament sites are in what are modern-day Iran and Iraq. At the time of writing, visiting the remains of Nineveh, Babylon and Ur is tricky, to say the least.

Israel & Palestine Today

'That man will get a clearer grasp of Holy Scripture who has gazed at Judea' wrote Jerome in the fourth century.

Today Israel still draws pilgrims and travellers who want to see the place for themselves. The meeting point of three of the great religions of the world—Christianity, Judaism and Islam—the so-called 'Holy Land' has had, at times, a very unholy history; today stories of suicide bombings, uprisings and military oppression still dominate the headlines.

For all that, Israel is a wonderful place to visit and few things help you explore the Bible more than exploring the land.

St Jerome was right.

Some key sites

1. Jerusalem. One of the great cities of the world, it is the city of David, home of the Temple, place of the crucifixion and resurrection. (See pp.136–7)

2. Jericho. Possibly the world's oldest continuously inhabited city. A city of green oasis in the midst of the Judean wilderness.

3. Bethlehem. Birthplace of Jesus and David.

4. Qumran. Home of the Essenes; the Dead Sea Scrolls were found in the caves nearby.

5. Masada. One of Herod's fortresses and site of a desperate last ditch-stand by Jewish rebels.

6. The Dead Sea. The lowest point on the surface of the earth. Its high concentration of minerals mean that nothing can live in it. Hence the name.

7. Caesarea Maritime. Expanded by Herod the Great in honour of Caesar Augustus, it was a famous port.

8. Nazareth. The place where Jesus grew up.

9. Galilee. The centre of Christ's ministry, where he taught and performed miracles in villages such as Capernaum and Chorazin.

The desert outside Jericho; one of the most stunning places in the world.

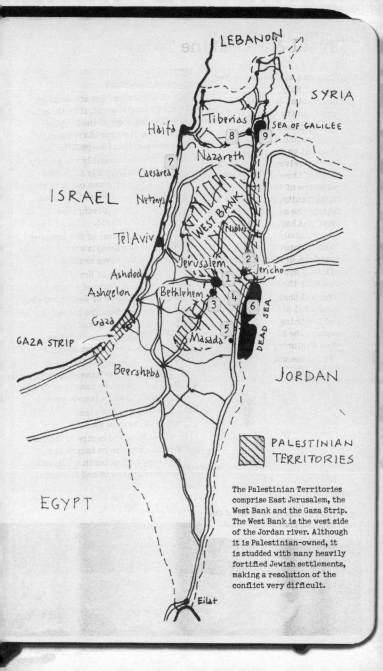

LEBANON

SYRIA

ISRAEL

Haifa

Tiberias

SEA OF GALILEE

8

9

Nazareth

7

Caesarea

Netanya

WEST BANK

Nablus

Tel Aviv

Jerusalem

2

Jericho

Ashdod

1

Ashqelon

Bethlehem

4

3

6

DEAD SEA

5

Masada

Gaza

GAZA STRIP

Beersheba

JORDAN

PALESTINIAN
TERRITORIES

The Palestinian Territories
comprise East Jerusalem, the
West Bank and the Gaza Strip.
The West Bank is the west side
of the Jordan river. Although
it is Palestinian-owned, it
is studded with many heavily
fortified Jewish settlements,
making a resolution of the
conflict very difficult.

EGYPT

Eilat

Jerusalem Today

Some key sites

Jerusalem is an amazing city with an atmosphere like no other. The **Old City**, within the walls, is split into four quarters: Jewish, Muslim, Christian and Armenian. Each has their own characteristic feel.

The city is dominated by the golden-crowned **Dome of the Rock**, which is on the old Temple Mount. Below it, tucked just off the bustling **souk** (market), is the **Church of the Holy Sepulchre**. Outside the city on the eastern side is the **Mount of Olives**.

1. Church of the Holy Sepulchre
2. Dome of the Rock
3. Wailing Wall
4. Roman Steps
5. Upper Room
6. Church of Ascension
7. Church of Pater Noster
8. Garden of Gethsemane
9. Church of St Anne and Pools of Bethesda
10. Garden Tomb
11. Citadel

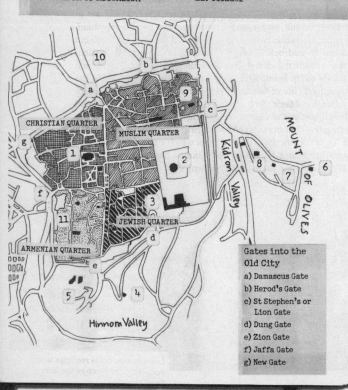

Gates into the Old City

a) Damascus Gate
b) Herod's Gate
c) St Stephen's or Lion Gate
d) Dung Gate
e) Zion Gate
f) Jaffa Gate
g) New Gate

Jerusalem

The **Church of the Holy Sepulchre** (also known as the **Church of the Resurrection**) was built over the traditional site of Jesus' crucifixion, burial and resurrection. The site was outside the city during the time of Jesus, so could have been used as a crucifixion and burial site. Other first-century tombs are still preserved inside the church. It is generally agreed that this place has an extremely strong claim to be the authentic site.

Jerusalem street scene: a porter making his way through the souk with a tray of bread.

Originally built in 330AD, it was destroyed by the Persians in 614AD, rebuilt, and then destroyed again in 1009 by the 'mad' caliph Al-Hakim bi-Amr Allah, who had the original tomb cut down to bedrock. When the Crusaders captured Jerusalem they rebuilt the church and it is mainly this structure which stands today. Inside the church is a rocky outcrop which is the traditional site of **Golgotha**. The tomb is encased in a structure called the **Edicule** (from the Latin *aediculum*, meaning 'small building') in the centre of the church. The running of the church is split between various Christian denominations with a lot of arguments over who owns which part. (Things are so sensitive that a ladder on the window has been there since 1860 as no-one can agree who owns it.)

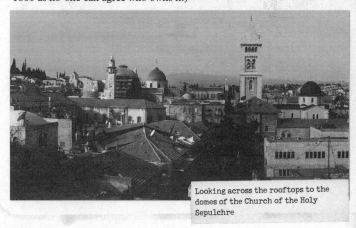

Looking across the rooftops to the domes of the Church of the Holy Sepulchre

The Dome of the Rock in Jerusalem, looking across from the Jewish cemetery on the Mount of Olives.

Ancient Jerusalem was dominated by the Temple; modern Jerusalem by the **Dome of the Rock**. This Islamic shrine occupies the place where Herod's temple once stood. It was built between 687–691AD by Greek Byzantine architects working for Caliph Abd al-Malik. The rock in the centre of the dome is believed by Muslims to be the place from which Muhammad ascended to God to receive the Islamic prayers before returning to earth. It is one of the most beautiful buildings in the world. Sadly, access to the interior is, at the time of writing, denied for non-Muslims.

Below the Dome stands perhaps the holiest place in Judaism: the **Western** or **Wailing Wall**. It contains the only remnants of Herod's temple, in the huge blocks of stone which made the original Temple Mount. Jews go there by their thousands, to worship at all that is left of their once-magnificent temple.

South of the city on the slopes of the Hinnom valley is the church of **St Peter Galicantu**, which commemorates Peter's denial of Jesus. Below the church is a flight of Roman steps that lead down the valley and on which Jesus probably walked when he crossed the city and went out to the Mount of Olives. Near here, the tomb of Caiaphas the High Priest was found.

Westwards, up the hill, is the **Upper Room**—a place traditionally associated with the Last Supper and the coming of the Holy Spirit at Pentecost. There is a strong tradition linking this site with the Pentecost events and from very early on (c. second century AD) Christians were used to meeting here.

The Mount of Olives lies to the east of Jerusalem, across the **Kidron valley**. This was one of the places that Jesus visited the most; he taught on the mount and the road from Jerusalem to Bethany led over the ridge. At the top of the Mount of Olives stands the **Church of the Holy Ascension**. Since 1187AD, this has been a very small mosque. It was the Crusaders who decided that this was the site of the Ascension; the early Church placed the site further down, in a cave beneath the **Church of the Pater Noster**. The summit of the mount offers a great view across Jerusalem. Zechariah implies that the Mount of Olives is the place where God will begin to raise the dead [Zech 14.4] making it a prime burial place for Jews. Much of the mount, therefore, is covered by a **Jewish cemetery**, containing some 150,000 graves.

At the foot of the mount is the **Garden of Gethsemane**, where Jesus watched and prayed the night before he was crucified [Mt 26.36]. Gethsemane means 'olive press' and the garden contains ancient olive trees. This was a place of prayer for Christians from earliest times and the church there now—the **Church of All Nations**—was built in 1919.

From the Mount of Olives, the main entrance to the city is through **St Stephen's Gate**. Near here starts the **Via Dolorosa**, or 'road of sorrow', which commemorates the journey made by Jesus carrying his cross on the way to Golgotha. It crosses the old city from east to west, ending inside the Church of the Holy Sepulchre. This route is marked by the fourteen **Stations of the Cross**—nine outside in the streets and five inside the church. This recent tradition dates from the sixteenth century.

This route takes you past the beautiful crusader church of **St Anne**, where you can see the remains of the **pools of Bethesda**. You can also visit the cheerfully-named **Monastery of the Flagellation**, in the basement of which there is a Roman pavement from the time of Christ.

On the opposite side of the city, by the Jaffa Gate, stands the **Citadel**, which, along with some remains of Herodian building, contains the Museum of the History of Jerusalem. Herod's Palace—where Pilate probably stayed when visiting Jerusalem—was just to the north of the existing remains.

To the north of the city is the **Garden Tomb**: an alternative site for Jesus' crucifixion and burial. It was discovered by General Gordon in 1838, who, startled by the resemblance of certain rock formations to a skull, thought that this must be *golgotha*, the place of the skull. It's probably not the site, but many find the tranquil atmosphere more conducive to reflection than the bustle of the Holy Sepulchre. In this crowded, vibrant city, it's a good place to sit and think and pray.

Galilee

The Mount of Beatitudes. It's a great place to gaze over Galilee and imagine what it was like when Jesus spoke to the crowds.

Much of Jesus' ministry took place in the region of **Galilee**. A trip on the sea itself can give you a good idea of the changeable weather conditions, while around the edge you can see many natural amphitheatres. It was in places like these that Jesus taught from a boat rowed a little way offshore.

Capernaum has a fantastic synagogue, the base of which is the synagogue where Jesus walked and talked. It also houses the ancient ruins of Peter's house, which has been used as a Christian meeting place since the first century.

Chorazin, set high on a hill overlooking Galilee, contains first-century houses, and the remains of a fine synagogue.

Tabhga has a beautiful rebuilt Byzantine basilica. Nearby is a church commemorating the miraculous catch of fish, and just round the shoreline is the **Mount of Beatitudes**, commemorating the Sermon on the Mount.

Nazareth, the town where Jesus grew up, is a bustling, rather nondescript city, dominated by the enormous Franciscan basilica. Below the **Convent of the Nazarenes** is a first-century street which, given the smallness of Nazareth, Jesus must have walked. Take the chance to visit the wonderful **Nazareth Village**, a recreation of a first-century village; few places give a better impression of what the Nazareth of Jesus' time was really like. And just a few miles away are the remains of **Sepphoris**, the city built by Herod Antipas where Jesus probably worked. There are remains of the theatre and streets and a magnificent collection of mosaics.

Tel Dan is the ancient city of **Dan**. The remains include some gates and gatehouses, and the probably site of the 'High Place' set up by Jeroboam to house the golden calf [1Kings 12.29].

Caesarea Maritime is a magnificent site on the coast, featuring the remains of Herod's great city. It has what was left of his huge artificial harbour, a stadium, a theatre and the remains of the palace where Paul appeared before Felix.

Elsewhere in Israel

One of the oldest church buildings in the world, the **Church of the Nativity in Bethlehem** was built in 330AD over the traditional site of Jesus' birthplace. The current building dates back to 530AD. (In 614AD it escaped destruction by the Persians, because they saw pictures of Persian magi on the walls.) The cave where Jesus is believed to have been born is beneath the church, and reached by a flight of steps. The traditional site of Jesus' birth is marked by a star on the floor.

Hebron has been inhabited for at least 5,000 years. The main site is the tombs of the patriarchs—the traditional tombs of Abraham, Isaac, Jacob and their wives.

Samaria was built by King Omri of Israel in 876BC and was captured by the Assyrians in 721BC. Herod the Great renamed it Sebaste (the Greek version of Augustus) and built many new public buildings, the remnants of which can be seen today.

Masada is an amazing cliff-top fortress built by Herod the Great overlooking the Dead Sea. It was the site of a famous mass suicide, when 960 Jewish rebels refused to surrender to the Romans in 70AD.

Qumran, on the west shore of the Dead Sea, is famous for the discovery of the Dead Sea Scrolls in the caves surrounding the site. This was an Essene community on the western shore of the Dead Sea. The scrolls were discovered in 1947 in jars in the surrounding caves.

Just to the north of the modern city of **Jericho** are the city's ancient remains, which date back thousands of years. A cable car takes you to the **Monastery of Temptation**, which marks the place where Jesus was tempted by the devil. In the wilderness to the west of Jericho is **St George's Monastery**.

The spectacular Monastery of St George, which clings to the side of a ravine on the Wadi Qelt.

Beersheba is a large, well-preserved site, rebuilt as it was in the eighth century under King Hezekiah.

Turkey

Antioch on the Orontes, also called Syrian Antioch, is situated on the Orontes River, in the far south-eastern corner of Asia Minor. By the second century AD, it was the third largest city of the Roman Empire. Paul made it his base of operations and there is an ancient church of St Peter.

Ephesus is one of the greatest archaeological sites in the world. The remains are stunning. Even the few fragments of the Temple of Artemis—once one of the seven wonders of the world—have a certain wistful beauty. There are streets and houses and the huge theatre, on an earlier version of which the silversmiths stood and shouted for their goddess. The Ephesus museum has some fantastic statues and there is also the church of St John, on a hill overlooking the Temple.

Now just a hill, **Colossae** is still a moving spot and with a bit of delving around you can trace the route of the three rivers that used to surround the city. The acropolis mound can be clearly seen against the background of the mountains. Maybe they'll excavate one day.

Set high on a hill, **Pisidian Antioch** is a bit off the tourist trail, which makes it all the more nice to visit. There is a fine main street, the remains of a theatre and a temple at the top of the hill, built into the hillside.

Perge marked a kind of turning point for Paul; it was where he set foot in truly Gentile soil and started to take the gospel to them. Today, the extensive remains give you a great idea of what a first-century city was like. From the acropolis hill you can look back and see how extensive the city was [Acts 13.13].

Ancient **Iconium** is now modern Konya, and there's not much left for the Biblical explorer. What used to be the main acropolis of Iconium is now a kind of cross between a small park and large traffic island. Most visitors here go to the mosques of the Whirling Dervishes, but the intrepid Bible explorer can take a five-minute taxi ride to the Archaeological Museum. There you can see some wonderful statues and sarcophagi, and some inscribed stones that are the remains of **Lystra** and **Derbe**.

It's worth exploring some of the ports that Paul used, notably places like **Miletus**, where he said his farewell to the elders of

Ephesus, knowing he would not see them again. Today the harbour is silted up, but there is a magnificent theatre. One of the seats has the greek inscription: 'For the Jews and the God-fearers' showing that the seats were reserved. You can also see places like **Patara**, where he set sail for his last, fateful visit to Palestine. Although heavily silted up, there are places you can climb to make out the original size of the ports.

The **Seven Cities of Revelation** are worth a trip. Well, five of them, anyway; there's nothing much at what were **Philadelphia** and **Thyatira**. And not much more at ancient **Smyrna**, which is buried beneath the modern, sprawling city of Izmir. (There are a few fragments of the ancient Agora right in the centre.) However, **Sardis** has some impressive remains, including the large synagogue, the rebuilt gymnasium and the Temple of Artemis, which stood below the ancient citadel.

Pergamum was a major city in New Testament times. The extensive remains include an acropolis, an ancient temple dedicated to Serapis—the Egyptian god of the underworld—and the Aesclepium, a kind of first-century hospital.

Laodicea is a huge, mainly overgrown, site. Laodicea was a wealthy city. Don't miss the ancient water pipes which show the calcium deposits building up on the inside. The water for the city came a long distance, by which time it was lukewarm and tasted foul because of the mineral deposits. Hence Jesus' warning to the Laodiceans about their 'lukewarm' faith.

Laodicea in Turkey where, among the extensive ruins, you can see the calcified water pipes which fed this 'lukewarm' city.

Greece

The main site for tourists is obviously **Athens**, although Paul only went there once. Just below the Acropolis is **Mars Hill**, where Paul addressed the men of the city [Acts 17]. You can also see the **Temple of Zeus**, and the rebuilt **Stoa of Attalus**, which many experts take as the model for the Stoa at the south end of Temple Mount in Jerusalem. There is also the famous **Acropolis** with the **Parthenon Temple** (although most of the sculptures from here are in the British Museum).

There are few visible first century remains at **Thessalonica**, (largely because modern-day Thessaloniki sits right on top). However, you can see the remains of the forum, and a pavement, and more interestingly, an inscription from the first century uses the word *politarches*—the word Luke uses for the city officials [Acts 17:6] (This word doesn't appear in any other Greek literature, thus reinforcing Luke's credibility as a historian.)

The remains of **Nicopolis** ('city of victory') include a stadium, theatre, odeum, nymphaeum, baths, gymnasium, basilicas, aqueduct, and city walls. Paul almost certainly visited the city, probably spending the winter there [Titus 3:12].

Outside **Philippi** is the Gangitis River where Paul met—and converted—Lydia, thus starting the first church on European soil. There is a large forum, a theatre and one of the earliest churches known in Greece.

The **Corinth** of Paul's time had an upper and lower city. The upper city—or **Acrocorinth**—rises 1800 feet above the plain around it and housed the large **Temple of Aphrodite**. You can see the Bema or judgment hall where Paul probably stood before Gallio and the Agora where Priscilla and Aquila may have had their tent-making business. There are also the remains of the Lachaion road, which ran to the northern port of **Lachaion**. In 1929, archaeologists found an inscription mentioning Erastus, who paid for a street to be repaved in exchange for being appointed as a city official. This could easily have been the Erastus mentioned by Paul as sending greetings to Rome [Rom 16:23]. The southern port of Corinth was at **Cenchraea**, where Paul cut his hair because of a vow [Acts 18:18].

Italy

The main Biblical site in Italy is **Rome**, where Paul spent at least two years and where he and Peter were probably martyred. The **Church of St Peter** in the Vatican is built over the traditional site of Peter's grave. Below the church are **catacombs**, and, in particular, the ancient shrine which is said to house the bones of the apostle. The Vatican museum also has a selection of art and relics from the early Church. There are other catacombs in the city (or under the city to be precise), the best of which are probably **San Callisto, San Sebastiano** and **San Domitilla**. A visit to these will also bring you along the ancient Appian Way, the old road leading into Rome from the south. Paul's bones are reputedly under the church of **San Paoli Fuori le Mura**. The church was rebuilt in the nineteenth century after a fire destroyed the old one.

The **Colosseum** was the huge arena where Romans enjoyed the spectacle of gladiatorial combat and seeing Christians eaten by various wild animals. Built by Jewish prisoners under Vespasian in 72AD and completed under his son, Titus, it could even be filled with water to recreate naval battles.

The church of **San Clemente** is a fantastic church which demonstrates how churches grew and developed in the first two centuries AD. Named after Clement I (according to tradition the third leader of the Roman church after Peter), the church is a beautiful building with mosaics dating from around 1100AD. But downstairs you find an earlier church—a fourth-century basilica. Go down yet again and there's a first-century Roman insula or apartment house and a temple to the god Mithras. So, we can trace the history: Christians first met in the apartment house. As they grew more numerous they purchased the buildings around. When Mithraism was outlawed in 395AD, they took over the Temple, filled the lot in and built the basilica. Around 1100AD this was filled in and the present church built. You can see a similar example at the church of **San Pietro et Giovanni**, where there is an old Roman road running up the side of the hill. Other churches associated with Biblical characters are **San Prisca** (traditionally the site of Priscilla and Aquila's house) and **San Pudens** (traditionally on the site of Puden's house, where tradition asserts that Peter stayed when he came to Rome).

Index

Numbers in **bold** indicate maps, diagrams or photos